Acc
01

D0994209

HOW LITERATURE
WORKS

HOW LITERATURE WORKS

Kenneth Quinn

1417988

CHESTER COLLEGE

ACC. No.	DEPT.
01094954	

CLASS No.

801 QUI

LIBRARY

MACMILLAN

© Kenneth Quinn 1992

All rights reserved. No reproduction, copy or transmission of
this publication may be made without written permission.

No paragraph of this publication may be reproduced, copied or
transmitted save with written permission or in accordance with
the provisions of the Copyright, Designs and Patents Act 1988,
or under the terms of any licence permitting limited copying
issued by the Copyright Licensing Agency, 90 Tottenham Court
Road, London W1P 9HE.

Any person who does any unauthorised act in relation to this
publication may be liable to criminal prosecution and civil
claims for damages.

First published 1982 in Australia by
Australian Broadcasting Corporation

Published in Great Britain in a new edition
with revisions 1992 by
THE MACMILLAN PRESS LTD
Houndmills, Basingstoke, Hampshire RG21 2XS
and London
Companies and representatives
throughout the world

ISBN 0–333–56833–8 hardcover
ISBN 0–333–56834–6 paperback

A catalogue record for this book is available
from the British Library

Printed in Hong Kong

For Gamby

Contents

Acknowledgements

The author and publishers wish to thank the following for permission to use copyright material:

Collins/Angus and Robertson Publishers for 'Nationality' by Mary Gilmore from *Selected Verse*, copyright © 1948 by The Estate of Mary Gilmore; and extract from 'An Absolutely Ordinary Rainbow' by Les Murray from *The Vernacular Poems*, copyright © Les Murray; Farrar, Straus & Giroux, Inc. for 'Visit to St. Elizabeths' from *The Complete Poems, 1927–1979* by Elizabeth Bishop, copyright © 1957 by Elizabeth Bishop, copyright © 1979, 1983 by Alice Helen Methfessel; New Directions Publishing Corporation for a poem from *A Coney Island of the Mind* by Lawrence Ferlinghetti, copyright © 1958 by Lawrence Ferlinghetti; New Statesman and Society for competition entry poem by Edward Blishen, *New Statesman*; Oxford University Press for 'Tigers' from *Tigers* by Fleur Adcock, 1967; and Oxford University Press, New Zealand, for 'The Condition' from *Selected Poems* by Lauris Edmond, 1984; Laurence Pollinger Ltd and Alfred A. Knopf, Inc. for 'Dead Boy' from *Selected Poems*, 3rd ed. revised & enlarged by John Crowe Ranson, copyright © 1927 by Alfred A. Knopf, Inc. and renewed 1955 by John Crow Ransom; Random House, Inc. for an extract from 'Fleet Visit' and 'The Cave of Making' from *W. H. Auden: Collected Poems* ed. E. Mendelson, copyright © 1955 by W. H. Auden; Alan Roddick, Literary Executor of the Estate of Charles Brasch, for extracts from 'Ambulando' and 'Why?' from *Collected Poems* by Charles Brasch, ed. A. Roddick, 1984; The Society of Authors on behalf of Mrs Iris Wise, for 'The Snare' by James Stephens; Myfanwy Thomas for 'The Owl' from *The Collected Poems of Edward Thomas*, Oxford University Press; A. P. Watt Ltd on behalf of The Trustees of the Robert Graves Copyright Trust and Oxford University Press, Inc. for an extract from 'The Halls of Bedlam' from *Collected Poems 1975* by Robert Graves.

Every effort has been made to trace all the copyright holders, but if any have been inadvertently overlooked the publishers will be pleased to make the necessary arrangement at the first opportunity.

Preface

This book is intended as a general introduction to the subject called literature. Its object is to describe and illustrate how a novel or a poem works; to show how it differs from a report in the newspaper, a scientific article or a textbook, or the minutes of a meeting. It works that way, of course, only because we know how to read it: there is a good deal, therefore, in the following pages about what is usually called the psychology of the reading process. A good deal also, to put all this in proper context, about what is usually called the social function of literature.

Literary theory and practical criticism are commonly treated as if they were separate subjects. I have tried to stress their interdependence. As R. S. Crane said in beginning his third Alexander Lecture in University College, Toronto, in March 1952:

> The final test of any critical language is what its particular scheme of concepts permits or encourages us to say, in practical criticism, about individual works.[1]

Hence the length of some of the passages quoted: they are examples of literature at work, not examples cited only to make a theoretical point.

Here and there a quick foray into literary history seemed profitable, but the student is left to master the basic anatomy

1. *The Languages of Criticism and the Structure of Poetry* (University of Toronto Press, 1953), p. 115.

of literary history (the details of who wrote what when) from the many books which offer this information.

How Literature Works was written during my tenure of a Connaught Senior Fellowship at Toronto as a first statement of a critical position, and presented in a series of two-hour radio programmes by the Australian Broadcasting Corporation in 1982. The present text differs considerably from that published by ABC Books, Sydney.

Raumati, New Zealand
Easter 1991   K.Q.

1

A Particular Use of Words

The fact is, there is something special about literary texts. Not necessarily something specially good: bad novels, bad poems, are commoner than good ones. The fact remains that reading a novel or a poem (any novel, any poem that *works* – however imperfectly – as a novel or a poem) is a different kind of experience from reading other texts (a news item in the paper, an article in an encyclopaedia, the minutes of a meeting). Reading a novel or a poem gets you involved in a particular use of words.

* * *

Words are the starting point for any systematic analysis of what we say, read or write. In a society of illiterates it would have to be different. *We* have learnt to hear what we hear as a string of words (or, more precisely, as a series of strings) which we can take apart whenever, for any reason, we wish to separate from its context a word that has caught our attention. Words are what *you* focus your attention on as you read this book. Not letters; not syllables; not sounds; words. Words separated from one another on the printed page which arrange themselves in strings in your mind as you read.

Words taken singly won't tell you much, however, or get you far. Words listed in a dictionary are words waiting for a context. The words strung along the lines of the printed page of a novel or a poem are words at work. Words in a dictionary have only definitions; words at work acquire meaning. They make statements; ask questions; describe scenes, express feelings, formulate ideas.

*   *   *

Poets tell us inspiration comes in phrases, not complete sentences. All who write have felt, on occasion, the magic of this happening: suddenly, the string of words is there, its shape implanted on it by its grammatical structure; the rhythm, the intonation, the tone of voice which the words take on when strung together in that structure – all lend the string of words its own unique sound and meaning. The phrase is more than a string of words, the sentence more than a string of phrases. The terms we use to describe this magical act aren't easily pinned down, but the reality they describe is familiar to all who work with words, to all acquainted with words in action. The difference it makes, the extent to which this matters when it happens, vary with different types of writing. It is above all a property of literary texts. Novels are never quite what they pretend to be; all who read poetry know the thrill of feeling the rhythms of phrase and sentence play across the formal pattern of line and stanza – 'the sounds of sense', as Robert Frost put it, 'breaking across the regular beat of the metre'.

*   *   *

You wouldn't call this literature:

> The need for determined efforts to accomplish substantial waste reduction objectives must be strongly supported by the University community. The fundamental principles of the University's new waste reduction policy are (1) Reduction: reduction at source is of primary importance in avoiding the generation of waste altogether; (2) Reuse: the use of an item again in its original form for the same, or for a different purpose; (3) Recycling: the separation of material at source to facilitate its return to reusable material. These three are known as the waste management hierarchy. Reduction is better than reuse, and reuse is better than recycling.
>
> (University of Toronto Staff Newsletter, 1990)

Or this:

> Until Section VI, where the concept of anomaly was first introduced, the terms 'revolution' and 'extraordinary science' may have seemed equivalent. More important, neither term may have seemed to mean more than 'non-normal science', a circularity that will have bothered at least a few readers. In practice, it need not have done so. We are about to discover that a similar circularity is characteristic of scientific theories. Bothersome or not, however, that circularity is no longer unqualified. This section of the essay and the two preceding have educed numerous criteria of a breakdown in normal scientific activity, criteria that do not at all depend upon whether breakdown is succeeded by revolution.
>
> (Thomas S. Kuhn, *The Structure of Scientific Revolutions*, 2nd edn 1970, 90)

Both passages display skill in the use of words; both are dominated by the conviction that the matter in hand is worth making as clear as possible. If I invite you to regard them as what I shall call 'everyday uses of language', that is not to deny or ignore these properties. Nor is there any suggestion that they deal with topics we should want to discuss every day. I call them everyday uses of language because they are examples of the way words work when no more than practical, everyday, down-to-earth matters are at issue. No layers of meaning, no secret meanings; these texts mean what they say, not more, not less. None of the tricks that poets use. Nothing to warn us of more going on than meets the eye's first glance.

* * *

Literature is more than words at work at everyday tasks:

> To be or not to be – that is the question:
> Whether 'tis nobler in the mind to suffer
> The slings and arrows of outrageous fortune,
> Or to take arms against a sea of troubles,
> And by opposing end them . . .
>
> (Shakespeare, *Hamlet*, Act 3, Scene 1)

Hamlet is arguing with himself, not putting a case to others. Can he justify his present failure 'to be' (his failure to take decisive action; to act, as we say, 'like a man')? Is Stoic, silent endurance not perhaps 'nobler' than open useless defiance when defiance can result only in death? Defiance, death, in Hamlet's present mood of frustration, represent the attractive way out – if only Hamlet could be sure death did mean an end to it all. All sorts of things are going on in these powerful, compact lines. Their object is not to put a case (still less, to settle the issue), but to represent the state of mind of a dramatic character. The conventions of dramatic monologue, the poetic form, permit, encourage, a compression, an imaginative richness beyond what would be possible, or good manners, in everyday objective prose.

Take this poem by D. H. Lawrence:

> And who has seen the moon, who has not seen
> Her rise from out the chamber of the deep,
> Flushed and grand and naked, as from the chamber
> Of finished bridegroom, seen her rise and throw
> Confession of delight upon the wave,
> Littering the waves with her own superscription
> Of bliss, till all her lambent beauty shakes towards us
> Spread out and known at last, and we are sure
> That beauty is a thing beyond the grave,
> That perfect, bright experience never falls
> To nothingness, and time will dim the moon
> Sooner than our full consummation here
> In this odd life will tarnish or pass away?
> (D. H. Lawrence, 'Moonrise', *Complete Poems*, 193)

Lawrence's poem is a kind of non-sonnet, in which, for all his passionate commitment to his theme, Lawrence places himself at an ironic distance from the grand manner he affects. The rhetorical opening 'who has seen the moon? . . .' is impatiently thrust aside by common sense ('who has not seen her? . . .'). The splendid, compelling sensuous imagery of the following lines challenges, mocks almost, the conventions of sonnet form: thirteen lines instead of fourteen; resonant internal rhymes ('seen', 'rise', 'chamber'); the transition from opening octet to moralizing sestet displaced to the middle of line 8 ('and we are sure . . .'); the conclusion structured by the traditional rhetorical device of the expanding triad of parallel clauses ('That beauty is a thing . . .', 'that perfect, bright experience . . .', 'and time will dim the moon . . .') – it would be too much of a good thing if we did not sense the mockery in Lawrence's surrender to his own eloquence. His starting point, I suspect, is Keats's sonnet 'When I have thoughts that I may cease to be'; he wants to show he can beat the Romantics at their own game – hands down; at the same time, his poem is a rejection of Romantic pessimism, and a passionate statement of Lawrence's belief in the enduring nature of human experience.

Shakespeare writes in the grand manner, Lawrence affects the lush Romantic style as an ironic strategy. Not all literary texts proclaim their status so openly. Let's take now three more matter-of-fact texts. Each is close to everyday English. And yet all three have this quality of more going on than meets the eye's first glance, the imagination (the writer's, then ours in response) made to work harder, the words made to play more complicated tricks than we expect from everyday texts.

First, some lines from a poem by Fleur Adcock:

> . . . We do not, in fact, fight like tigers.
> Look, the cubs are only playing . . . .
>   We hurt. We draw blood.
> The grown ones, too, do not fight. We may
> See them gliding out softly, at night,
> Together. They are going to kill
> Something else: not to hurt each other.
> Why should they tear gold and black striped fur,
> Gulp tigers' blood? They have other prey.
> We must admire their common sense . . . .
>   (Fleur Adcock, 'Tigers', in *Tigers*, 1967, 35)

A conversation piece. Lover says to lover, perhaps, 'Why must *we* fight like tigers? (the stress on *we* because somehow, in fact or in imagination, there are tigers there before them to watch). But the stress on *we* is already a first acknowledgement of a familiar cliché. The conversation piece becomes an ironic exploration of that cliché. Words working the way words work in a poem. Look at the last line: in real conversation, 'we must admire their common sense' (another cliché) would be thrown out as a rattle of syllables ending with a strong stress on *sense*, the tone of voice hardly rising above sarcasm (everybody knows tigers don't have common sense). In Fleur Adcock's poem, the beat of the iambic meter imposes a different rhythm, evens up the stresses, introduces a note of whimsy and ironic detachment: a stress on *admire* and on *common*, the stress on *sense* no stronger than the others.

Now take this:

> The word goes round Repins, the mumur goes round Lorenzinis,
> At Tattersalls, men look up from sheets of numbers,
> The Stock Exchange scribblers forget the chalk in their hands
> And men with bread in their pockets leave the Greek Club:
> There's a fellow crying in Martin Place. They can't stop him.
>
> The traffic in George Street is banked up for half a mile
> And drained of motion. The crowds are edgy with talk
> And more crowds come hurrying. Many run in the back streets
> Which minutes ago were busy main streets, pointing:
> There's a fellow weeping down there. No one can stop him.
> (Les A. Murray, 'An Absolutely Ordinary Rainbow')

Martin Place is the centre of downtown commercial Sydney. Les Murray imagines the almost unimaginable: a man weeping there inexplicably, uncontrollably while a crowd gathers round him; men drop what they are doing in the betting shop and the Stock Exchange, the habitués jump up from lunch in their clubs – all pour out to watch. You need only consider for a moment how you might go about structuring this idea as a short story to see that, what Murray has given us is words working as words work in a poem.

Finally, this:

Hale knew they meant to murder him before he had been in Brighton three hours. With his inky fingers and his bitten nails, his manner cynical and nervous, anybody could tell he didn't belong – belong to the early summer sun, the cool Whitsun wind off the sea, the holiday crowd. They came in by train from Victoria every five minutes, rocked down Queen's Road standing on the tops of the little local trams, stepped off in bewildered multitudes into fresh and glittering air: the new silver paint sparkled on the piers, the cream houses ran away into the west like a pale Victorian water-colour; a race in miniature motors, a band playing, flower gardens in bloom below the front, an aeroplane advertising something for the health in pale vanishing clouds across the sky.

(Graham Greene, *Brighton Rock*, Chapter 1 opening lines)

Prose, this time: the opening lines of the story of the murder of a seedy journalist by a teenage gang, and the strangely moving drama Greene weaves around that hypothesis. But a novel, not something that actually happened. Something more than report of fact. Hence the striking opening sentence, the coolly selective picture of the sort of mindless society aimlessly enjoying itself; the sort of milieu, we have been conditioned to suppose, in which the violence that is to follow easily takes root. Ostensibly, the details of the scene are those which are no more than casually observed by Greene's hero (he notes the 'aeroplane advertising something for the health' without troubling to take in the name of the product, or its nature).

Greene draws, of course, upon a well-established tradition:

Bishop Grantly died as he had lived, peaceably, slowly, without pain and without excitement. The breath ebbed from him almost imperceptibly, and for a month before his death, it was a question whether he were alive or dead.

A trying time was this for the archdeacon, for whom was designed the reversion of his father's see by those who then had the giving away of episcopal thrones. I would not be understood to say that the prime minister had in so many words promised the bishopric to Dr Grantly. He was too discreet a man for that. There is a proverb with reference to the killing of cats, and those who know anything of either high or low government places, will be well aware that a promise may be made without positive words, and that an expectant may be put into the highest state of encouragement, though the great man on whose breath he hangs may have done no more than whisper that 'Mr So-and-so is certainly a rising man'.

(Trollope, Barchester Towers, Chapter 1)

Trollope, on his favourite subject, the Church of England by law established. But even if we didn't know that, we'd recognize this at once as fiction – not a true account of things that actually happened. Not even Lytton Strachey (whose attempts to 'debunk' biography by replacing the ostensibly impartial judgement of traditional history and biography with the more intimate approach of the novel) treats his eminent deceased with such urbanely irreverent amusement.

* * *

Many uses of words aren't literature, some are. What makes it so easy to tell the difference? What is it that is particular about the use of words we call literature? You can't say that literary texts have been put together with more care than other texts because that isn't always the case:

If any Fellow of the College shall pertinaciously disturb the concord or discipline of the College, or shall wilfully violate or neglect to comply with any of the Statutes of the College for the time being, it shall be the duty of the Council, on proof of such misconduct, to admonish such Fellow, and if, notwithstanding such admonition, such Fellow shall contumaciously persist in such misconduct, it shall be competent for the Council (other than the Fellow whose conduct is impugned, if a member of the Council) to suspend such Fellow from the enjoyment of the benefits and advantages

of his Fellowship for such time as they shall think fit or to deprive him altogether of his Fellowship.
(St John's College, Cambridge, *Stat.* XXVIII[4])

The Fellows who put that text together plainly took more than ordinary care: the matter was important; they were men trained to value words put together well; they were particular about the words they used. That doesn't make it literature.

We expect poets or novelists to be particular about the words *they* use. The more particular they are about the words they use, the better the novel or poem is likely to be. But there's more to it than that. A bad novel is still a novel of sorts. A silly, sentimental poem, though worthless as poetry, is still a poem; shoddy as the writing is, its only claim on our attention is as a poem. Whether good or bad, whether the claim on our attention is justified or not, novels, poems, plays deal with the writer's experience of the world in a way which sets such texts apart from other texts; whatever the form – novel, poem, play – whatever the differences between this novel and other novels, this poem and other poems, all such texts have something in common: *they work*, in so far as they work at all, *in a particular way*. If they didn't work that way, there'd be no novel, no poem; it's because they work that way that reading them constitutes a literary experience.

* * *

The difference between literary texts and other texts is like that between cars and trucks. Cars come in all sorts of shapes and sizes; many of the things they have in common (wheels, tyres, engines, windscreens . . .) are found also in trucks. And yet, for us, cars and trucks are two quite different kinds of vehicle. A visitor from Mars might find the distinction hard to grasp. But for us the difference is obvious because cars and trucks occupy different places in our lives: the different use we put them to keeps them apart in our minds. It's the different place literary texts occupy in our minds that makes it easy for us to keep literary texts and non-literary texts apart.

Recognizing a text as literature means recognizing that what we're being offered is a literary experience, one that calls for a different kind of *attention* to the words used. The way we read a poem or a novel differs from the way we read an article in a newspaper or an encyclopaedia. We prepare ourselves to think harder, more imaginatively – more responsively. The structure of words which makes up a literary text not only has *meaning*, it is meaningful in a special kind of way; reading it involves exposing our minds to an unusually complex use of words; in that structure there has, somehow, been captured, waiting for us to release it, something different from everyday uses of words.

Reading the newspaper, reading letters – these are things we do all the time, they're as easy and as natural as walking; it isn't usually necessary to spend time explaining what's involved. Reading a poem or a novel is like swimming: it's an activity that has to be learnt; doing it well means training and practice. The experience, the pleasure to be got from it, aren't there waiting for us; they're only there if we know how to bring the text on the page before us to life by the way we read it.

Only the reader who has discovered how novels and poems work can read a novel or a poem with responsive enjoyment: some discover it for themselves in a flash of enlightenment; for most of us it is something that dawns slowly upon us; we improve with practice, find it useful to think and talk about what we're doing.

* * *

A novel or a poem works the way it does because it has been put together to work that way. That needn't mean it has been put together according to rules consciously present in the writer's mind: most writers work by instinct – an instinct that comes from long practice; with that instinct goes a very special ability (which comes into operation at the height of the process of composition and which we call inspiration) to draw upon and adapt everything they've ever read, and make of it something which is fresh and their own, a structure of words which is both complex and unique.

Reading such texts is a matter of practice. Only practice can build up the mental stamina needed to read with responsive enjoyment. It's a matter of trained expectations. Untrained readers have no expectations. They meet *Paradise Lost* as they meet a visiting celebrity from another country; they are in no position to tell what is strange to them from what is peculiar to the individual. Where so much is strange, discriminating reaction to what is distinctive is impossible. Many readers never get beyond this initial, exhausting confusion.

Reading a novel or a poem is an acquired skill. But the process can be helped if you understand what's involved. Because natural readers are in the minority, because most readers work less hard at reading than most good writers work at writing, explanation of the typical ways in which poems and novels work (explanation, not laying down rules) is worth while – worth while because it helps.

II

When you read a novel or a poem, the meaning you read into the string of words before you on the printed page exists only in your mind. It comes into existence because you can respond – not just to the words, but to the grammatical links between the words. To do only that, however, is to do no more than scan the text; to skim through it as you skim through a newspaper – or a novel that has started to bore you and has ceased (or never started, perhaps) to work as a novel. For a text to work in your mind as a novel or a poem, you have to feel as well the *rhythm* of thought and syntax – the way the text would sound if you read it aloud; the way, if you read it silently, it sounds to some inward ear; the movement, the phrasing of the thought; the variations in pitch and tempo, the hesitations, the accelerations, the meaning you read into the text demands. We lack precise words to describe the experience; probably, that hard-worked word 'rhythm' will serve as well as any as a shorthand description. (See *List of Critical Terms*.) For we know what we are talking about. Just as we know how it feels when we get lost in a text; when the rhythm falters, or seems to go astray and we have to begin again; or when we listen to a reader stumble through a text the meaning of which has eluded his grasp.

A sentence from a novel by Margaret Drabble can be as elaborately structured syntactically and rhythmically as a Shakespearean sonnet. Liz Headland's friends are streaming, dozens, scores of them, to her New Year's Eve party in her huge London house; they are the symbol of her success, after twenty years of marriage (a marriage now threatened, though Liz does not know it yet – but will know it before the evening and the chapter are over); for the moment, all that nags her thoughts, mars her pleasure in her success, is her mother far away in the North, the mother who symbolizes all that Liz has had to struggle all her life to leave behind. The sentence is built around a succession of 'therefore's ('therefore' because Liz has set it all in motion by her invitation):

> And *therefore* grumbling couples complain in cars on their way to Harley Street from the Home Counties and beg one another not to let them drink too much: *therefore* Esther and Aliz meet and laugh on a street corner a few hundred yards away: *therefore* stepchildren muster and stepparents-in-law assemble: *therefore* Liz Headland's mother sits alone, ever alone, untelephoned, distant, incomprehending, incomprehended, remote, mad, long mad, imprisoned, secret, silent, silenced, listening to the silence of her house.
>
> (Margaret Drabble, *The Radiant Way*, Chapter 1)
> [italics added]

A virtuoso passage, slipped in as the novel begins to gather momentum – a whole novel pitched at this level of intensity would be intolerable. First, three clauses each introduced by 'therefore', each with two verbs ('complain . . . and beg', 'meet and laugh', 'muster and . . . assemble'), each clause shorter than the one before (the third, only two subjects and their verbs). Then, a fourth 'therefore' and an abrupt change of key, the rhythm broken, the syntactical structure reduced to a single verb (the stark 'sits alone') and an audacious, savage string of adjectives and participles (thirteen of them), the phrasing of which we are left to find for ourselves – one possible reading is to group them in a four plus three threes, leading up to that final cruel alliteration; then, a less tightly tensioned phrase to round off the paragraph:

alone, ever alone, untelephoned, distant,
incomprehending, incomprehended, remote,
mad, long mad, imprisoned,
secret, silent, silenced,
listening to the silence of her house.

The sentence is a representation of Liz's thoughts as she sits at her dressing table; but the representation of the stream of consciousness is given a structure of its own.

* * *

What comes into existence in your mind is never the same as what existed in the mind of the person who put the text together. How could it be? No human being ever understands what another says quite in the way the speaker intends. Though the need to explain our actions to others, to receive an explanation of theirs, requires us to conduct our lives as if it were otherwise, there are times when we feel in our heart of hearts, no less than Henry James's Strether, that 'nothing ever was in fact – for anyone else – explained. One went through vain motions, but mostly it was a waste of life'. However hard writer and reader try, the writer never quite gets across to the reader what the writer thinks or feels. Writer and reader are always to some extent at cross-purposes: for the reader, the text is a starting-point, for the author the text is the final product of a process of thought – in the end, the writer settled for those words, in that order, making those statements.

Readers differ, moreover. You and I set out from the same structure of words, and make different things of it. Even though we've the same printed text in front of us, the understanding each of us takes from it, each time we read it, is always to some extent our creation. T. S. Eliot's paradox that every new novel or poem modifies our understanding of all the poems or novels we've read is well known.[1] We can put it the other way round: our understanding of every new novel or poem (new, that is, to us) is expanded, filled out, by our memory of all the other novels or poems we've read. Each new significant addition modifies our understanding of all we've

[1] 'Tradition and the individual talent', 1917.

read; each addition is interpreted in the light of the system to which we admit it when we read it.

* * *

These are basic facts of language. In everyday life they may be exasperating. But that's the way it is. 'We have to cease to think', said Nietzsche in a characteristic over-statement, 'if we refuse to do it in the prison-house of language.' However, original the thought, the formulation of it is bound down by the way our language works (its grammar) and the limits to what words can be made to mean. There are those for whom all expression is a reduction to cliché, to stereotyped, second-hand, shop-soiled phrase and opinion. Fortunately, there are also those who strain at their bonds, who can take liberties, force concessions from their enslaver; work outside or beyond what it occurs to the rest of us to attempt; can exploit cliché with an ironic detachment. If words had fixed, clear-cut meanings, if all statement were clichés, if we all said exactly what we meant, we should all think like computers, and the world would be a duller place than it is. The inexactness of language, the impossibility of pinning words down, the free-dom within the prison-house – these are what makes literature possible.

   This is as true of the larger structures as it is of word and phrase. No writer of genius hopes to write a work that is wholly original: complete originality is the dream of the artistically naive, the refuge of the artistically incompetent. All literary creation (all art – all social behaviour of any kind for that matter) is a balance struck between the expected, the conventional (the prevailing conventions of that literary form, the prevailing conventions of the community) and the expres-sion, or assertion, of his (or her) individuality by the indi-vidual. All genuine creativity demands, in some measure, resistance to convention, challenge, provocation, invitation to accept what is new, strange, confusing or disturbing by reason of its failure to conform – and is yet so good, so undeniably successful, as not to be easily rejected. The provocation need not be strident; it may be subtle (more a refinement of technique than a flagrant rejection of techniques). And of course it may *not* be successful. But artistic expression wholly within the prevailing conventions (unless the object is to mock those conventions by pretending to adopt them) is sterile.

The trick is to make your chosen form work for you; to 'make the form your own', so that *your* sonnet isn't just a reduction of your thought to the conventions of sonnet-form, but a structure of words, syntax and metre with a rhythm of its own (a rhythm that signals *your* presence within the form), tensioned by the energy of the meaning restrained within it, straining against those conventions. The extreme case, perhaps, is ironic exploitation of form: Coleridge's exploitation, for example, of the archaic conventions of border-ballad in the *Ancient Mariner*.

* * *

'What comes into existence in your mind is never the same as what existed in the mind of the person who put the text together.' If the poet is a maker, we the readers of the poem are makers too; the poet puts the words together, we read meaning into those words; the two acts of creation are complementary; reading the poem is a process of construction, of building a consistency out of the string of statements; it is also a process of *deconstruction*, of taking the built thing apart; a reduction, a selection, between all the text has to offer, of what to concentrate our attention on; a process of submission to the expansions of the text touched off as we read – some central to the act of expression itself, many purely personal to the reader.

A reflective silent reading of Hamlet's soliloquy may suggest as you read the line:

Or to take arms against a sea of troubles . . .

the tale of King Canute's futile defiance of the advancing tide. The words:

And by opposing end them . . .

may perhaps suggest Virgil's Aeneas rushing 'mindlessly into battle' (*arma amens capio*) against the Greek invader, courting

death; or some other of the many passages in Virgil's poem
where surrender to the heroic impulse – because death is the
easy way out – is shown as the natural reaction of the trained
soldier to a situation he cannot otherwise cope with. It cannot
be said that these are irrelevant reactions; they may even be
historically 'correct' (associations in Shakespeare's own mind,
associations he wished to provoke, perhaps). But it cannot be
said they are necessary deconstructions of Shakespeare's text;
or even, for that matter, deconstructions that will, or should,
occur to us in subsequent readings.

Every reading of a text is, in some degree, individual,
unique, unrepeatable. We do not read a novel or a poem a
second time merely to repeat the experience; every reading is a
fresh experience, a fresh, provisional limitation of the potential of the text, accepted in order that we can hold the text in
our minds that way this time. Not merely do our reactions
change from one reading to the next: our own performance of
the text, the rhythm we give it as we read it, will also change,
adapting itself to a new emerging understanding of the text.

It's quite a different case from listening again to a recording
of the poem. Because the recorded performance never varies,
because the recording represents a performance we have
outgrown, it quickly comes to bore or irritate us. Because it is
completely predictable, it stands in the path of any fresh
understanding.

*   *   *

The fact that a poem is not something to be pinned down does
not mean that you and I are free to make what we like of it;
can take out of the text any meaning we see in it. True, there
are those who seem to come close to maintaining this. Indeed,
few issues in contemporary criticism have generated more
heat, or more confusion.

To read into a line or a sentence a meaning that goes
against the syntax (to take a noun as a verb, a subject as an
object) may open up intriguing avenues of meaning; but to
persist in the mistake, once you realize it, is cheating. To
entertain a sense a word could not have had for the writer (a
sense that alters the meaning but does not destroy it) is a

different case. The mistake is less clear-cut, perhaps unavoidable. Shifts of meaning, new overtones of meaning that do not threaten the meaning the words must bear in their context, may add a fresh dimension which we may feel reluctant to discard; to confine our understanding of a work of art to that which the artist who made it possessed of it, is, most critics writing today would agree, an unjustifiable limitation of the work, even if it were achievable.

The ground may seem to be slipping from under the feet of any critic who maintains our first duty is to respect (as far as we can) the meaning the maker of the text built into it. There is, however, an argument which we can bring forward here, one which is increasingly heard from critics. The argument appeals to what I have called the rhythm of the text, the rhythm of the thought as expressed by the words of the text. A sentence in a poem or a novel is not like a proposition in logic – a self-contained structure of words related only by syntax, divorced from any context, which we can bend any way words and syntax will allow. In the 'real' world in which poets write poems, and novelists write novels, no sentence is fully meaningful until the reader has discovered a way of reading it that brings the inert words and syntax into active life. This is true of all statements that reach out beyond the immediately obvious into some frame of reference to the 'real' world, but particularly true of the statements we find in poems and in novels, the point of which is often less than obvious – unexpected, even paradoxical, until we can relate it to an attitude hinted at or implied.

Take Robert Frost's sonnet 'Acquainted with the Night':

I have been one acquainted with the night.
I have walked out in rain – and back in rain.
I have outwalked the furtherest city light . . . .

There is no way short of outright violence to the text to read Frost's poem as though it were something said to the rhythm of casual conversation ('I've always liked a long walk on a wet night'). No way of distorting the slow, plangent rhythm into the breezy, relaxed rhythm of Robert Graves's lover striding round a whole mountainside to work off his feelings after a lovers' tiff:

> Some of you may know, others perhaps can guess
> How it is to walk all night through summer rain . . .
> To circle a mountain, and then limp home again . . . .
> ('Around the Mountain', opening lines)

confident, six stanzas later, that, next morning, he can expect the sun to shine again:

> His house looms up; the eaves drip drowsily;
> The windows blaze to a resolute sunrise.

What we make as readers of these two poems is dictated by the rhythm of thought each imposes: Graves's poem is a splendid exercise in the Donjuanesque; Frost's poem is a moving, disturbing, oblique expression of a deep-seated anguish left unstated.

* * *

To claim that Frost's poem, or Graves's poem, 'means what it means to me', if by that we mean we are free to read into the text any meaning we like, is plainly untrue. We are not free agents; we have to come to terms with the restraints the text itself imposes.

Like the famous slogan of the 1940s and 50s (devised to deride the New Critics) 'there are no poets, only poems', the slogan 'a text means what it means to me' first gained currency as a mischievous simplification of a critical position conservative critics found it impossible to take seriously. The new avant-garde accepted the challenge, and adopted the slogan as a provocative statement of a position they were prepared to defend. The slogan caught on. That it was a provocation to see things in a new light was lost sight of: it quickly acquired the status of revealed truth, the complexities of the issue forgotten in the heat of battle.

Backed up by equally heady catch-phrases ('all readings are misreadings', 'some misreadings are more interesting than others'), the slogan 'a text means what it means to me' became the rallying cry for a revolt of intellectuals against a sterile intellectualism which, it was claimed, had come to dominate the critical establishment; it was part of the general revolt of the 1960s and 70s. In particular, it was a revolt against the fashion for reducing a literary work to a summary of its supposed imaginative content; in pursuit of a recurring, dominant image (the symbol of a single basic idea), isolation of which was supposed to function as the key that unlocked the whole work, the work itself was left behind, or tossed aside. Finding the image and turning the key was called 'interpretation' – a sense of the word that had little connection with the detailed explication of a literary text to which the term 'interpretation' had traditionally been applied. It was this sense Susan Sontag (a product of the Chicago New Critics of the 1950s) had in mind in her essay 'Against interpretation' which became famous in the late 60s and 70s. (See *List of Critical Terms*.)

Not unreasonably, it was protested that such a reduction was a high-handed, arbitrary, élitist way to deal with a work of the creative imagination. A poem or a novel is more than a puzzle to be solved. It is a complex sensory experience as well as an intellectual experience; any reduction of it is partly to destroy the experience; drastic reduction means total destruction.

* * *

Those who play any critical game that distracts them (and us) from constant reference back to the structure of words before us on the printed page and the experience that structure has to offer, who set themselves any goal other than full possession of that structure of words, break of course no law of the land, however ruthlessly they put theory before practical criticism.

But to maintain seriously that a text means whatever it means to you, the reader (intending by that – not an obvious truism about the limitations of individual readers, but an assertion of your right to read into the text any meaning that occurs to you) is to trample on the claim – the claim of literary texts in general – to be taken as a social act. Not an act of communication in any straightforward sense of the word 'communication'; but a structure possessing constant reference to the world of things and ideas outside itself; a structure which is accessible, which rewards acceptance, as the product of an articulate human intelligence. To disregard this status of a novel or a poem as a social act is to put the pleasure we get from reading it on a level with the pleasure we get from a sunset, or a mountain-top covered in snow.

* * *

In every sentence of a novel or a poem, if we know how to read it, we feel the speaking voice of the writer, determined by the rhythm of the text itself, the way the words demand to be read – not the way these words might be read in a context that worked differently. This is true even of things quoted by the writer: though not (we are invited to believe) the writer's own words, we hear them inflected by the writer's speaking voice, given overtones, an emphasis, they would not otherwise have. George Steiner calls this the 'real presence' of the writer. Umberto Eco, in a recent recantation of earlier, more 'permissive' attitudes and approaching the problem from within a more 'objective' conceptual framework, speaks of the 'intention of the work'. The word 'intention' is charged of course by Eco with ironic overtones: it had been a major objective of the 1940s and 50s to expel 'authorial intention' from critical consideration, to assert the independence of the finished work from the will of its author. The new conventional wisdom, which Eco seeks to consolidate, is that the text has a will of its own: there is a way it seems to us to *want* to work; we feel we do violence to the text if we read it differently.

A poem or a novel is a structuring of experience by one human being which becomes a structuring of experience in the mind of another human being. A well written text is complex enough to promote variations in the way we read it; but we are not free to read it in any way we choose. If there is no one right way, there are wrong ways: embark on one of these and the text begins to sound false to your inward ear, warning you of the violence you are doing to the poem (or whatever it is you are reading) by reading a meaning (whether exciting or

simply inadequate) into a line or a sentence where it does not
fit.

True, the obligation to read a text as a social act is never
absolute. Writers, if they do not often think as other people,
think none the less within a conceptual framework (what I
shall call a 'field of significance') which their creation can
outlive, or transcend. The really powerful works of the
creative imagination often puzzle their contemporaries; it
takes a generation, or longer, before they begin to explode in
the minds, to fire the imagination, of those who read them.

They possess too a curious capacity to adapt themselves to
circumstances. The generation that lived through the war in
Vietnam read Virgil's *Aeneid* differently from Victorian
England, saw in it a 'message' (that the need to win corrupts
moral standards) to which Victorians were blind. The truly
powerful text works like a virus, adapting itself to different
resistances through a series of mutations. We don't just read
Henry James's *The Ambassadors* differently from the way
Americans read it in 1900: the work adapts itself to our
capacity to understand it – or to be provoked by it. To see
James's novel in a different light (remembering, for example,
all those Americans who, since James's time, have made Paris
their spiritual home) is not to deny, or diminish, James's
presence in the text. Our changed perspective, our altered
sensibilities, are more likely to enhance that presence. Inevitably, our new reading (our changed 'reception', as some
critics call it, of the text) borders sometimes on a misreading.
But it is one important, legitimate way in which literature
works.

* * *

The fact is that literary texts offer more than a message
transmitted and received. The transmission of information is
neutral, impersonal – these at any rate are the goals aimed at;
it is a wholly artificial use of language, if one increasingly
common in the technological society in which we live. Literature is not concerned with the transmission of information,
but the sharing of experience between author and reader,
within a context of feelings and attitudes invoked in support of

a point of view, sometimes presented for reappraisal, sometimes passionately challenged.

Take Shakespeare's sonnet 'When I have seen by Time's
fell hand defac'd':

> When I have seen by Time's fell hand defac'd
> The rich proud cost of outworn buried age;
> When sometime lofty towers I see down raz'd,
> And brass eternal slave to mortal rage;
> When I have seen the hungry ocean gain
> Advantage on the kingdom of the shore,
> And the firm soil win of the watery main,
> Increasing store with loss and loss with store:
> When I have seen such interchange of state,
> Or state itself confounded to decay,
> Ruin hath taught me thus to ruminate –
> That Time will come and take my love away.
>   This thought is as a death, which cannot choose
>   But weep to have that which it fears to lose.
>
> (Shakespeare, Sonnet 64)

The sonnet is 'about' (we might say) the conflicting
emotions of the lover in the face of the evidence all around him
that nothing lasts. But to say that is a poor substitute for
Shakespeare's poem. If it were only a matter of getting that
message across, we'd expect him to go about the matter more
efficiently. The sonnet is more a process of reflection; the
emotions are more complex, more sombre, the expression of
them more measured than in – say – Herrick's tongue-in-
cheek advice to young girls to show themselves more co-
operative before it is too late – advice which calls for a
sprightlier rhythm, a more confidently assertive syntax, a less
disturbing imagery:

> Gather ye rosebuds while ye may,
>   Old Time is still a-flying:
> And this same flower that smiles today
>   Tomorrow will be dying . . . .

Then be not coy, but use your time,
 And, while ye may, do marry;
For, having lost but once your prime,
 You may forever tarry.
       (Herrick, 'To the Virgins, to make much of Time')

* * *

What makes a text a literary text isn't that it has a definite, fixed structure; that it's there, written down, waiting to be read; that it's clear, well put together (supposing it is these things). The memorandum on recycling shares these properties with Shakespeare's 'When I have seen by Time's fell hand defac'd'. The difference isn't that the memorandum is the product of a humbler artistry. It is that it is an artistry that could have been dispensed with.

An academic administrator can take pride in drafting recommendations to colleagues, can go to some trouble to make them elegant as well as clear. But he (or she) need not do this. Indeed, the result, as in the present case, is apt to strike us as an overkill. In a different context (a novel by Robertson Davies perhaps) the same words might work as parody (the academic who dots every i and crosses every t) or as satire (a betrayal of academic standards, an over-diligent revision of priorities in pursuit of the trendy). The encouragement to read the words that way would come from that context. It would be the capacity of the narrative to make them work that way which would justify the pseudo-quotation. Normally, administrative memoranda, newspaper reports, books on scientific subjects have a more self-evident justification: clear statement of what is proposed or recommended; clear statement of what took place; clear exposition of a theory, or the arguments against an existing theory. Such texts have an evident social function: even if clumsily written, dully expressed, they'd discharge that function – as is often the case. Legal texts in particular often strike the layman as dull or clumsy because those who drafted them wanted to plug every loophole, wanted to leave no doubt about what was intended.

Such texts have, in short, a practical use. They are a means
to an end. That's not to say literary texts have no practical
use. Though there are many, no doubt, who would say that, it
is a philistine view of existence to regard all that stimulates the
life of the mind as unimportant. What we can say is that there
is a very drastic reversal of priorities: a literary text exists in its
own right; it need serve no immediate, easily stateable
practical end; our normal impulses to act on what we read are
suspended. A novel can enhance, deepen, extend our
understanding of the way the world works; a poem, however
paradoxical, if it works as a poem, may somehow force us to
admit the essential truth of the paradox asserted. These are
qualities we may expect; but, even denied them, we will not
abandon a novel or a poem that works as a novel or a poem.
What is indispensable is a quality which can readily be
dispensed with in a newspaper report, an administrative
circular, a legal text, or the like: the intellectual pleasure, the
quickening of our emotional life, the compulsion to surrender
to the process of reading a text that will not let us go. If a novel
or a poem fails here, it fails as a novel or a poem.

III

A literary text demands from us a particular kind of attention.
The layout of Keats's poem 'To Autumn' on the printed page,
our expectation that we're going to listen to a *poem* touches off
in our minds an instant change of gear – we are no longer
cruising, but taking an interesting, complicated stretch with
care:

> Where are the songs of Spring? Aye, where are they?
>   Think not of them, thou hast thy music too –
> While barréd clouds bloom the soft-dying day,
>   And touch the stubble-plains with rosy hue;
> Then in a wailful choir the small gnats mourn
>   Among the river sallows, borne aloft
>   Or sinking as the light wind lives or dies;

And full-grown lambs loud bleat from hilly bourn;
  Hedge-crickets sing; and now with treble soft
  The red-breast whistles from a garden-croft;
  And gathering swallows twitter in the skies.

Every time we take up a poem or a novel, we tune into the text we are about to read, as we tune into a television channel, with a quick flip of our mental controls: for each text we read we choose the setting of our mental controls experience has taught us to adopt for that kind of text; the *mental set* (as psychologists call it) determines both *what* we react to, what seem to us the *significant* characteristics of the text, and *how* we react to those characteristics. The practised reader knows how different types of text work; you become extraordinarily sensitive to small details in a text which make it different from all others you've read and can thus *place* a text – place it not only on a scale of quality, but place it in the tradition to which it claims allegiance; can judge its originality, the extent to which the text exploits the possibilities of that tradition; can react with a tuned sensitivity to *all* those properties which together make up the experience the text offers.

We can also misread a text – read it with the wrong mental set: usually a misreading is accidental; but not always. Take the following extract from a marine insurance policy:

And touching the Adventures and Perils which the said Company are made liable unto or are intended to be made liable unto by this Insurance they are of the Seas Men-of-War Fire Enemies Pirates Rovers Thieves Jettisons Letters of Mart and Counter Mart Surprisals Takings at Sea Arrests Restraints and Detainments of all Kings Princes and Peoples of what Nation Condition of Quality soever Barratry of the Master and Mariners and of all other Perils Losses and Misfortunes that have or shall come to the Hurt Detriment or Damage of the aforesaid subject matter of this Insurance or any part thereof.

And in case of any Loss or Misfortune it shall be lawful to the Insured their Factors Servants and Assigns to sue labour and travel for in and about the Defence Safeguard and Recovery of the aforesaid subject matter of this Insurance . . .

The significance you read into a text as a result of the mental set you choose can turn studiously neutral statement aimed at covering every possible contingency into deadpan irony (you read the clauses of the policy in that case in the bored tone of one for whom such language is all part of the day's work), or social satire – or comic extravaganza (emphasizing all the repetitions, making the most of all the unfamiliar technical terms). With some effort of conscious self-deception, you can transform the dispassionate legal text into one that is hilarious, laden, even, with lascivious overtones.

It is the way we read a text which brings the text to life; this is as true of our silent reading of a text to ourselves as it is when we read the text aloud to others. Normally, the choice of mental set doesn't lie with us, but is selected for us by the text itself; though we haven't seen this text before, we recognize the *form* (the kind of text it is), and read it accordingly. The process is so familiar, so much a matter of course, we can even be tricked by the form of a text into reading meaning into words where no meaning exists. Nonsense verse works this way:

> Sweet Hernia on the heights of Plasticine
> Sings to the nylon songs of Brassière:
> The very aspirins listen, as they lean
> Against the vitreous wind, to her sad air.
> I see the bloom of mayonnaise she holds
> Coloured like roofs of far-away Shampoo.
> Its asthma sweetens Earth! Oh, it enfolds
> The alum land from Urine to Cachou!
> One last wild gusset, then she's lost in night!
> And dusk the dandruff dims, and anthracite!
>   (Edward Blishen, reprinted in *New Statesman Competitions*,
>   ed. Arthur Marshall)

Sham poets often play this trick on us: impressive-sounding matter essentially worthless as poetry – or even meaningless – is made to look like poetry by setting it out in lines with a ragged right-hand margin as if it were poetry, thus inviting the mental set appropriate to poetry. This is what Harold Stewart and James McAuley did when they perpetrated the Ern Malley poems which hoodwinked many people, including the editor of the literary periodical who published them in 1944. The victims of the hoax were guilty of a mistake in mental set, accepting as meaningful and significant texts which were neither.

The opposite mistake is to read poetry with the gear control locked in overdrive (the setting appropriate for reading the newspaper, or the kind of novel that can be consumed casually in the train); we skim along the line of sense (looking for the 'meaning', or just trying to decide whether we like the poem) – and then, by misreading the poem (by reading it with the wrong mental set), we miss the experience the poem has to offer. Many good novels (the kind that aren't written to be casually consumed) are misread by many readers in much the same way.

* * *

Mental set involves a decision by the reader about both the *form* and the *significance* of the text. (See *List of Critical Terms*.) the text is a poem (or a text the reader takes to be a poem), it's largely a matter of deciding how to recapture the *tone* of the poet's speaking voice. With a novel, it's more a matter of piecing together, as we go, a coherent understanding of the narrative we're reading: we don't any longer even imagine ourselves performing a novel to an audience. The decisions we take about the text affect the nature of our response to it. The mental set with which we watch a play isn't the one we'd adopt if it were all happening in real life: our sense of emotional and intellectual involvement may be intense; the dramatic experience may be totally absorbing; yet always, at the back of our unconscious minds, we're aware that what's happening on the stage is only make-believe; this almost totally submerged awareness inhibits our normal reactions, detaches us from the events being enacted, places a barrier between them and us. Nobody jumps on the stage to prevent Othello from murdering Desdemona. When the murder is over, instead of our normal impulse to action, the feeling that justice must be done, the wrong righted, we watch the play end with that curiously relaxed mental response which Aristotle calls catharsis. Those who minimize the danger of TV incitement to violence make much of this – perhaps more than is justified.

When we read a novel, our mental set similarly inhibits our reaction to what has supposedly happened. The literary experience isn't necessarily less intense. However, many novelists encourage a sense of detachment by implying a tone in the narrator's voice which would be offensive if the events narrated (with their consequences for the happiness or the misery of the participants) were real; the tone produces in us the literary counterpart of dramatic catharsis. Critics usually call this 'distancing'. (See *List of Critical Terms*.) Trollope's archly ironic narrative of the political manoeuvring behind the election of his bishop shows the distancing process at work:

Such a whisper had been made, and was known by those who heard it to signify that the cares of the diocese of Barchester should not be taken out of the hands of the archdeacon. The then prime minister was all in all at Oxford, and had lately passed a night at the house of the master of Lazarus. Now the master of Lazarus – which is, by the bye, in many respects the most comfortable, as well as the richest college at Oxford, – was the archdeacon's most intimate friend and most trusted counsellor. On the occasion of the prime minister's visit, Dr Grantly was of course present, and the meeting was very gracious. On the following morning Dr Gwynne, the master, told the archdeacon that in his opinion the thing was settled.

At this time the bishop was quite on his last legs; but the ministry also were tottering. Dr Grantly returned from Oxford happy and elated, to resume his place in the palace, and to continue to perform for the father the last duties of a son; which, to give him his due, he performed with more tender care than was to be expected from his usual somewhat wordly manners.

(Trollope, *Barchester Towers*, Chapter 1)

Distancing is perhaps even commoner in poems. The argument of a poem might strike us as ridiculous, scandalous, unacceptable in all sorts of ways, if we mistook the significance of the poem – didn't *accept* it as stringing a line of sense along which the poet's intellect can dance, *involving* us, while the poem does to us what a witty, ingenious poem can do. Take Donne's poem upbraiding the rising sun for disturbing lovers' pleasures:

> Busy old fool, unruly Sun,
> Why dost thou thus,
> Through windows, and through curtains, call on us?
> Must to thy motions lovers' seasons run?
> Saucy pedantic wretch, go chide
> Late school-boys and sour prentices,
> Go tell Court-huntsmen that the King will ride,
> Call country ants to harvest offices;
> Love, all alike, no season knows, nor clime
> Nor hours, days, months, which are the rags of time . . .
>
> (Donne, 'The Sun Rising')

IV

A text has *form*: it is a novel, or a poem, or a play; it's probably a particular kind of novel or poem – a historical novel, a novel written in the tradition of social realism, a thriller, perhaps; an epic poem, a lyric, or perhaps a sonnet; there are many more forms, some large and comprehensive, some quite specialized. In addition a text has its own individual *structure*: it is those words, those sentences, those lines of verse, in that order; it's that particular novel, that particular poem.

Form is what a text has in common with other texts put together according to the same rules or conventions; it's because we recognize the form of a text as one we've met before that we know how to place the text now in front of us and prepare to read it accordingly. *Structure* is the detailed working out, within the conventions of the adopted form, of an original idea: structure is what makes a text unique, different from any other text we've read before.

In a poem that works as a poem, the form is fundamental; take the form away and the experience dissolves. If what is said could really be said equally well in prose, then the poem is a fraud. Form not backed up by structure likewise collapses: if the structure is not original, unique, but only a cheap, shoddy copy of other poems, the poem does not justify the pretensions of its form.

This is as true of novels (or plays) as it is of poems. We submit to Trollope's arch irony, we submit to Donne's intellectual fireworks, because we recognize the irony, the wit, as an integral part of the structure appropriate to that form. Take this passage from Defoe's *Moll Flanders*:

> He held me in talk so long, till at last he drew me out of the raffling place to the shop-door, and then to take a walk in the cloister, still talking of a thousand things cursorily without anything to the purpose. At last he told me that without compliment he was charmed with my company, and asked me if I durst trust myself in a coach with him; he told me he was a man of honour, and would not offer anything to me unbecoming him as such. I seemed to decline it a while, but suffered myself to be importuned a little, and then yielded.
>
> I was at a loss in my thoughts to conclude at first what this gentleman designed; but I found afterward he had had some drink in his head, and that he was not very unwilling to have some more. He carried me in the coach to the Spring Garden, at Knightsbridge, where we walked in the gardens, and he treated me very handsomely; but I found he drank very freely. He pressed me also to drink, but I declined it.
>
> Hitherto he kept his word with me, and offered me nothing amiss. We came away in the coach again, and he brought me into the streets, and by this time it was near ten o'clock at night, and he stopped the coach at a house where, it seems, he was acquainted, and where they made no scruple to show us upstairs into a room with a bed in it. At first I seemed to be unwilling to go up, but after a few words I yielded to that too, being indeed willing to see the end of it, and in hopes to make something of it as last. As for the bed, etc., I was not much concerned about that part.

Form and structure are indispensable to the success of Defoe's novel: the social realism is suspended in a web of fantasy – the irrepressible, opportunist, unscrupulous, successful whore whose hedonistic, self-centred moral vision bolsters up her belief in her own integrity, however unscrupulous she seems to us in her treatment of the men who come her way. A social historian who makes it his business to read *Moll Flanders* in pursuit of evidence about eighteenth-century social conditions must do so warily: his is a mental set which would normally be inappropriate, a misreading justified by special interest.

Or take these lines:

As the carriage drew away from the Circular Wharf Mr Stafford Merivale tapped the back of his wife's hand and remarked that they had done their duty.

'No one', Mrs Merivale replied, 'can accuse me of neglecting duty.' She might have pouted if inherent indolence had not prevailed, and a suspicion that those acquainted with her must know that her claim was not strictly true.

So she smoothed the kid into which her hands had been stuffed, and added, 'At least we were, I think, agreeably entertained. And that is always compensation for any kind of inconvenience. Miss Scrimshaw,' she asked, looking not quite at her friend, 'weren't we entertained?'

'Oh yes, *most* agreeably,' the latter answered in a rush, which transposed what must have been a deep voice into a higher, unnatural key. 'Living at such a distance nobody can fail to be refreshed by visitors from Home. The pity is when their visits are so brief.'

(Patrick White, *A Fringe of Leaves*, opening lines)

The first hundred pages of Patrick White's novel *A Fringe of Leaves* are, among other things, an elegant parody of the eighteenth- or nineteenth-century novel of manners: we have Fielding, or Jane Austen, transposed to early nineteenth-century Sydney; the double detachment of time and distance makes the irony of White's narrative manner more pointed when we read his novel knowing it was written in the 1970s. *A Fringe of Leaves* is a very literary text: one that appeals to connoisseurs as well as those who like a story well told.

But not all novels suggest other novels; the formal models don't have to come from literature: they can come, or seem to come, from life. Take the opening lines of Joyce Cary's *Not Honour More:*

> This is my statement, so help me God, as I hope to be hung. My name is Latter, James Vandeleur, late Captain 21st Hussars and District Officer Nigerian Political Service, retired, resident at Palm Cottage near Tarbiton, Devonshire, England, with wife and one child; also a visitor, Lord Nimmo, who occupied one room on ground floor.

The parody this time is of the kind of honest, no-nonsense, factually accurate report an officer in the British Colonial Service might attempt to write; he 'hopes to be hung' because he has killed Lord Nimmo, believing him to be his wife's lover. Joyce Cary takes trouble to do what Defoe took little trouble to do: he gives his character a speaking voice which is entirely plausible, entirely in character; 'the style is the man', as we say; we read Captain Latter's would-be factual record as unconscious deception of himself by a man incapable of comprehending the nature of the experience he has lived through, or the bizarre qualities of the man he killed. Form and structure are put to work – they're not just a garment thrown over crude prose. The prose is not in fact crude, but remarkably clear, fast-moving, compelling; the parody is more than parody; it has unmistakable features which mark it as literature.

Take the opening lines of D. H. Lawrence's first novel, *The White Peacock*:

> I stood watching the shadowy fish slide through the gloom of the millpond. They were grey, descendants of the silvery things that had darted away from the monks, in the young days when the valley was lusty. The whole place was gathered in the musing of old age. The thick-piled trees on the far shore were too dark and sober to dally with the sun; the weeds stood crowded and motionless. Not even a little wind flicked the willows of the islets. The water lay softly,

intensely still. Only the thin stream falling through the millrace murmured to itself of the tumult of life which had once quickened the valley.

I was almost startled into the water from my perch on the alder roots by a voice saying:

'Well, what is there to look at?' My friend was a young farmer, stoutly built, brown-eyed, with a naturally fair skin burned dark and freckled in patches. He laughed seeing me start, and looked down at me with lazy curiosity.

'I was thinking the place seemed old, brooding over its past.'

He looked at me with a lazy, indulgent smile, and lay down on his back on the bank, saying:

'It's all right for a doss — here.'

'Your life is nothing else but a doss. I shall laugh when somebody jerks you awake,' I replied.

He smiled comfortably and put his hands over his eyes because of the light.

'Why shall you laugh?' he drawled.

'Because you'll be amusing,' said I.

We were silent for a long time, when he rolled over and began to poke with his finger in the bank.

'I thought,' he said in his leisurely fashion, 'there was some cause for all this buzzing.'

I looked, and saw that he had poked out an old papery nest of those pretty field bees which seem to have dipped their tails into bright amber dust. Some agitated insects ran round the cluster of eggs, most of which were empty now, the crowns gone; a few young bees staggered about in uncertain flight before they could gather power to wing away in a strong course. He watched the little ones that ran in and out among the shadows of the grass hither and thither in consternation.

'Come here — come here!' he said, imprisoning one poor little bee under a grass stalk, while with another stalk he loosened the folded blue wings.

'Don't tease the little beggar', I said.

'It doesn't hurt him — I wanted to see if it was because he couldn't spread his wings that he couldn't fly. There he goes — no he doesn't. Let's try another.'

'Leave them alone,' said I. 'Let them run in the sun. They're only just out of their shells. Don't torment them into flight.'

He persisted, however, and broke the wing of the next.

'Oh dear — pity!' said he, and crushed the little thing between his fingers. Then he examined the eggs, and pulled out some silk from around the dead larva, and investigated it all in a desultory manner, asking of me all I knew about the insects. When he had finished he flung the clustered eggs into the water and rose, pulling out his watch from the depth of his breeches' pocket.

'I thought it was about dinner-time,' said he, smiling at me.

Lawrence's novel begins with a scene which shows the English countryside run down, tawdry, trivial — no longer 'lusty', vital, vibrant with energy; an idle conversation springs up between two friends whose value systems are deeply opposed. Every statement is loaded with implications, every action is symbolic; the farmer 'put his hands over his eyes because of the light' when the speaker hints at a coming social revolution that will destroy the farmer, perhaps, with the same bored, callous indifference that the farmer shows to the bees. The opening description of rural peace and beauty, 'old, brooding over its past', the rapidly sketched-in evocation of a time when religion and the simple passions of man were strong and healthy, lay the ground for the contrast between past use of the land and the present day. The farmer places himself by everything he says and does: his cruelty in trivial things (wantonly killing the harmless bees) implies a larger cruelty. The speaker, in judging him, places himself: his sensitivity comes close to hyper-sensitivity. A text like this offers an intensified simulation of life. In real life, we do not really place ourselves by everything we say and do; certain actions reflected on afterwards may be seen as symbolic, certain statements as pregnant with a significance afterwards brought to birth; the concentration of significance in Lawrence's opening lines is, if we choose to apply simple standards of realism, wildly implausible; but that is to misread the text; we must adjust to the pseudo-realism; knowing the conventions of the form, we can read the resultant structure appropriately, respond as intended to the literary experience offered.

V

We're getting somewhere: literature is a particular use of words; literature consists of texts put together to work in a particular way; what sets a text working that way is a decision by the reader to read it with the appropriate mental set. The text must work at a level of intensity which makes the reader feel the more responsive attention the text demands is justi-fied; justified not simply as a kind of mental gymnastic exercise, but justified by the feeling we have as we read that the text isn't limited to what it says in as many words; justified because things are conveyed that couldn't equally well be spelled out in simple, straightforward prose.

I'm setting limits to what I regard as literature which not all would accept without argument; limits which a couple of hundred years ago would have seemed artificial and unnecess-ary. There's a problem here. Now's the place, perhaps, to tackle it.

The *word* 'literature' goes back to the Romans; when a Roman talked about *litterae* ('letters'), he meant any kind of writing — verse or prose — that was worth taking seriously and could be expected to last — whatever the subject. For the Greeks, the intellectual life had meant argument, discussion, the theatre, the public performance of poetry or prose; the symbol of the intellectual life was the spoken word; a written text was merely the record of a performance, heard or imagined. For the Romans, the symbol of the intellectual life was a written text; *litterae* meant reading books, thinking about books, the writing which was the natural outcome.

The area covered by the intellectual life was smaller then than now: Cicero could pride himself on being conversant with the whole of human knowledge — all, that is to say, that mattered. The practical arts and crafts didn't get much into books — except, of course, farming, which even got into poetry. It is unlikely Cicero knew much about making shoes

or even swords — or ploughshares for that matter, since it
wouldn't have occurred to him to make any of these with his
own hands. About architecture or medicine he probably knew
little; though these were subjects that did get into books, they
weren't the kind of books Cicero spent much time on. The
great subjects were poetry and philosophy; history, being a
comparative newcomer, ran a bad third.

It was much the same in our English eighteenth century. In
the age of Johnson, the republic of letters is fully re-
established. Writers in Johnson's day are no longer what they
had been in Elizabethan times — aristocratic dilettanti,
courtiers or professionals dependent on the patronage of
courtiers. Johnson is the product of a new, more generally
available education: a writer who had made a living of sorts
by writing, and risen to preside over a new middle-class
intelligentsia that consciously recreated the attitudes of the
Roman Augustan age. For Johnson, 'literature' meant pretty
much what *litterae* had meant for Cicero; there were the same
gentlemanly exclusions. It seems improbable that Johnson
would have thought of the transactions of the Royal Society as
literature. Johnson's contemporary Bishop Percy was doubt-
ful whether the popular songs and ballads which he collected
deserved to rank as literature. There was the same confidence
that poetry, philosophy (moral philosophy), history were
what mattered; each called for some measure of genius, but all
were within the grasp of common sense. The explosion comes
in the nineteenth century. There is a swing of the pendulum
away from this gentlemanly view of literature; the industrial
revolution and the spectacular advance of science transformed
society; new universities sprang up on all sides, new subjects
were devised, studied, written about; a new class of intellectuals came into existence; the professional scholar (as opposed
to the dilettante) was elevated from the social status of
eccentric, more or less harmless, to that of gentleman, and
even that of public celebrity. Writers, novelists especially,
were also professionals; they wrote for a public instead of
posturing in public; they were often women.

*   *   *

By the end of the nineteenth century, no individual could seriously claim to be conversant with the whole of human knowledge, the whole of human achievement; even if one left out the practical arts, the new technology, the area covered was too vast to correspond to any individual's aptitudes or interests. The growth, in prestige as well as scope, of science meant a fragmentation of intellectual activity. C. P. Snow's two cultures were already a fact of nineteenth-century Western life. With the two cultures went two different ways of describing reality: on the one hand, the traditional concepts and the traditional ways of presenting these concepts in literature; on the other hand, the new descriptive techniques of science; it became customary to speak of the latter as 'objective' and the former as 'subjective'. The two accounts weren't just complementary: they were in large measure mutually contradictory; what brought them into open confrontation, of course, was the growth of the social sciences.

I shall come back to the alleged objectivity of the social sciences in Chapter 4. My concern here is with an emerging consciousness that literature was a term applicable to certain kinds of writing only: what these had in common was that they were subjective, not objective — not scientific; in compensation, such texts offered a particular kind of æsthetic experience; the value you placed on that experience depended on the camp you belonged to. There were those who resisted this tighter definition of literature. Matthew Arnold was one. In the public controversy between Arnold and T. H. Huxley in 1880 it is Huxley (the scientist) who sees how things must go: for Huxley, literature means what it means for us; Arnold was fighting a rearguard action which had to fail because of its refusal to admit the reality of social change.

We see in operation here a process which is common to the whole life of society: expansion means diversification and therefore fragmentation. In the intellectual life of Western man, it is the process by which, in the course of two and a half thousand years, first, the natural sciences and, more recently, the social sciences hived off from philosophy and became separate disciplines, leaving philosophy today as a subject with more sharply defined, narrower frontiers than even a

century ago. Where literature is concerned, the shrinking of
the frontiers has not meant the steady advance which we like
to think of as characteristic of scientific thought: Homer, the
Greek tragedians, Virgil, Dante, Shakespeare aren't easily
improved upon. What it has meant is concentration on those
forms which have proved most hardy, and greater complexity
and individuality within those forms: the eighteenth-century
novel is a kind of fictional cousin of history; the modern novel
possesses a much more distinctive structure — more individual, more tightly organized.

So long as literature can be defined as 'all forms of writing',
the thing is easy; 'all forms of writing worth taking seriously' is
already tricky, but you could get away with that, probably,
until the middle of the seventeenth century; people got away
with it, indeed, until the middle of the nineteenth century by
choosing to disregard the growth of science; by the middle of
the nineteenth century, science and its tool for coping with
reality, a way of writing that is consciously non-literary,
become too prominent a feature of the intellectual landscape
to be ignored with comfort.

*   *   *

A history of English literature, in discussing the seventeenth
or eighteenth century, takes in a good deal of prose which
would seem to us to belong more properly to history, or
philosophy, or politics, or journalism; a passage from Richard
Hooker's *Ecclesiastical Polity*, an article from the *Spectator*
possess certain qualities which we associate with serious
literature. Take this example.

> There is no antidote against the opium of time, which
> temporally considereth all things: our fathers find their
> graves in our short memories, and sadly tell us how we may
> be buried in our survivors. Gravestones tell truth scarce
> forty years. Generations pass while some trees stand, and
> old families last not three oaks. To be read by bare
> inscriptions like many in Gruter, to hope for eternity by
> enigmatical epithets or first letters of our names, to be
> studied by antiquaries, who we were, and have new names

given us like many of the mummies, are cold consolations
unto the students of perpetuity, even by everlasting languages.

(Sir Thomas Browne, Urn Burial)

Urn Burial was published in 1658. We'd not expect anyone
writing on such a subject today to write so urbanely; those
who write on this sort of subject don't today think of
themselves as contributing to literature, and write accordingly: such works now form at most part of the context for
literature. Browne writes in the tradition of Montaigne and
Bacon, the tradition that takes as its model the philosophical
prose of Seneca. We find it disconcerting to hear such things
talked about in prose that seems to call for the kind of
response we are more accustomed to make to a Shakespearean
soliloquy.

The implicit claim of such texts to be taken as literature
seems to us misplaced. Henry James is perhaps the last major
figure in English who can get away with using rhetoric
flamboyantly, unashamedly, for the exposition, outside a
novel, of an idea:

It is difficult to speak adequately or justly of London. It
is not a pleasant place; it is not agreeable, or cheerful, or
easy, or exempt from reproach. It is only magnificent. You
can draw up a tremendous list of reasons why it should be
insupportable. The fogs, the smoke, the dirt, the darkness,
the wet, the distances, the ugliness, the brutal size of the
place, the horrible numerosity of society, the manner in
which this senseless bigness is fatal to amenity, to convenience, to conversation, to good manners — all this and
much more you may expatiate upon. You may call it
dreary, heavy, stupid, dull, inhuman, vulgar at heart and
tiresome in form . . . But . . . for one who takes it as I take
it, London is on the whole the most possible form of life.

(Henry James, Notebooks)

* * *

If we ask ourselves what we today consider as literature, we
discover, I think, some confusion in our minds.

It is unlikely we will have in mind only what writers write today: the latest Margaret Drabble or García Márquez; the latest Seamus Heaney or Charles Simic. Unless our interest is very specialized, we will want to include, alongside what you might call *the current output*, works such as Shakespeare's *Hamlet*, Coleridge's *The Ancient Mariner*, Trollope's *Barchester Towers*, Henry James's *The Wings of the Dove*. Suppose we call this second group *the repertoire*: those poems and novels from previous generations or centuries with which all seriously interested in literature can be supposed to possess some kind of familiarity. What else?

Traditionally, all talk and writing about literature has tended to follow the model of political history. The structuring principles, that is to say, are chronological and nationalistic. Literary historians have had difficulty in coming to terms with the fact that much of what extends and revitalizes imaginative writing in English has come from elsewhere. The modern reading public is internationalist in outlook. Novel readers in particular read, enjoy, discuss writing wherever it comes from. Try drawing up a list of the ten best novels of the last ten years – the ten you have enjoyed most: it is certain you will want to include writers from several countries; equally certain that your list will include translations. So that the 'current output' means increasingly the best (or at any rate the most talked about) new writing available in English. This change of perspective does not seem to have affected our thinking about the repertoire to the same extent, no doubt because few readers possess a working knowledge of more than a handful of past classics from any national literature other than their own. We still think about literature in quite different terms from the way we think about music.

What the current output and the repertoire have in common is that both are made up from works that are read for their own sake. Despite the huge, unmanageable size of the current output, the number of novels or poems which get talked about is surprisingly small — easily manageable by serious readers. This is even more the case with the repertoire, where time has carried out for us an even more drastic sorting out of what will last and what will not. Like other gamblers, publishers pick no more than the occasional winner.

In addition to the current output (or that part of it which catches on) and the repertoire, there are those past works which have dropped from the repertoire and are no longer read for their own sake, or which never quite made it. These also form part of the history of English literature, or French literature, or Spanish literature (as the case may be) and are still studied by students for that reason; along with the works which make up the repertoire, they form part of what is called the *canon* (a term normally used especially when speaking of a particular national literature). The canon of English literature is made up by a somewhat arbitrary reduction of the immense amount written to those works still judged to be worth remembering. Defoe wrote some 400 pamphlets; he appears in histories of English literature as the author of the half dozen works that caught on; he appears in the contemporary repertoire as the author of *Robinson Crusoe* and *Moll Flanders*.

* * *

Repertoire (unlike canon) is a concept that largely ignores time. The works which constitute it aren't lined up in our minds in a receding perspective according to the time they were written. Take three classics at random, *Hamlet*, *The Ancient Mariner*, *Barchester Towers*: *Barchester Towers*, the most recent of the three, was written over a hundred years ago; but for those of us who are familiar with the classics of English literature, it looms larger on our mental horizon than many novels written much more recently; *Hamlet* feels closer to us, more immediately present than Shaw's *Major Barbara*, *The Ancient Mariner* closer than, say, *Dauber* (a long narrative poem by Masefield). Chaucer, Shakespeare, Dickens are not diminished, as lesser writers are diminished, by the passage of time; the best of what they wrote continues to live in our minds, continues to serve as an active inspiration to those who write today. This isn't to say the repertoire remains static: the works which loom largest in our minds today aren't those which loomed largest fifty years ago; another fifty years will, beyond doubt, mean fresh changes.

A history of English literature must also take account of works that don't have this special property of timelessness.

The repertoire and the list of works we should want to draw up as important for the development of English literature overlap but do not correspond: there are different priorities, different criteria for rejection or retention. Students of English literature have to read the lesser poets and novelists of a period in order to have some standard of comparison; they have to read works on subjects we'd not think of today as belonging to literature, in order to familiarize themselves with the ideas and opinions, the attitudes and prejudices of a period which concerns them for other reasons. There are works which can be read now only in this spirit: though of crucial importance to the history of English literature, they strike us as old-fashioned, or feeble, not worth reading for themselves; others, though interesting for the subject matter, don't strike us as offering the literary experience at all.

* * *

One way round the problem is to present English literature (or French literature) as a series of *traditions* (the tradition of the novel, the tradition of the short personal poem, etc.) and confine ourselves to those works which seem to constitute what F. R. Leavis called (in connection with the English novel) 'the great tradition'; the sum of the great traditions would make up what I have called the 'repertoire'. I fancy most of us who read serious literature for pleasure in effect do this: we perhaps sample works which fall outside the repertoire, but we probably spend more time reading the masterpieces that belong to repertoires other than English. For any form there is a living tradition (in Eliot's sense of the term in 'Tradition and the individual talent') — living and therefore subject to that constant process of reordering of which Eliot spoke. That tradition isn't confined to a single language or period: Homer, Virgil, Horace have more to do with the tradition of English poetry than the minor English poets of the seventeenth or eighteenth century: *Madame Bovary* is more important to our understanding of the tradition of the novel than a host of Victorian novels. It might be sensible if the teaching of literature were to concentrate more on the great traditions: as it is, students are encouraged to pay lip service to works (historically rather than intrinsically interesting) which privately they find unreadable or boring. I'm not suggesting we should read only those past works that are easily appreciated. Many masterpieces require considerable mental persistence; appreciation is never quite free from a sense of the past; but their impact, when we've got to know them, can become immediate, rewarding, exciting.

It isn't the critic who decides that history, for example, no longer belongs to the territory called literature: it's the historian. Gibbon, like Johnson or Pope, thought of himself as a man of letters. Modern historians, however much they think of themselves as artists, think of themselves first as professionals in a recognized discipline. Good history shares many qualities with good novels, even good poems. But we don't any longer think of historians as engaged in writing literature.

* * *

Literature is writing of a particular kind, involving a particular use of words; writing that works in a particular way, makes different (usually more exacting) demands upon the reader from other types of reading. Writing that exploits the potentialities of words; the words become more than words. Writing that renews, extends, revises, refreshes, by characteristically non-logical, non-objective techniques, our perception of the world and our moral understanding. Or does some of these things.

Sometimes the function of literature is to intensify the awesome majesty and mystery of the universe we live in. Take the great storm scene in Hardy's novel *Far from the Madding Crowd*; there is a party that night given by the new master of the farm; all the men are drunk except the farm-manager Gabriel Oak; he leaves the men to their drink, and goes out into the night, to cope with the rising storm:

> Gabriel proceeded towards his home. In approaching the door, his toe kicked something which felt and sounded soft, leathery, and distended, like a boxing-glove. It was a large toad humbly travelling across the path. Oak took it up, thinking it might be better to kill the creature to save it

from pain; but finding it uninjured, he placed it again among the grass. He knew what this direct message from the Great Mother meant. And soon came another.

When he struck a light indoors there appeared upon the table a thin glistening streak, as if a brush of varnish had been lightly dragged across it. Oak's eyes followed the serpentine sheen to the other side, where it led up to a huge brown garden-slug, which had come indoors to-night for reasons of its own. It was Nature's second way of hinting to him that he was to prepare for foul weather . . .

Gabriel Oak goes to his sheep:

They were crowded close together on the other side around some furze bushes, and the first peculiarity observable was that, on the sudden appearance of Oak's head over the fence, they did not stir or run away. They had now a terror of something greater than their terror of man. But this was not the most noteworthy feature: they were all grouped in such a way that their tails, without a single exception, were towards that half of the horizon from which the storm threatened. There was an inner circle closely huddled, and outside these they radiated wider apart, the pattern formed by the flock as a whole not being unlike a vandyked lace collar, to which the clump of furze-bushes stood in the position of a wearer's neck.

This was enough to re-establish him in his original opinion. He knew now that he was right, and that Troy was wrong. Every voice in nature was unanimous in bespeaking change. But two distant translations attached to these dumb expressions. Apparently there was to be a thunderstorm, and afterwards a cold continuous rain. The creeping things seemed to know all about the later rain, but little of the interpolated thunder-storm; whilst the sheep knew all about the thunder-storm and nothing of the later rain.

This complication of weathers being uncommon, was all the more to be feared. Oak returned to the stackyard. All was silent here, and the conical tips of the ricks jutted darkly into the sky. There were five wheat-ricks in this yard, and three stacks of barley.

He goes back to the scene of the drinking party:

> All was silent within, and he would have passed on in the belief that the party had broken up, had not a dim light, yellow as saffron by contrast with the greenish whiteness outside, streamed through a knot-hole in the folding doors . . .
>
> He put out the expiring lights, that the barn might not be endangered, closed the door upon the men in their deep oblivious sleep, and went again into the lone night. A hot breeze, as if breathed from the parted lips of some dragon about to swallow the globe, fanned him from the south, while directly opposite in the north rose a grim misshapen body of cloud, in the very teeth of the wind. So unnaturally did it rise that one could fancy it to be lifted by machinery from below. Meanwhile the faint cloudlets had flown back into the south-east corner of the sky, as if in terror of the large cloud, like a young brood gazed in upon by some monster.

But literature doesn't have to be as grand as that: it is also the function of literature to sharpen our perception of what for most of us is no more than ordinary experience by restructuring it as a poem:

> Although I shelter from the rain
> Under a broken tree,
> My chair was nearest to the fire
> In every company
> That talked of love or politics,
> Ere Time transfigured me.
>
> Though lads are making pikes again
> For some conspiracy,
> And crazy rascals rage their fill
> At human tyranny,
> My contemplations are of Time
> That has transfigured me.

There's not a woman turns her face
Upon a broken tree,
And yet the beauties that I loved
Are in my memory;
I spit into the face of Time
That has transfigured me.
(Yeats, 'The Lamentation of the Old Pensioner')

* * *

By literature I mean in short very much that the Greeks called 'poetry'; that is to say, 'creative writing'; writing as a creative act; making something built to last, something striking, something worth remembering, something worth going back to. The term 'poetry' won't do for us, however, because in modern English 'poetry' has come to mean verse — good verse, but verse as opposed to prose; so that to talk of poetry in prose sounds paradoxical, a contradiction in terms. The Elizabethan critic Sir Philip Sidney, some four hundred years ago, in his *Apologie for Poetrie* could use the term as the Greeks had used it because creative writing in English in his day *was* still chiefly in verse; the Germans have a word *Dichtung*, which covers creative writing in both prose and verse; the best we can do in English seems to be 'creative writing'.

* * *

In this book I'll have most to say about two forms of creative writing: novels and short poems. I shall have something to say about related forms — the long narrative poem, for example. But I shall concentrate on the short poem and the novel as the forms most practised and read in our own day. I shan't have much to say about plays: partly for reasons of space — to cover all means covering nothing properly; but also for another reason.

The status of plays as literature is unchallengeable: it would be absurd to say that the plays of Shakespeare are not literature. But a play is a play. It works differently. When we read a novel or a poem, we have to do the spadework ourselves. When we watch a play or a film, the spadework has been done for us by the producer of the play, the director of the film: we don't have to rely on words to bring the text to life in our minds; major interpretative decisions have been taken for us — what the characters look like, their reaction to what is said and done, the setting of the action. We see all this before our eyes. The dramatic experience is a visual experience; it depends at least as much on spectacle as it does on dialogue. The literary experience depends entirely on what comes into existence in the reader's mind as he reads. It is true that a special convention since ancient times has made available the text of plays to an audience of readers as well as to the audience physically present witnessing the spectacle in the theatre. Some writers, indeed, have adopted the dramatic form with no real intention of having their plays performed. Plays thus differ from films, radio and TV programmes, the scripts of which are not normally available to the public — the only form of publication is the performance.

The nature of the dramatic experience is something which has been discussed since the time of Aristotle; what happens when we read a text has only recently attracted critical attention; the need to understand how literary texts work is something we've only just become aware of. What's made the need acute is that the ability to read a serious novel or poem with the mental set it demands is no longer an accomplishment that can be taken for granted among educated people. That's why I've made the nature of the literary experience the subject of this book.

VI

Literary texts, like other things in life, can be good, bad or indifferent. A bad poem is still a poem, a bad novel still a novel; the kind of text it is is decided by the way it works, however badly it works. What makes the good ones good? Well, partly it's a matter of quality of *structure*; partly a matter of *significance* — the quality of the relationship which the text sets up between itself and the world outside the text of which it is, however simplified, distorted, enriched, made more interesting, a representation. That sounds very general. Can't we be more specific?

If we were talking about trucks, we might say the first requirement of a truck must be that it can carry a heavy load; requirement of a truck must be that it can carry a heavy load; a second that it must be able to maintain traction on rough terrain; a truck that won't do these things is still a truck; but it isn't any good as a truck. Can we deal like this with novels and poems? The answer is we can't: what makes a poem or a novel good is the totality of its impact, the quality of the literary experience it has to offer; the best we can hope to do is to identify components of that total impact which are not easily dispensed with; we can't insist that a poem or novel, to be good, must possess all these components, be better in all these respects than other texts. To talk like that is to ignore the complexity of what we're talking about.

To my way of thinking, the component to put first is quality of the *verbal texture*. Every competently written text sets up (and maintains, with variations) its own distinctive rhythm. That rhythm, a counterpoint of the natural rhythm of word and phrase and the rhythm of the syntax (which is the rhythm of thought), establishes a level of seriousness — what is sometimes called the tone. It is this rhythm, this level of seriousness, which, more than anything else, distinguishes a good novel, or a good poem, from a bad. When rhythm goes wrong, everything goes wrong. A gauchely written novel (gauche from the point of view of its rhythms), as well as displeasing the ear, simply fails to convince.

Readability is one aspect of what I have in mind — a good novel holds your attention, won't let you put it down. It's one of the qualities which stamped the opening lines of *Brighton Rock* at once as a literary text:

Hale knew they meant to murder him before he had been in Brighton three hours. With his inky fingers and his bitten nails, his manner cynical and nervous, anybody could tell he didn't belong — belong to the early summer sun, the cool Whitsun wind off the sea, the holiday crowd. They came in by train from Victoria every five minutes, rocked down Queen's Road standing on the tops of the little local trams, stepped off in bewildered multitudes into fresh and glittering air . . .

Readability is one aspect only, however; the most obvious, not the most important — and a dangerous quality, which can get out of hand; conspicuous readability is usually achieved by limitation of significance; all bestsellers are readable. You wouldn't want to single out Henry James or Patrick White as a writer who held his readers' attention: both expect their readers to work hard; the spring which draws us along the line of narrative, though we sense its power, is controlled by a delicately balanced escapement. By quality of the verbal texture I mean the pleasure derived from reading a text put together by a skilled and sensitive craftsman.

I don't mean 'fine writing': fine writing will irk if it lacks the punch, the onward thrust, the compulsion of plot, the sensuous richness of thought and image. Fine writing is usually writing that is too fine for the sense. Equally, I prefer, in this connection, to avoid the term *style*: style suggests something added afterwards, something stuck on to ornament the sense; for me, the verbal texture has the sense embedded in it; sense and the expression of it expand together in the writer's mind. One doesn't expect even the greatest masterpieces to move or startle all the time: but when they don't move or startle, they should still possess the unobtrusive freshness of newly constructed statement — not seem strung together from the second-hand material of cliché. Good fiction, in its quieter moments, suggests to me always the crispness of fresh linen. Jane Austen is a better writer in this respect than George Eliot.

Even when the writer writes in the character of somebody unskilled in writing, the text, while sounding as we'd expect that character to sound, must generate the special excitement we look for in literature. In *Not Honour More* Joyce Cary asks us to accept that we're reading the clumsy, unimaginative prose of a former officer in the colonial service: the verbal texture perfectly expresses the character Cary wishes to create. If we turn to the concluding lines of Cary's earlier novel, *Prisoner of Grace*, we hear a different version of how it all came about. This time it is Captain Latter's wife who speaks. A different way of talking (a different verbal texture) expresses the quiet, probing, intellectual candour of a very different mind — a mind anxious to face facts (whereas Latter's mind manipulates facts until they seem to prove what he wants to believe). Where Latter is superficial and impulsive, able to think and write only in clichés, Nina writes with simple honesty; she is anxious to be fair, willing to believe her first husband's accusation that she is the victim of the instinctive prejudices of her class. The cause of all the trouble is Chester Nimmo, whom Latter loathes and Nina secretly despises. Nimmo is the hypocrite with a streak of genius, whose instinct for the politically advantageous move never fails him. He too writes the story of his life (or part of it) in a third novel, *Except the Lord*; as with Latter's account, the opening words are the man — Nimmo peddles, however, a different kind of cliché:

> Yesterday, an old man nearing my end, I stood by the grave of a noble woman, one of the three noblest I have ever known, my mother, my sister, my wife. If I draw back now the curtain from my family life, sacred to memory, I do so only to honour the dead, and in the conviction that my story throws light upon the crisis that so fearfully shakes our whole civilization.

* * *

Verbal texture is a property of *structure*: the second component, therefore, I expect of a decently written literary text is quality of structure; where verbal texture looks to the way the text is working at any given point — the capacity of the words, at that point, to bring the text to life in the reader's mind — structure looks to the text as a unified whole. In a well constructed text, our progress along the line of sense creates an illusion of inevitability: there is a beginning and an end and some kind of connection between them, even when the end is inconclusive or disturbing. If the text is a poem, it may be the logic of a line of thought, running in harmony with (or in contrapuntal tension against) the metrical pattern, that gives the poem its structure. If it is a novel, we must feel the compulsion to surrender to an illusion we might otherwise reject. Even so loosely episodic and rambling a narrative as *Moll Flanders* is shaped, held together by structure. The narrative gathers momentum in the second half; the episodes become longer, more interesting. As her experience of life increases, Moll finds words come easier, she becomes less honest — less honest with us, less honest with herself. She started as a 'whore', a woman who easily surrendered to passion; she will end a common, if enterprising thief. She claims to have treated her successive husbands honestly, but she never really tells the truth to any of them. Yet throughout this process of increasing sophistication and concern with respectability, she retains her old disarming candour about her weakness for any man who comes her way:

I was now left in a dismal and disconsolate case indeed, and in several things worse than ever. First, it was past the flourishing time with me, when I might expect to be courted for a mistress; that agreeable part had declined some time, and the ruins only appeared of what had been; and that which was worse than all was this, that I was the most dejected, disconsolate creature alive. I that had encouraged my husband, and endeavoured to support his spirits under his trouble, could not support my own; I wanted that spirit in trouble which I told him was so necessary for bearing the burthen.

But my case was indeed deplorable, for I was left perfectly friendless and helpless, and the loss my husband had sustained had reduced his circumstances so low, that though indeed I was not in debt, yet I could easily foresee that what was left would not support me long; that it wasted daily for subsistence, so that it would be soon all spent, and then I saw nothing before me but the utmost distress; and this represented itself so lively to my thoughts, that it seemed as if it was come before it was really very near. Also my very apprehensions doubled the misery, for I fancied every sixpence that I paid for a loaf of bread was the last I had in the world, and that tomorrow I was to fast, and be starved to death.

My third component is *integrity*. A novel or a poem may possess a verbal texture which is rich and exciting, a well planned structure — and still be worthless because the verbal skill, the skill with which the bits are fitted together, is not backed up by any integrity of purpose; is not the expression of anything we can recognize as worth our taking seriously. Integrity is not the same thing as sincerity. To expect a poet to be always sincere, to believe what he says in his poem in any straightforward sense of the word 'believe', is naive: he may be arguing tongue-in-cheek for the poetry to be got out of an idea, in hot imaginative pursuit of a promising fancy. A novel writen in the first person may be planned to leave us with the conviction that the character is a hypocrite. To possess integrity, a text must play fair with the reader, not lay claims upon his attention which aren't backed up; mustn't aim at crude manipulation of opinion, or pander to the reader's appetite for sexual stimulus. Popular songs, advertising texts often offend in this way: they display skill, imagination, complete lack of integrity. Take this jeweller's advertisement for a diamond ring:

> We want you to love happily ever after! If a diamond ring is sparkling somewhere in your plans for a beautiful future, let Birks help you choose wisely and well. Buying a diamond might easily be the most important and most meaningful purchase you'll ever make. Your Birks diamond will give you a feeling of happy confidence. Because you'll always know that you bought it from people you can trust — implicitly. Birks diamonds have the look of love.

The plot of a novel may be wildly improbable, obviously contrived and yet hold the reader: it may do so only because the action is too compelling to allow us to stop and think about the improbability; but if the novel is any good, it's more likely to be because we feel that these characters, held together though they may be by an obviously contrived, wholly implausible plot, nevertheless ring true as people; that our understanding of human beings, of life, is deepened, extended, enhanced. The literary experience isn't just a matter of words well used; there has to be an emotional, even a moral component to back up and justify the verbal artistry. A text can ring false on any of these levels: we can have the reaction that a phrase (sometimes even a single word), an emotion, a moral judgement (expressed or implied) does not fit — and we feel the text fall apart; the unity of the experience dis-integrates. The feeling is immediate and can be very strong, as can be the feeling of excitement which is produced when, on all these levels, the text hangs together.

I don't mean literature must uplift or improve; obviously, it need not. But before we can recognize a text as worth the time and attention it asks of us, it must have an impact on our moral self; it may be only that the challenge to make sense of a difficult poem renews our mental alertness and our sense of values; we get involved, and the world ceases to be quite the same place. Reading a poem may be as refreshing to our minds as a walk on the beach. The person who takes no pleasure in either is missing something in life. Usually, however, the claim made upon our attention by a well constructed poem or novel is more ambitious, more audacious, not easily resisted: it sets us re-examining our moral beliefs or prejudices, our assumptions about what is important in life. There is a revision of our priorities called for, suggested, implied.

A serious writer doesn't have to be solemn; comedy, satire, if it is any good, possesses this quality of artistic seriousness as much as tragedy. The writer of that kind of popular novel which we consume in trains, or when we don't feel up to the challenge of the literary experience (the kind of novel which for many people is the only contact with literature), does not possess it.

There is a moral shoddiness as well as shoddiness of the verbal texture. Serious writers face the truth of the human condition: they tell it, if you like, the way it is. That's not to say they have to tell it in as many words. The function of literature is not to prove but to unsettle.

VII

It's time to draw together some of the threads I've scattered through this first chapter.

The core of my argument has been that literary texts, despite all the things they have in common with other texts, are essentially different from other texts. The difference isn't one of quality: there are good novels and bad ones, good

poems and bad ones. What makes good and bad alike
different from other kinds of writing is that they work
differently. They involve 'a particular use of words', different
from other uses we make of words: their purpose is different
(they don't have the same straightforward objectives as other
texts); they achieve their purpose by different techniques (the
nature of the experience they offer us is different); for them to
work as they are designed to work, they have to be recognized
as different by those who read them; having recognized them
as different from everyday texts, we read them with a different
mental set from everyday texts.

Today, we no longer think of literature as including those
kinds of writing which set out to deal directly and 'objectively'
with human beings and their environment (the physical and
the social sciences). As we understand the term today,
'literature' implies a kind of artistic creation associated in our
minds with certain forms of writing (novels, poems and the
like) which we have learnt to recognize as working differently
from other forms of writing. A poem, a novel — or a play — is
a structure of words infused with meaning. An important part
of the reader's pleasure, of the critic's business, is the recovery
of that meaning — the felt presence of the author, the
distinctive sound of that sense. A poem or a novel has other
properties. It is an event in time, with a beginning and an end:
where you begin and where you end is dictated by the
structure of the text (confronted with a painting on a wall you
can begin and end anywhere). The event takes place within a
field of significance, alluded to or taken for granted. Within
that field, the meaningful text (the text whose meaning has
been recovered by the reader) adopts a position: acquiescence,
provocation — more often, provocation (calling into question,
challenging our ideas or accepted values) than acquiescence.
The possibilities of acquiescence are platitude and rhetoric,
the echo, stirring or boring, of what we already believe or take
for granted.

A poem or a novel shares this property of provocation with
other works of art: a building, a painting, a symphony. These,
too, can provoke, challenge our accepted ideas, our expectations about what a building or a painting should look like, a
symphony sound like. It is this property which justifies the

metaphorical use of the term 'meaning' of such structures, like the metaphor implied by the term 'statement' in connection with non-verbal structures.

If you ask me to pin it down more clearly, the best I can manage is to say that *literature is experience reorganized as a structure of words that can be perceived both as artistic creation and as a representation of life that is essentially true*. By reorganization I mean using words, sounds, images, rhythms, as a painter uses shapes and colours to form a structure which in its totality is a fresh organization of what the painter saw or imagined. But analogy can mislead here, too: a painting can make a 'statement' of a kind about things outside itself; but that statement is vague, unformulated; the statements poems and novels make *are there*, not to be ignored, challenging us to make of them what we can.

Take Wordsworth's 'Daffodils':

I wandered lonely as a cloud
That floats on high o'er vales and hills,
When all at once I saw a crowd,
A host, of golden daffodils . . .

By reorganization of experience I mean the image of the cloud, which conjures up a manner, a context and a mood of wandering; I mean the placing of 'crowd' at the end of the line, the emphasis given 'crowd' by the echo of 'cloud' (the words rhyme, but it's a strong rhyme); I mean the shift at the next line from 'crowd' to 'host', and the suggestion 'host' carries with it of the daffodils lined up like an army of soldiers uniformly dressed; I mean the challenge in 'golden' to see the line of yellow daffodils as a line of soldiers decked in gold for some mediæval pageant. There is an element of paradox, challenge, contradiction, surprise in the reorganization: we perceive it, not as an aberration of the poet's mind, but as essentially true, in the way that a good picture is essentially true, though 'objectively' a distortion; 'true' not by reference to a logical standard of true or false, but true by reference to the way our minds work.

The unity of what are usually called 'form' and 'content' is fundamental to this reorganization: a philosopher may take pains to offer his understanding of the world in pleasurable form; he tries to write clearly, decently; but his understanding, and our understanding of his understanding, are independent of the words he uses; his case is logically argued, paraphrasable, can be restated in other words. A literary text *is* the organization of experience which it offers: it can't be paraphrased, stated in other words, or it becomes a different organization. A translation of a novel or a poem is, necessarily, a fresh act of creation. Which is why all translations, to some degree, mislead, and many fail.

VIII

In the world we live in, literature is faced with a struggle for survival: ruthless competition for attention, survival of the fittest — the fittest to cope with the social environment, not what we might like to think of as the best, or the most intensely rewarding.

The threat is of various kinds, and comes from more than one quarter. There is the threat from the scientific view of the world, which tends to treat literature (especially poetry) as trifling with words, dealing at best in half-truths and clichés, and dealing with them 'unscientifically' (that is, not 'objectively'): I shall come back to this in Chapter 5. There is the threat to literature in general which results from the transformation of society by technology. There is the threat to which literature has exposed itself by becoming too specialized — too specialized for the kind of society we now have.

How many people today understand what literature is and how it works? Let's suppose the number larger than it ever was, the percentage of the total population not much different from a hundred years ago: we are still worse off than we were; the distribution of that percentage has altered; the audience for English literature is fragmented — spread over the English-speaking world, scattered, geographically and socially, across a large city like London, New York or Sydney. The individual readers might amount to a lot if you could put them together, but they don't amount to much because they never meet; they hardly count as a cultural force; in economic or political terms, they are only marginally worth catering for — or that at any rate is the view publishers and politicians take more and more. Even within the ranks of its potential audience, literature has to contend with other cultural activities which offer easier, more facile alternatives: literature is vulnerable; all of us find it easier to watch a mediocre TV programme than to read a serious novel; many have never known the literary experience, never learnt to read a book.

There is no sign that the social revolution of our time will nourish a revival; that literature, any more than religion, will in the foreseeable future once again be a dominant force. I don't want to sound too gloomy: there have been crises before. I believe in the unpredictability of the human spirit, but am apprehensive of blind economic forces and the power of technology to change our lives. Of course the agony may be more protracted than we sometimes fear: already in the 1930s Q. D. Leavis claimed serious literature was being driven out of existence by popular, meretricious books; that didn't happen, or hasn't happened yet; but now literature has more powerful, more alluring rivals than the lending libraries.

We have reached the point where there can seem little hope. Many already console themselves, like Auden in his last years, by treating poetry as an indefensible adornment of existence they happen to have got addicted to, like old furniture or a glass of sherry at the end of the day:

> . . . After all, it's rather a privilege
>   amid the affluent traffic
> to serve this unpopular art which cannot be turned into
>   background noise for study
> or hung as a status trophy by rising executives,
>   cannot be 'done' like Venice
> or abridged like Tolstoy, but stubbornly still insists upon
>   being read or ignored . . .
>   (W. H. Auden, 'The Cave of Making')

We need not be without hope. The satisfaction, the pleasure we take in words is oddly deep-seated in human nature. We see it given expression on all sides — in the media, in advertising, in everyday talk. In such contexts the literary instinct operates most often at a trivial level, because those who respond to it do not know how to do better; the verbal structures they produce are naive; they are like clumsy children splashing round in a sea of words because they have never learnt to swim. But the instinct is there.

Literature is too important to see lost — because it makes, really makes, life worth living; not just agreeable, but tolerable. Tolerable because the chaos of universal semi-literacy will be intolerable. I'm not going to pretend not to care whether literature survives. I do care. It's for that reason that I've made it my object to give an account, as clear as I can make it, of what literature is and how it works.

It isn't easy to be clear. A first chapter must simplify questions as complex as these, in order to talk about them at all. A first chapter is largely a personal statement of a position. That seems to me as it should be: we must begin somewhere. The false emphases, the over-simplifications can be corrected later. Being clear isn't just a matter of stating the facts. There is a measure of obliqueness in all human communication. The ostensible logic of a novel, the name of the game, is narrative; the writer's real object may not be to tell a story, but to have the story affect us in a particular way. The ostensible logic of a poem may be systematic step-by-step argument — the poet behaves as if trying to convince us; but persuasion may not be, often isn't, the object of the exercise. In an analysis like that attempted here, the ostensible logic has to be systematic discussion, one point after another. Literary criticism is a subject, however, whose terminology is notoriously ambiguous, where one has to resort constantly to metaphor; where the critic is attempting to account rationally for intuitions (and perhaps giving an account of them that is misleading). No critic has read everything, or even everything that matters; nothing I can say can ever seem quite right for you, because you will remember things I've never read, and haven't read at all things I know intimately; my view, as one who has never read the Icelandic sagas, of the development of narrative, will seem distorted to someone who has. Like any reader, I have my likes and dislikes. Critical judgements are never wholly right, never absolute. Never even wholly intelligible: the process by which you begin to see what I mean is more osmotic than dialectical — a matter of my ideas seeping through the talk until they no longer sound strange or confusing, but start to sound like ideas you can understand and don't reject. If it were easier, everything worth proving would have been proved a long time ago.

2

How Fiction Works: the Text that tells a Story

To tell a story, to listen to a story being told — these are things that belong to the very core of social life; to put into words 'what happened' ('what I said to him', 'what she said to me'), if not something older than the beginnings of song, or the first crude attempts at drama, is incomparably older than argument about ideas, reaction of the moral self to what happens around us, or objective description of the way the world works. Western literature begins with two of the greatest stories ever told, Homer's *Iliad* and *Odyssey*. In antiquity, in the Renaissance, the predominant literary form was the poem or the play that told a story. For the last two hundred years it has been the novel.

It's not hard to see why this should be: to tell a story like Defoe's *Robinson Crusoe*, or Milton's *Paradise Lost*, or a story like Henry James's *The Wings of the Dove*, Proust's *Looking for Lost Time*, or Margaret Drabble's *The Radiant Way*, means adding to the creative impulse a sustained effort of the imagination; means putting together in words something that has the dimensions of a major structure; means offering the reader the experience of literature in its most massive (if not its most intense) form. Homer's *Iliad*, Virgil's *Aeneid*, Dante's *Divina Commedia*, a novel by Dickens or Dostoievsky, Umberto Eco or Patrick White, reflects the interests, standards, aspirations, absurdities of a whole society; puts them in a fresh light; calls in question, even, the value system upon which that society rests.

The adventures of Odysseus on his way back from the Trojan War, how Oedipus blinded himself because he could not bear to look at the children he had got upon his own mother — these are only the raw material of literature. Before the raw material can become a literary text it has to be shaped by the conventions of a particular *form*; it has to be given, within the conventions of that form, the *structure* of a particular telling; it has to be brought to life by the play of the writer's imagination and his skill with words. More often than not, the writer provides both the raw material and the finished product. I don't imagine the story of Pinkie and his gang existed at all until Graham Greene began work upon an idea which had come to him: out of that idea came *Brighton Rock*, a novel with an elaborately structured plot — terse, matter-of-fact, stylish — which moves within a carefully calculated larger structure of moral implication. A story can be given any one of a variety of forms: *Robinson Crusoe* is a series of adventures loosely strung together; *Paradise Lost* is structured according to the formal conventions of the epic tradition; *The Radiant Way* is a novel which lends ironic, elegant structure to the everyday lives of a group of people in twentieth-century England.

The primary appeal in all stories is to our natural human appetite for narrative. Things happen, characters are created, scenes described; people talk. The simple, primary appeal of the story as it unfolds is made complex; it is sustained, amplified by the action of the text upon our minds as we read. We do not have to reflect long upon a poem like Virgil's *Aeneid* or *Paradise Lost*, or a novel like *Far from the Madding Crowd* or *Brighton Rock* — any text that hits us hard and holds our interest — before we stumble upon factors fundamental to our understanding of how literature works. To sort out some of these factors will be the subject of this second chapter.

II
FIELDS OF SIGNIFICANCE

The movement of a narrative through time is its most easily grasped characteristic: there are readers whose only motive in reading a novel is to find out 'what happened to the fellow';

they judge a story by its capacity to sustain excitement about what is happening; when the line of narrative pauses for description of a character or a scene, these readers skip.

It is a poor story, however, or a misreading of a good one, that generates only narrative excitement. To be taken seriously, a narrative text must get our minds working, reacting to the text, not just assimilating it, not just treating it as a commodity to be consumed.

In all but the crudest stories, the onward movement of the narrative is not continuous. It stops for dialogue: a novel speaks with several voices, those of the novelist's characters as well as that of the narrator; we find it natural to be told, at length, not only what people did, but what they said; the conversational exchanges between guests and hostess at Liz's New Year party in Margaret Drabble's *The Radiant Way* are part of a carefully contrived strategy for getting the novel launched on its course. The onward movement of the narrative stops also to take in texts other than the narrative proper — letters, newspaper reports and the like; ostensibly, the object is documentation of the narrative, but in a good novel the quoted material undergoes usually an adjustment of emphasis, takes on new overtones in order to match the rhythm of the narrator's speaking voice. The onward movement stops also for detailed description of an object or a place, or how a character looked. Description, like dialogue, doesn't just add variety: it helps the narrative take on another dimension, as in this description of a rustic bonfire:

> The brilliant lights and sooty shades which struggled upon the skin and clothes of the persons standing around caused their lineaments and general contours to be drawn with Düreresque vigour and dash. Yet the permanent moral expression of each face it was impossible to discover, for as the nimble flames towered, nodded and swooped through the surrounding air, the blots of shade and flakes of light upon the countenances of the group changed endlessly. All was unstable; quivering as leaves, evanescent as lightning. Shadowy eye-sockets, deep as those of a death's head, suddenly turned into pits of lustre: a lantern jaw was cavernous, then it was shining; wrinkles were emphasized

to ravines, or obliterated entirely by a changed ray. Nostrils were dark wells; sinews in old necks were gilt mouldings; things with no particular polish on them were glazed; bright objects, such as the tip of a furze-hook one of the men carried, were as glass; eyeballs glowed like little lanterns. Those whom Nature had depicted as merely quaint became grotesque, the grotesque became preternatural; for all was in extremity.

(Hardy, *The Return of the Native*, Book I, Chapter 3)

We read any decent story with the expectation that the story, as we read it, will take on this other dimension, will assume a *significance* that justifies the claim the story makes on our attention. The sequence of events doesn't unwind in a vacuum; we begin to see what it's all about. And we begin to react to what we read. I'm not talking about our impressions of the story after we've read it; nor am I talking about the reader's purely personal associative processes. I'm talking about the reading process itself; the compulsion we feel in the words, as we read them, to surrender to the reaction they set up in our minds. Or which we don't feel: a story, a whole novel even, may leave our minds numb, like a witty remark the point of which escapes us. Total non-reaction is the exception. True, some modern novels seem designed to bring the reader to the verge of complete frustration; usually, however, the text expands in our minds, moves sideways as well as forwards, invites an appraisal which we keep under constant reappraisal as we advance along the line of narrative. Significance is, if you like, the orchestration of the line of narrative. But it's also what makes the writer's story the expression of the writer's moral perspective.

* * *

I'm going to call this sideways movement a movement into the 'field of significance' of the text: 'field' in the sense in which we talk of a magnetic field; the area within which the magnet, or magnetic coil, exercises its power over responsive objects (iron or steel responds, lead doesn't); the text is the magnet, the responsive object is the reader's mind. It's not, of course, an analogy to be pressed too far: we're dealing with a psycho-logical phenomenon, not one that can be measured and described according to the laws of physics. The field of significance is something that exists only in the reader's mind. And yet, the starting point, the stimulus to react, is built into the words themselves. As we move along the line of narrative, the text reaches out into particular areas of our minds, draws ideas to the surface of consciousness as we read. Because the text keeps changing as we advance, the field of significance also keeps changing: the associations set up by earlier words and phrases aren't switched off as we advance; they diminish only gradually – sometimes persisting, sometimes needing to be reactivated as our perception of the text broadens; we look back over the text as we extend, or revise, our comprehension of it. While all this is going on, we have to continue to submit to the forward movement of the text, or we lose the thread. The experience is not unlike a guided tour through some royal palace: as we move along the route determined for us, perspectives are glimpsed, corridors glanced along, doors opened. We may linger, look back, for a moment, because something has caught and held our interest; but we must keep moving, or we shall be left behind.

Recognition of the text as a literary text entails a special setting of our mental controls, a setting which leaves us prepared for a sideways expansion of the text limited only by our sense of what the process of tuning in calls for. In a short poem, the process is usually more intense, more far-reaching than in a novel; within a particular novel there's usually considerable variation. Non-literary texts, what I shall call *objective prose* (the kind of prose appropriate to good reporting, or to a scientific article), make a characteristically different demand upon our attention: the asserted objectivity of this kind of text invites a corresponding objectivity in the reader, an objectivity which we consciously maintain as we read, often against the pull of our emotions or prejudices; tempta-tion to surrender to a sideways expansion is inhibited, damped down, resisted as straying from the text. All texts expand outwards to some extent; all texts place themselves within an area of implication and shared knowledge for those who know the subject. But in objective prose the sideways expansion is minimal. It is the line of statement, the forward movement of the sense, which is important. In a literary text, the line of statement may be relatively unimportant; its chief function may be to generate the sideways expansion.

What we are talking about is the *significance* of a text as opposed to its *meaning*. Meaning is a property of the line of statement: meaning is formulated, it is there in as many words; all we have to do is to recapture the rhythm that makes them meaningful. Significance is a property of the sideways expansion: significance is unformulated; what comes into existence in our minds is the result of a collaboration between the author and us, significance is *our* response; it is what *we* make of the text.

The response to a text which has been the common property of a culture for centuries keeps acquiring fresh dimensions; each generation brings to it a different capacity to respond. For totally unresponsive readers, significance doesn't exist at all: they read with their mental controls set for reading an item in the newspaper or a scientific article; and because they misunderstand the nature of the transaction proposed, the literary experience passes them by. For the responsive reader, significance is the most exciting thing about reading a narrative text.

Significance is controlled, all the same, as meaning is, by the text, though less directly: significance is the charge laid in the words of the text by the writer who put the text together; reading the text activates that charge, sets up the field of significance of the text, causes the text to reach out into particular areas of our minds as we read. The *degree* of control is less than with meaning: the reactions which are drawn to the surface of consciousness are ours. It is the text, none the less, which generates these reactions: we are not free to make of a text what we choose. Our reactions have their source in our ability to respond; but they are kept under control by a sense of obligation to the text which all practised readers learn to adopt as a necessary condition of the literary experience. We dismiss as irresponsible readings which the text itself won't support. Our reactions, though individual, can be discussed, therefore: readers can, and do, reach a working agreement about the field of significance of a text.

* * *

The field of significance of a narrative text has two aspects. First, it relates the text to a society and a set of social attitudes; in describing the way of life of a group of characters, a value system is set up without usually being directly described; we come to see why what is talked about is important. That is the *first* aspect: the text controls *what we think about while we read*; it sets our minds working in a particular direction; the narrative acquires point, *significance*, outside itself. The story takes on then that more general relevance which intrigued Aristotle when he praised fiction (poetic fiction) as more 'philosophical' than history (which he thought of as dealing only with individuals). Second, the field of significance relates the story which is being told to other stories — places it in a tradition of storytelling, controls *how we are to think about what we read*. This aspect is sometimes referred to as the 'tone' of the text; you might call it the 'flavour' of the text. A literary text suggests its own interpretation: it disposes our minds to receive what we read in a particular way. Partly it's a matter of perceiving that the text takes up a position, as it proceeds, with relation to other texts. But it's a matter also of perceiving *how* what is said is to be taken. A literary text manipulates our thinking, makes us see what is talked about in a particular light.

A good novel, in short, doesn't just tell us what happened to X or Y: we see X and Y as representing more than themselves; we see 'what happened' to X and Y as possessing a claim on us outside and beyond the particular story told. But that's only one aspect of its field of significance: a story that stopped at typical characters in typical situations would strike us as crude. What holds our interest, or excites our admiration, is deciding *how to take* the story we're reading. Guided by the text itself, we fit together an interpretation as we read (what critics call a 'reading'); we find ourselves challenged to determine the nature and extent of the manipulation to which we are being exposed.

Critics usually appeal here to that hard-worked word 'irony'. 'Irony' is, however, perhaps the best word: for it is the essence of irony that the value system asserted is not the value system implied; the text, while nowhere saying so in as many words, works in such a way as partly to detach the reader from the value system which it apparently takes for granted. If we were reading objective prose, that would be an intolerable state of affairs; with a literary text, the challenge to fit together and keep under constant revision, while we read, our interpretation of the text before us is a fundamental component of the literary experience.

III

Strether's first question, when he reached his hotel, was about his friend; yet on his learning that Waymarsh was apparently not to arrive till evening, he was not wholly disconcerted. A telegram from him bespeaking a room 'only if not noisy', reply paid, was produced for the enquirer at the office, so that the understanding they should meet at Chester rather than at Liverpool remained to that extent sound. The same secret principle, however, that had prompted Strether not absolutely to desire Waymarsh's presence at the dock, that had led him thus to postpone for a few hours his enjoyment of it, now operated to make him feel he could wait without disappointment.

(Henry James, *The Ambassadors*, opening lines)

There are many ways of telling a story. For *The Portrait of a Lady* James had chosen the grand manner, spending several pages on description of scene and how his characters looked before anything actually happened, or anything actually was said. Twenty years laters, in *The Ambassadors* and *The Wings of the Dove*, James's mastery of the form finds expression in an abrupt change in technique. Instead of leaving his readers time to settle into the story, he takes off to a flying start, relying on them to accept the challenge of a story hundreds of pages long in which every word appears to count; where the clues to who is who, and where, and why, are slipped into the text at intervals, as they might be in a short personal poem — or in real life.

The opening of *The Ambassadors* is deceptively casual, almost conversational. The imagined scene is sketched in with the incisive economy of a cartoonist. The first word is the name of a character, who is simply named — a trick adopted by

Graham Greene (a great admirer of James) in beginning *Brighton Rock*. Common sense suggests we shall find out all we need to know about Strether before we are through, that he is likely to prove the hero of the novel. And so it *will* prove: though Strether is an odd sort of hero, it is around Strether that the story turns; it is Strether who has the last word ('"Then there we are", said Strether'). Description of what he looks like will come later (in half a dozen pages or so) when we have had time to get interested in him for other reasons:

> . . . a man of five-and-fifty, whose most immediate signs were a marked bloodless brownness of face, a thick dark moustache, of characteristically American cut, growing strong and falling low, a head of hair still abundant but irregularly streaked with grey, and a nose of bold free prominence, the even line, the high finish, as it might have been called, of which had a certain effect of mitigation. A perpetual pair of glasses astride on this fine ridge, and a line, unusually deep and drawn, the prolonged pen-stroke of time, accompanying the curve of the moustache from nostril to chin . . . .

For the present James's concern is for us to see Strether as he sees himself, as a man whose first thought is for his old friend; though the second half of the opening sentence suggests that Strether's first thought is more a matter of good breeding than genuine anxiety: the question once asked, no real disappointment follows the answer received.

A few hints next about Strether's friend. Waymarsh has not arrived, but the hotel has had a telegram from him 'bespeaking' a room. The word is not idly ponderous: we shall discover that Waymarsh is a man who bespeaks rooms. When James gets round to describing him, late that night in the room he had bespoken, it is a formidable personality he will describe:

> He had a large handsome head and a large sallow seamed face — a striking significant physiognomic total, the upper range of which, the great political brow, the thick loose hair, the dark fuliginous eyes, recalled . . . the impressive

image . . . of some great national worthy of the early part of mid-century . . . .

We begin to realize why Waymarsh spends four words in his telegram reserving a room 'only if not noisy' where a less wary traveller might have been incautious enough to ask for a 'quiet' room, even a 'comfortable' room. Waymarsh has learnt to be wary, to spell out precisely his minimum requirements; and to do it all, in the grand manner, reply paid. Perched on the edge of his bed with the glare of the gaslight in his eyes, 'almost wilfully uncomfortable', Mr Waymarsh of Milrose, Connecticut, is plainly not a man who expects Europe to be enjoyable; it is an experience to be endured, the discomforts anticipated and provided against to the extent that is possible. We shall discover that Waymarsh personifies Strether's Puritan conscience, as his patroness Mrs Newsome represents his surrender to Yankee cultural refinement. James's novel is largely the story of Strether's progressive emancipation from both these long-endured shackles upon his intellectual and emotional development. The pieces of the puzzle that are Waymarsh will be passed out, will fit into place, later. Enough is said to intrigue, to arouse and support our curiosity, about the friend Strether was not exactly anxious to have meet him as he stepped onto the dock at Liverpool, and could now wait to see 'without disappointment'.

* * *

She waited, Kate Croy, for her father to come in, but he kept her unconscionably, and there were moments at which she showed herself, in the glass over the mantel, a face positively pale with the irritation that had brought her to the point of going away without sight of him. It was at this point, however, that she remained; changing her place, moving from the shabby sofa to the armchair upholstered in a glazed cloth that gave at once — she had tried it — the sense of the slippery and the sticky . . . .

(Henry James, *The Wings of the Dove*, opening lines)

The Ambassadors is, pretty much, a transposition into narrative form of a comedy of manners. The repudiation of New England social and intellectual values is sharp, deep, total. But the tone is that of urbane irony. *The Wings of the Dove* is closer to tragedy than to comedy.

Its main character (hardly its heroine) is the English girl Kate Croy; its main theme is the English middle class, where upward mobility is possible, but the road to success harsh, vicious, unscrupulous. Milly, the American heiress doomed to an early death, is the exploited victim. Like Strether, it is Kate who will have the last word. The narrative this time is more compelling, more staccato. The implication is the same, however: we shall find out all we need to know about Kate in good time.

> She waited, Kate Croy, for her father to come in . . . .

Why the inversion? Is it just conversational mannerism? We have to read James's opening paragraph more than once, to puzzle over it as we might puzzle over the text of a poem, before the run of the sense and the distribution of the emphases which the sense dictates become clear. We end up, I suggest, with something like:

> Shé wáited, Kàte Cròy, for her fáther to còme ìn . . .
> (´ denotes a strong stress, ` a weaker stress)

Not just a simple statement that Kate remained in the room till her father appeared — nearly three pages later: *waited* is the ostentatious, self-righteous waiting of the chairman of a meeting who does not expect to be kept waiting by stragglers, and shows it. Kate has come to see her father: he knew she was coming, he could have had the grace to wait in for her; instead, *she* has to do the waiting; *shé wáited*, therefore, out in front, with a strong double stress. But *Kate Croy* is stressed too, if less strongly — a first hint that Kate, whatever she was once, is not now somebody to be kept waiting. Not at any rate by her father — by such a father: a strong stress on *father*; a secondary stress on *come in*, to make the point that his coming in isn't something to be taken as a matter of course.

but hè kept hèr uncónscionably . . .

Once again, the thought is Kate's; a further pointer to the way
she feels about the father with whom she has come (we shall
discover) to propose a somewhat bizarre reconciliation.

> and there were moments at which she showed herself, in the
> glass over the mantel, a face positively pale with the
> irritation that had brought her to the point of going away
> without sight of him . . . .

After two short, heavily stressed, probing clauses, the narrative expands into a third, much longer clause. The expanding
triad (or *tricolon crescendo*) is a traditional rhetorical device.
Here, it establishes the rhythm of the narrative, launches the
story on its way; at the same time it brings the scene into
sharp focus. A lesser writer might have had Kate striding up
and down the room. James brings the camera to bear upon
her at rest, surrendering to a typical feminine instinct, pausing
to look at herself 'in the glass over the mantel'. What the
mirror shows us is 'a face positively pale with irritation'. But
that is not what Kate sees. What she sees is a proof that she
has escaped from her sordid past; she is well dressed, handsome; not 'pretty', not 'beautiful'; 'handsome'; the phrase 'the
handsome girl' will recur, time after time, in the ensuing
pages. To say all this at once, now, is not the way James has
chosen to go about it. He holds his hand for a page or so.
When he has described the scene from which Kate has
escaped, he will come back to her:

> . . . the girl's repeated pause before the mirror and the
> chimney-place represented her nearest approach to an
> escape. . . . . Wasn't it in fact the partial escape from this
> 'worst' in which she was steeped to make herself out again
> as agreeable to see? She stared into the tarnished glass too
> hard indeed to be staring at her beauty alone. . . .

> It was át thìs poìnt, however, that she remáined; . . .

James's opening sentence suggested, perhaps, a fixed tableau
— Kate seated in a chair, say, looking at her reflection, about

to get up and go. It is part of the business of the second sentence to correct this: 'át thìs poìnt' (not, we realize on a re-reading 'at this poínt') picks up 'to the point of going away' but adds a note of irony, for we now see that 'remained' is to be read — not in the straightforward sense 'didn't go away', but in the sense 'paused' — kept deciding to leave, kept turning on her heel, perhaps, away from the mirror toward the door; then turning back again into the room, or toward the window. The words 'changing her place' add a further corrective. She *does* sit down, but she keeps getting up (to go to the mirror), and then returning to a different seat — because each time she sits down, she feels she has to escape:

> moving from the shabby sofa to the armchair upholstered in a glazed cloth that gave at once — she had tried it — the sense of the slippery and the sticky.

A few deft touches sketch in the repulsive scene. But the repulsion is Kate's: 'she had tried it' focuses on the exploratory touch of Kate's hand once she has sat down. Note that James does not say that the armchair *was* slippery and sticky, but that it 'gave at once . . . the sense of the slippery and the sticky'; 'slippery' and 'sticky' become — not so much a description of the chair, as the keynote of the whole sordid scene, and by implication (an implication soon to be confirmed) a symbol of the character of Kate's father.

IV

If novelists always wrote like that, reading novels would be hard work. James writes for readers who will read more than once — will, at any rate, turn back, on their way through his long story, to that opening paragraph, expecting to make more of it than they did the first time, gratified to discover how much they had been told without realizing it. Few readers would have the patience to build up the picture, detail by detail, implication by implication, on their first time through; more than you might suppose slips into the practised reader's subconscious, controlling the reader's expectations at some subliminal level. The difficulty of James's last novels is often exaggerated: by the end of his career James had developed a quite extraordinary sense for the stresses and inflections of the speaking voice (perhaps in part because the last novels were actually dictated); to read them aloud takes practice; but when you've got the knack, you will find them easier to read aloud than silently. The fact remains, of course, that, though we read poems that way, we expect novels to be plainer sailing.

* * *

Let's take a longer example. At the beginning of Book 4 of Virgil's *Aeneid*, attention shifts from Aeneas, the Trojan refugee whose narrative of his adventures occupied the previous two books, to his royal hostess, Queen Dido of Carthage, and the scene at the banquet in his honour over which she has been presiding. The banquet is at an end, the handsome adventurer has finished his tale, Dido is left to her thoughts and feelings:

> But the Queen, long since crippled by love's blow,
> nourishes the wound with her veins, is torn at by a hidden
>   fire.
> Much the manliness of the man to her thoughts keeps
>   coursing back,
> much the honour of his line: in her mind his face, his words
> stick fast, passion denies her limbs the peace of sleep.
> Next day's dawn was ranging the earth with Phoebus'
>   torch,
> had pushed apart the damp darkness in the sky,
> when, barely sane, she addressed her sister (always like-
>   minded) thus:
> 'Sister Anna, what dreams reduce me to fear and indeci-
>   sion!
> What a man this stranger is who has come newly to our
>   house!
> What a countenance is his, what a chest and shoulders on
>   him!

I do believe, it is no fancy, he is of the race of gods.
Ignoble spirits are by fear betrayed. Oh, how tossed
by fate, what wars drained to the last he told of!
If it were not settled in my mind, unshakable,
never again to bind myself with the marriage bond,
after my first love failed me, deceived me by his death,
if I did not loathe marriage beds, marriage torches,
I might perhaps have surrendered and failed this once.
Anna, I will confess it, since my poor husband Sychæus
died, his blood shed in his own house by a brother's hand,
this man alone has upset my feelings, set my thoughts
tottering. I acknowledge the old fire. It smoulders still.
But I had sooner the earth opened up before me,
or that the all-powerful father blasted me to the deep
night of hell, hell that the pale shades inhabit,
than ravish honour or undo honour's laws.
He who first joined himself to me has taken love
away: let him have it for his own, let him keep it in the
    grave.'

Dido is desperately in love. Nothing like this has happened to
her since her husband died; it takes time for her to come to
terms with the situation which confronts her, time to prepare
herself for the consequences; *we* need time to understand
Dido's reaction; Book 4 begins slowly, therefore. Her first
impulse is to break the vow she had made not to remarry; then
her sense of how a queen must behave reasserts itself and she
struggles to dismiss the idea. Not much happens in these
twenty-nine lines. And yet the complexity of the sideways
process generated by them is almost inexhaustible; every time
you read them you see more in them.

The responsive reader feels pulled different ways (the
sideways expansion operates in different planes so to speak);
the components of a complex field conflict, but don't cancel
one another out: they interact, a tension is established, an
associative complex that gives the story depth, interest (dynamic, compulsive interest), the illusion of truth to the human
condition; we are challenged to reconsider conventional
notions about how queens and heroes (in and out of legend)
should behave.

Take the opening words, *But the Queen*: cool, almost casual, not in the least melodramatic; not, say, 'Meantime most lovely Dido' or the like; Dido is going to be 'most lovely' later when she stands asking her gods for permission to remarry; the adjective will emphasize then the contrast between the woman in love and the role of queen and chief priestess which she struggles to enact; 'Queen' sets resonating one key theme in the coming tragedy — Dido *is* a queen, not an ordinary woman; she cannot forget it, struggles to reconcile what she wants with her concept of what queenliness demands — and loses. The phrase 'But the Queen' will recur at the beginning of the quarrel scene (it is an outraged queen who confronts the lover who is about to walk out on her) and at the beginning of the death scene (it is Dido's concept of herself which causes her to stage-manage her spectacular suicide). 'Queen' sets the sideways process working.

The basic component is that which sets up and sustains the epic framework: it is a matter of the décor (the magnificence of the banquet, implanted in our minds by the narrative of a previous book), a matter of diction (formal, dignified), a matter of the metrical structure; a matter of the long, formal opening speech: in an epic poem a character usually speaks for at least ten lines, more often twenty, each time he opens his mouth. All these features emphasize the allegiance of Virgil's text to the tradition of Homeric epic. The heavy assonance of the opening k's and w's in the original Latin emphasizes his allegiance to the old Roman tradition of narrative poetry. 'But the Queen', in a different context, might be dry and flat: here it rides on a crest of remembered majesty; these are not ordinary people and these are not ordinary events.

But there are components of the field which pull other ways, transforming what might have been dead pastiche into a living tension. The fresh day dawning is Homeric:

> Next day's dawn was ranging the earth with Phoebus'
>   torch,
> had pushed apart the damp darkness in the sky,
> when, barely sane, she addressed her sister (always like-
>   minded) thus . . .

Conceptually, however, the scene belongs to tragedy. People get up early in Greek tragedy; they come out into the light of the new day to cast off the pollution of night, to unburden themselves to the cosmos. Dido unburdens herself — not to the world of nature, but to her sister; she is a civilized, sophisticated woman (not a barbarian like Euripides' Medea); she acknowledges the obligation to be rational, to sort things out, to act in accordance with moral standards; but she is 'barely sane'; rational decision is now beyond her.

Virgil is loading the dice against Dido. Not openly, but by the calculated resonance of a key word, by our sense of the field of significance which is building up around the narrative. The twin metaphors of the physical wound and the hidden fire with which the narrative began were explored as if literally true:

> But the Queen, long since crippled by love's blow,
> nourishes the wound with her veins, is torn at by a hidden
>   fire.

Dido's love for Aeneas is love in its simplest, most conventional form (the sudden, irrational infatuation verging on madness); conventional imagery can serve to state it; the metaphors belong to the stock imagery of love poetry. But the coolly rational exploration of the metaphors introduces overtones suggesting precise, dispassionate, scientific explanation. We feel the sideways expansion take on a further component: the rational exploration of the imagery recalls the Roman materialist poet and philosopher Lucretius. Clear echoes of Lucretius reinforce our sense of the presence of this further component: Lucretius, too, describes love as a physical wound but he is contemptuous of the fuss men make about love; he derides lovers who see visions of their beloved flit before their eyes; Virgil's 'in her mind his face, his words stick fast' crisply evokes Lucretius' more diffuse 'if the object of your love is absent, at once there are images of her present, her sweet name rings in your ears'.

With the echoes of Lucretius comes the implied invitation to see Dido — not in tragic terms as the victim of searing, irresistible passion, but as a headstrong woman made foolish by a transitory madness; indulging passion, willing to resort to self-deception. Virgil isn't debunking Dido; his account of her infatuation and suicide isn't simplistically Lucretius. The components of the field of significance co-exist: the epic form generates one component; the familiar tragic situation, a second; overtones of intellectual materialism elicited by the echoes of Lucretius, a third.

The opening eight lines set the tone of the book. Then we listen to Dido as she tries to justify herself to her sister: by the time she has finished, she has a powerful claim upon us; but along with sympathy goes a critical appraisal which is not part of the mental set of a normal reading of an epic or a tragic text; her words are designed to reveal her thoughts, as though she were not a figure of epic or tragedy, but a real person whose conflicting emotions we could sense and analyse.

She begins 'What dreams reduce me to fear and indecision!' After the banquet, Dido has spent a short, troubled night. What has she been dreaming about? Once again we have Lucretius at hand to help us: we see the dead in dreams; that too, he tells us, can be explained in materialist terms; we dream of those things which most occupy our waking minds; that also has a rational explanation. Prepared to think in Lucretian terms, we can fit together the hints provided: Dido has been dreaming of Aeneas, of being in love with him, of marriage with Aeneas; the dream terrifies her; she also sees her dead husband in her dreams; that dream terrifies her too; now, though 'crippled by love's blow', she has pulled herself together and, 'barely sane', she attempts to sort things out. She retreats in terror from the way she feels her thoughts moving; for her, the only logical step is marriage to the man for whom she feels as she has felt for no other since her husband's death:

> Anna, I will confess it, since my poor husband Sychæus died, his blood shed in his own house by a brother's hand, this man alone has upset my feelings, set my thoughts tottering. I acknowledge the old fire. It smoulders still.

But she panics at the logic of her own thoughts, ostensibly because of loyalty to her vow:

> But I had sooner the earth opened up before me,
> or that the all-powerful father blasted me to the deep
> night of hell, hell that the pale shades inhabit,
> than ravish honour or undo honour's laws.
> He who first joined himself to me has taken love
> away: let him have it for his own, let him keep it in the
>   grave.

What she had said a moment before suggested another, less commendable motive:

> If it were not settled in my mind, unshakable,
> never again to bind myself with the marriage bond,
> after my first love failed me, deceived me by his death,
> if I did not loathe marriage beds, marriage torches,
> I might perhaps have surrendered and failed this once.

Marriage let Dido down; her husband was murdered, she was cheated of his love; she resolved she would not let herself be cheated again. It is a clue to Dido's character — to the character Virgil will build up, hint by hint: this proud, wilful woman is utterly self-centred.

The epic tradition of Homer and the Roman Ennius, Greek tragedy, the Roman materialist Lucretius, these are the chief components of the field of significance through which these lines move. The first two are obvious enough: they are central to the tradition in which Virgil writes. I stress the third because the echoes of Lucretius aren't just verbal echoes — part of Virgil's reading which wells up in the heat of composition and is pressed into service. Lucretius is more than the greatest Roman poet of the preceding generation (perhaps even the greatest Roman poet before Virgil): he is also a source of ideas for Virgil and his contemporaries — new, exciting ideas about how the world works; the Epicurean philosophy which he expounds provides one of two powerful intellectual frameworks within which the minds of thinking Romans of Virgil's generation could come to terms with the world around them — Epicurean materialism and Stoic acceptance of fate. For those who were not philosophers by profession, professionally committed to one or the other, the two co-existed as familiar, challenging explanations of the world and our role in it. Rather as Marxism and the theories of Freud stand out among intellectual influences in the twentieth century. A writer doesn't have to be a committed Marxist or a committed Freudian to find the more familiar doctrines of either a convenient intellectual framework to draw upon: Marx or Freud provides a body of ideas that can be alluded to, exploited as a way of implying more than is said, a way of letting what is said expand into a complex structure of implied significance — the more powerful because the i's are not dotted and the t's not crossed, because the reader's collaboration is tactfully elicited.

When this is done with an old, familiar story, the old story is seen in a new light: it can then be thoroughly modernized the myth retold with all the names changed; or the story can be retold with the old names, but everything else modernized (as in Jean Anouilh's ironic modernization of Sophocles' *Antigone*); or — as in Virgil's *Aeneid* — the old story can exploit the traditional form, offering the reader a fresh depth of intellectual content. Virgil can represent Dido as believing in an avenging Jove armed with a thunderbolt to strike down the wicked, believing in an underworld peopled by shades of the dead:

> But I had sooner the earth opened up before me,
> or that the all-powerful father blasted me to the deep
> night of hell, hell that the pale shades inhabit,
> than ravish honour or undo honour's laws.

We shall see her later (in Book 6) condemned for all eternity, along with her husband, to that *hell that the pale shades inhabit*. The traditional framework enhances the poetry and the imaginative fiction. At the same time, Dido is a real woman, a woman we can think about, pity, judge as we judge the people in the living world around us.

V
NOVELS

Until you have told your story, it has no form, no structure; it is infinitely flexible; you can bend it any way you like, cut it off at any point you wish. As you tell your story, it takes shape; when you have finished, it is that story, that poem, that play; it is those words in that order, telling your story that way; a structure of words and syntax that sometimes forces itself upon the reader's attention more than the story told. Those words in that order, playing those tricks.

Narrative texts tend to be long — often very long. The Dido passage comes from a text almost 10 000 lines in length: that's about the length of *Paradise Lost* — the length of the average modern novel. Space is needed to construct a sequence of situations, in the course of which the story can take shape, develop and then come to an end.

That means an important difference between a novel and the sort of poem that normally comes into our minds today when we think of poems — a text a mere dozen lines long, perhaps, at most two or three dozen. The status of a short poem as story can never be more than marginal; the words must work fast, must generate a more powerful sideways thrust than would be necessary, or tolerable, in a novel or a long narrative poem. Reading a typical modern short poem is strenuous mental exercise: there is the challenge of a problem to be solved; you have to bring into some kind of organization in your mind resonant words in resonating combinations (contrasting, perhaps, with an illusion of conversational casualness), a rhythm that guides as well as compels, rhymes that highlight key words, producing an effect of incantation or magical utterance — you have to bring all that under control and make out of it something that hangs together as a structure of meaning. Reading a novel (most novels) or a long narrative poem is, by comparison, a leisurely experience.

You can see why. A novel can't work like a poem only twenty lines long: you may eventually read a novel two or three times — half a dozen times, even; but you can't postpone till you've done that your attempt to make of it something that hangs together. The nature of the literary experience is transformed by the difference in length. With a novel, you have to build your consistency as you go; even when you re-read a novel, it's like travelling a second time along a road you half remember from a previous trip. The novel, moreover, is an experience in graduated doses (chapters): a course of injections, rather than a single shot. But, above all, there is space: space for detailed account of what happened; space for detailed report of what the characters say to one another; space for detailed description of scene.

* * *

The novel remained for a long time a kind of non-form: it was fiction pretending to be autobiography (like *Robinson Crusoe* or *Moll Flanders*); fiction pretending to be history (like Trollope's *Barchester Towers*); fiction pretending to be a collection of letters (like Richardson's *Clarissa*) — anything but what it was in fact, a work of fiction. All these structuring devices are still used; others have been devised; we may be invited to imagine (as in Conrad's *Heart of Darkness*) that we are listening to a tale put together on the spur of the moment by a man talking to friends about his memories — and then lapsing into a story a hundred pages long.

The idea was to give the reader some explanation for the text: there was no intention to deceive; the reader was challenged to see the everyday transformed into something of more permanent relevance which could be accepted as a work of literature. The short personal poem began in much the same way: a poem claimed to be an actual letter to a mistress or a friend, or to have been written to commemorate an actual birthday, marriage or death. The difference is that a poem can never cease to be a poem — its structure won't permit that; a novel, not being written in verse, *can* almost get away with pretending to be a non-literary text. Almost, not quite: the disguise is seldom hard to penetrate.

Once people had got used to novels, the disguise didn't have to be adopted. Some novelists still keep up the pretence; others found different ways of doing things. Dickens favoured a novel which was an obvious fiction, a reorganization of reality, that made no pretence of reporting fact; a fiction which was whimsical, comic, discursive, bordered on fantasy — and was yet true to the human condition. There's never been, and still isn't, such a thing as the typical novel; no set of conventions has displaced all others, won acceptance as *the* way to write a novel. Any short list of major twentieth-century novels must include wholly eccentric, unprecedented, isolated masterpieces such as Proust's *Looking for Lost Time*, Joyce's *Ulysses*, Carlos Fuentes's *Terra Nostra*: we can't dismiss such works on the grounds that they're against the rules for writing novels, any more than we can dismiss the French novels of the *nouvelle vague*, or the experiments of the 1970s and 80s with magic realism, which seem to discard the novel form altogether. There are no laws such as those we formulate to describe the physical universe. Any writer who chooses can stand the traditional rules on their head, and perhaps get away with it.

A decision to stand the rules on their head implies of course an awareness that the rules exist. Poems and novels — the good ones — are more often the work of the artistically sophisticated than the artistically naive. Milton chose to write *Paradise Lost* in blank verse because he was aware that major poems had been written in the past without rhyme. Twentieth-century poets, when they in their turn discarded rhyme, knew what they were doing and why they wanted to do it. When, as a further assertion of a break with tradition, they allowed the sense to stray across the line-end to a degree nineteenth-century poets would have found intolerable, the aim was to create a tension between rhythm and syntax, which the reader would feel and would mark, in reading the poem aloud, by some kind of pause or change of inflection. Contemporary novelists play tricks with plot: because they are irked by conventions of plot that have outgrown their usefulness; but also as a provocation of their readers, to disconcert them by a narrative that does not work the way they have come to expect. Of course, the time comes when the reason for innovation and the nature of that innovation have been forgotten: today, poets and ordinary readers alike often read poems aloud as though the line-end were merely a convention of the printed page, a warning that you were reading poetry and might expect some rhythmical change, but not necessarily a pause or change of stress at the line-end. When the novelty of plots that have no clear beginning or end fades, it becomes necessary to go back to a conventional beginning and end (as

Umberto Eco does in *Foucault's Pendulum*, in which the narrative ends where it began 640 pages before).

There are fashions, however. Earlier novelists were fond of the massive novel which followed the adventures of a set of characters over a whole lifetime, sometimes literally from birth to death. One modern fashion which has lasted well is for the kind of novel that's built around a tightly woven plot: a structure closer to drama than to history. Such a novel resembles an attack of acute appendicitis: there is a clear-cut beginning, a rapidly evolving sequence of events which pushes everything else in the world aside; a crisis, during which the patient-hero is distraught, his perception of himself and all around him is distorted by fever; then, usually, the surgical intervention, and the sequence winds down to a more or less happy conclusion — it is all over; occasionally, the fever subsides of its own accord; sometimes, the surgeon's intervention fails and the patient dies.

Very different from this complusive, streamlined pseudo-realism is the technique, common in novels of the 1970s and 80s, of constructing the narrative in such a way as to frustrate the reader's expectation of a straightforward story progressing from definite beginning to definite end. The unexpected is not so much in the events narrated (which are often in no sense outlandish or bizarre) but in the manner of narration. In Milan Kundera's *The Unbearable Lightness of Being*, for example, the narrative begins in deceptively straightforward fashion: the style is simple; the tone, no more than urbanely philosophical; the characters, interesting, intriguing and plausible enough (such implausibilities as are attributed to them are spoken of in terms to disarm incredulity); everything takes place in a world we can believe in:

Tereza tried to see herself through her body. That is why, from girlhood on, she would stand before the mirror so often. And because whe was afraid her mother would catch her at it, every peek into the mirror had a tinge of secret vice.

It was not vanity that drew her to the mirror; it was amazement at seeing her own 'I'. She forgot she was looking at the instrument panel of her body mechanisms; she thought she saw her soul shining through the features of her face. She forgot that the nose was merely the nozzle of a hose that took oxygen to the lungs; she saw it as the true expression of her nature.

Staring at herself for long stretches of time, she was occasionally upset at the sight of her mother's features in her face. She would stare all the more doggedly at her image in an attempt to wish them away and keep only what was hers alone. Each time she succeeded was a time of intoxication: her soul would rise to the surface of her body like a crew charging up from the bowels of a ship, spreading out over the deck, waving at the sky and singing in jubilation.

> Milan Kundera, *The Unbearable Lightness of Being*,
> Part 2, Chapter 3)

But the narrative, once launched on its course, keeps changing course in a series of flashbacks, anticipations, repetitions, changes of context – each suggesting reinterpretation or reorganization of the story thus far told. As with Picasso's paintings of his cubist period, what, in different hands, might seem naive incompetence (heads that are triangular or quadrilateral, eyes in the wrong place) is in fact the product of a highly sophisticated technique. The Kundera speaking voice deprecates disbelief, as though to question what we are told were a failure, on the reader's part, to measure up to the writer's expectations. The object is to jolt us out of our confidence that we know the shape of the world around us, that what happens to human beings can always be assembled into a continuous narrative; we see the world around us and the people in it in, as we say, 'a new light', subjected to the distortion of a fresh perspective. Or simply to remind us that the business of art is not only, or always, to depict, or describe, for immediate recognition and instant acquiescence, the world of familiar, or readily imaginable, experience.

There's no end to the shape novels can take. What they have in common is something the reader can recognize as story — fiction so structured as to switch on the appropriate mental set. Attempts to structure novels without a story (or with token stories, stories that lead nowhere), in order to make fiction 'truer' to 'real life', like the kitchen-sink dramas of the 1950s, only work in so far as they can sustain a mental set in which pseudo-realism (in particular, crude, repetitious dialogue), in addition to working as farce (or heavy-handed social satire, perhaps), can lay the ground for something else. As the farcical realism of the conversations between Petey and his wife in Harold Pinter's *Birthday Party*, for example, helps to lend the pseudo-realistic fantasy of the thuggery scenes a kind of symbolic significance. The mental set with which we read fiction is not the mental set we adopt in dealing with everyday life. We take in life around us because it is there; it has to be coped with; action is demanded of us. To get interested in the doings of a set of characters who never existed, we need a structuring of events capable of generating around these characters a field of significance which arouses and holds our attention.

* * *

It isn't so much a clear-cut beginning and clear-cut end which make a novel: it is the total concentration on the events narrated and the field of significance which these generate to the exclusion of all else. The world stands still while Barchester looks for its new bishop, reacts to his reign, waits for the old dean to die, has his successor imposed. For weeks on end that Paris spring, nothing seems to impinge upon the consciousness of Henry James's characters in *The Ambassadors* beyond their relationship with one another. We know that in real life political or ecclesiastic intrigue, a love affair, even the pursuit of a murderer, seldom totally excludes all else from the minds and daily routine of the participants: in a novel, we accept the convention because, if well handled, it can give effective shape to, and intensify, the literary experience.

A common structuring device is to string together a series of episodes; a field is built up that is the representation of a way of life — or rather, the writer's vision of a way of life. Thus, in the opening chapter of Heinrich Böll's *And Never Said a Word*, the narrator, in the course of one afternoon, draws money from a city bank, buys himself a scratch meal at a hot-dog stand, visits a basement shoemaker (where he leaves money and a note for his wife), visits two middle-class homes (giving a lesson in mathematics to a son of the house in one, and a lesson in Latin to the daughter of the other), visits a fashionable married couple (from whom he attempts to borrow money), visits an old school friend (where he attempts again to borrow money), visits a city church, and finally ends up in a pub playing a pinball machine. By the end of the chapter we have built up a picture of a character (seedy, hard-up, unscrupulous, but with some depth to him) and can place him in the context of a way of life.

A work of fiction builds up its own reality. The reality built up may seem strange, bizarre; it may seem to contradict our own experience of reality. If we were actually reading the sort of text many novels pretend, or half pretend, to be, our mental controls would signal something wrong. In a work of fiction, all depends on whether the fiction can sustain the fantasy: if it can, we aren't disturbed. I don't mean it depends on whether the writer can get away with telling lies: I mean something more complicated and more intriguing. We read objective prose reluctant to go along with anything contrary to common sense; we refer what we read to our judgement of true or false; accept what's true, reject what's false; objective prose deals with *how it is, how it was or will be*. Fiction deals, most often, with *how it could well have been* (but in fact wasn't). It deals also, though more rarely, with *how it would have to be* — granted the hypothesis which the particular text invites us to grant: the test then is not the test of true or false — not even general truth to our experience of life; the test is, does the fantasy convince, or not convince?

The way one thing leads to another in a novel may be just too good to be true: we accept this as part of the writer's reorganization of experience; it doesn't detract from the essential truth of the fiction — and perhaps even enhances it by setting the essential truth against a contrasting background of formal convention or fantasy. No sensible reader minds if the characters in a novel keep running into one another with a frequency that would strike us as extraordinary in real life; no sensible reader is disturbed when just about every male character in Henry James's *Portrait of a Lady*, upon meeting James's heroine, promptly falls in love and proposes marriage to her. James has made things neater, more interesting, more challenging to the imagination than in real life.

There are novels in which the behaviour of the characters falls outside all norms of human behaviour. García Márquez's *One Hundred Years of Solitude* repeatedly invites us to accept what in a different context we'd dismiss as fantastic. I say 'invites', though there is of course no invitation extended in as many words. The fantastic is simply put forward as the most natural thing in the world:

> They went into José Arcadio Buendía's room, shook him as hard as they could, shouted in his ear, put a mirror in front of his nostrils, but they could not awaken him. A short time later, when the carpenter was taking measurements for the coffin, through the window they saw a light rain of tiny yellow flowers falling. They fell on the town all through the night in a silent storm, and they covered the roofs and blocked the doors and smothered the animals who slept outdoors. So many flowers fell from the sky that in the morning the streets were carpeted with a compact cushion and they had to clear them away with shovels and rakes so that the funeral procession could pass by.

In literature, nothing is impossible: pigs can fly, the dead can speak; gods, goddesses can be spoken of without apology or explanation as moving among human beings, unseen or in human shape. Things happen that no one in his right mind would accept. Take Milton's narrative of how Satan, the night after his arrival in Paradise, sets out upon his devilish temptation of Eve:

> So saying, on he led his radient Files,
> Daz'ling the Moon; these to the Bower direct
> In search of whom they sought: him there they found
> Squat like a Toad, close at the eare of *Eve*;

Assaying by his Devilish art to reach
The Organs of her Fancie, and with them forge
Illusions as he list, Fantasms and Dreams;
Or if, inspiring venom, he might taint
Th' animal spirits that from pure blood arise
Like gentle breaths from Rivers pure, thence raise
At least distempered, discontented thoughts,
Vain hopes, vain aimes, inordinate desires
Blown up with high conceits ingendring pride.

(Milton, *Paradise Lost*, Book 4)

Milton certainly believed in God; there was a sense in which he believed in the Devil. But to take *Paradise Lost* as Milton's notion of what happened in the Garden of Eden is a naive misreading: his story, like Virgil's story in the *Aeneid* or Coleridge's story in the *Ancient Mariner*, is a conscious fantasy, meant to be recognized as fantasy; any impulse to reject the story on the grounds that 'it didn't happen', 'it isn't true' springs from an equally naive misconception of the nature of fiction.

Coleridge called the psychological process involved 'a willing suspension of disbelief' (*Biographia Literaria*, Chapter 14, speaking of his contribution to *Lyrical Ballads*). But why should we be willing to suspend disbelief, willingly allow a writer to get away with things anybody in his right mind knows can't happen? Once again, it's a matter of mental set. But we don't just switch off common sense because we are reading a novel or a poem: the compulsion to believe must come from the novel or the poem. Involuntary belief might be nearer the mark than voluntary suspension of disbelief. The involuntary belief lasts of course only for the duration of the fiction which induces it. A thoroughly bad novel induces no compulsion. It is the narrative energy generated by *Paradise Lost* or *One Hundred Years of Solitude* which compels us to accept what we are told as plausible, convincing even, within a world which the narrative itself creates by a process of selective description built into the story as it unwinds; the field of significance set up is sufficiently powerful to hold together those things which are completely acceptable as part of our human experience and those which, if taken in isolation, we should have to reject as fantastic. In literature nothing is impossible. We don't read fiction in our right minds: we read prepared to surrender to the supernatural or the fantastic, not just as something we can let the writer get away with if his story is good enough, but because the supernatural or the fantastic creates and enhances the literary experience. We don't swallow all we're told simply because our mental controls are set at fiction: what we're told has got to be plausible by the standards that particular fiction sets; if the fiction cannot sustain the implausibility, our minds protest, the control of the text over our minds is threatened, or lost altogether.

The function of the fantasy in *One Hundred Years of Solitude* is, I think, to serve as a representation of the mental processes of a remote Spanish-speaking community in Central America for whom the frontier between what can happen and what can't isn't ours: the simple, apparently naive narrative invites us to accept, as a matter of course, what our experience of our kind of world would normally impel us to reject.

Rather different from this kind of open fantasy is what is sometimes called poetic truth. Take this paragraph from Conrad's *Heart of Darkness*; the scene is the River Thames at sunset, early this century:

The day was ending in a serenity of still and exquisite brilliance. The water shone pacifically; the sky, without a speck, was a benign immensity of unstained light; the very mist on the Essex marshes was like a gauzy and radiant fabric, hung from the wooded rises inland, and draping the low shores in diaphanous folds. Only the gloom to the west, brooding over the upper reaches, became more sombre every minute, as if angered by the approach of the sun.

And at last, in its curved and imperceptible fall, the sun sank low, and from glowing white changed to a dull red without rays and without heat, as if about to go out suddenly, stricken to death by the touch of that gloom brooding over a crowd of men.

Forthwith a change came over the waters, and the serenity became less brilliant but more profound. The old river in its broad reach rested unruffled at the decline of day, after ages of good service done to the race that peopled its banks, spread out in the tranquil dignity of a waterway leading to the uttermost ends of the earth. We looked at the venerable stream not in the vivid flush of a short day that comes and departs for ever, but in the august light of abiding memories. And indeed nothing is easier for a man who has, as the phrase goes, 'followed the sea' with reverence and affection, than to evoke the great spirit of the past upon the lower reaches of the Thames. The tidal current runs to and fro in its unceasing service, crowded with memories of men and ships it had borne to the rest of home or to the battles of the sea. It had known and served all the men of whom the nation is proud, from Sir Francis Drake to Sir John Franklin, knights all, titled and untitled — the great knights-errant of the sea. It had borne all the ships whose names are like jewels flashing in the night of time, from the *Golden Hind* returning with her round flanks full of treasure, to be visited by the Queen's Highness and thus pass out of the gigantic tale, to the *Erebus* and *Terror*, bound on other conquests — and that never returned. It had known the ships and the men. They had sailed from Deptford, from Greenwich, from Erith — the adventurers and the settlers; kings' ships and the ships of men on 'Change; captains, admirals, the dark 'interlopers' of the Eastern trade, and the commissioned 'generals' of East India fleets. Hunters for gold or pursuers of fame, they all had gone out on that stream, bearing the sword, and often the torch, messengers of the might within the land, bearers of a spark from the sacred fire. What greatness had not floated on the ebb of that river into the mystery of an unknown earth! . . . The dreams of men, the seed of commonwealths, the germs of empires.

We wouldn't accept that in our right minds either: the sustained personification of the River Thames is an open appeal to what critics called the 'pathetic fallacy' — treating inanimate nature as though it shared our human thoughts and feelings. True, the way is discreetly prepared (the mist 'was like' a gauzy fabric, the gloom in the west brooded, 'as if' angered); rivers are traditionally living creatures, gods even. But that only explains why Conrad can get away with what he does: it doesn't explain why he tries. This is more than fine writing. Conrad is building up a field of significance in which we can feel that normal rational attitudes are out of place. We can thus more easily accept the unstated implications of Conrad's story. Expressed in objective prose, the story would not be a story at all, but a rational attack on what we now call colonialism, backed up by an appeal to the argument that history repeats itself: as the Romans came to the end of the earth to conquer Britain, so modern Europeans have travelled to the end of the earth to conquer Africa; the Thames is the symbolic setting of the first conquest, the Congo of the second. Expressed as it is, the reorganization of experience takes on this privileged status of essential truth.

VI
PERSPECTIVE AND VERBAL TEXTURE

Why write novels, poems, plays, telling tales that aren't true? Why read them? Is it only a sophisticated form of entertainment? A game, a pastime, a form of escape from boredom? This is the place to say something more about two related properties of literary texts. One I shall call *perspective*; the other *texture*. Both terms appeal to an analogy with the visual arts. As I shall use them here, 'perspective' is an aspect of meaning; 'texture' is a property of the verbal structure itself.

Perspective is the angle from which a writer sees a character, an event, an emotional situation, a moral dilemma — or rather, how the writer invites us to see these by the words he uses. How, to extend the metaphor, the light falls from that angle, the highlights and the shadows; the emphases and exclusions which result if the narrator moves in closer, the ironic detachment if the distance is increased. The perspective from which you look at something determines the way you think about it, determines the understanding, the insight which the resultant organization prompts; determines the capacity of the narrative thus constructed to generate understanding and insight in us, its readers.

What we are talking about is often ascribed to the power of the writer's imagination, or to the writer's moral vision. But these terms focus attention on the writer rather than on the novel or the poem before us: the writer's mind is only accessible to us through the writer's text and the speaking voice we read into that text. If that text is competently constructed, it determines the area within which our response is given free, independent play (but never wholly free, never wholly independent). If we talk of 'insight' in connection with a novel or a poem, what is at issue is the writer's insight as evidenced by the perspective from which our thoughts are brought to bear upon the fiction as it falls into shape in our minds while we read. The quality of that insight, as evidenced in that fiction: it may be fresh, sharp, penetrating, convincing; or it may be conventional, blunt, undiscerning.

The quality of a writer's insight, in short, becomes of interest only if the writer can — not only organize insight into an unusually vivid, arresting perspective, but transpose that perspective into words. 'Transpose into words' rather than 'express in words': transposition demands capacity to exploit the potential of the chosen form; to construct a reorganization of reality within that form; to construct a way of seeing with words, syntax, rhythm, as a painter uses colour and shape to construct a way of seeing the world, a way of showing the world to us. I call this quality of a novel or a poem its verbal 'texture'.

I have argued in the previous chapter that every competent text sets up (and maintains, with variations) its own distinctive rhythm. That rhythm establishes the level of seriousness (what is sometimes called the *tone*) of the narrative; sets up a speaking voice and an attitude; holds together all that is striking, challenging, paradoxical in word and phrase (all that otherwise would merely catch the eye) in an articulated tension. Fiction isn't necessarily better written than history (or a poem better written than philosophical argument) — it may not be. It is differently written, however; different in its structure as well as its form. It is the texture of the verbal fabric which, more than anything else, distinguishes a good novel, or a good poem, from a bad. Exploitation of texture in the absence of any settled perspective upon the human condition degenerates into fine writing. Insight into the human condition in the absence of any special ability to create with words is clumsy, if possible at all.

Suppose we take a portrait many of you will know: Modigliani's portrait of a female nude in the Courtauld Institute in London, or his portrait of the bride and groom in the Museum of Modern Art in New York: in one case an unnamed woman; in the other, an unnamed couple. What we have before us is a structure of paint on canvas: the shapes, colours and texture of the paint constitute an aesthetic experience; the colours move us as colours, the shapes catch and hold our eyes as shapes, the texture of the paint has a sensuous appeal that has little to do with the person represented, but is a property of the painting as a painting.

And yet we have no difficulty in accepting them as human beings; no difficulty in feeling the artist has communicated to us his understanding of these human beings, though what Modigliani has drawn is more a caricature than a drawing aimed at getting shape or detail right — a startling, vivid, intriguing caricature whose truth to life we are compelled to concede almost against our will. Paint on canvas has forced us to come to terms with the artist's invitation to see those human beings that way.

The two aspects, aesthetic experience and intellectual experience (the communicated insight, if you like), are easily recognized; what is hard to account for is the way the portrait works. The colours and shapes aren't decoded in our minds into real people, our attention remains held by the painting itself; we don't mentally substitute something else, in order to think more easily about Modigliani's nude or his bride and groom as real human beings. A thing of paint on canvas can only be a simplification and a distortion — can't really look like a real man or woman; and yet, the thing of paint on canvas triumphs over its limitations by being — not a substitute for reality, but an aesthetic experience which possesses also some quality of essential truth.

A painting is a structure of paint on canvas: a novel or a poem is a thing of words, structured into statement. Some of what I've just said holds good in this case also. As before, the structure is the basis of an aesthetic experience: the novel or poem is, like the Modigliani portrait, an expression of the artist's understanding of his subject. The terms 'perspective' and 'texture' now need careful handling, however, or they will mislead us. We are now talking about something we can only read, not something we can see except as a string of words upon the printed page. Virgil's description of Dido in love is a verbal, not a visual, experience. A resonant word or phrase will touch off an image in the reader's mind; but the text isn't a series of instructions programming a sequence of mental images; the words aren't transposed by the reader into pictures upon a mental television screen. Some degree of transposition into mental images is likely enough, but the foreground of our attention remains under the control of the structure of words; we react continuously to that structure and to the meaning we read into it. It may hardly occur to us to think what Dido looked like. Such images as are conjured up belong to the field of significance of the text rather than to our reception of the text itself. When Dido speaks, her words take on a formal eloquence (structured by metre as well as syntax) remote from the real speech of human beings. They can do this because the words are the words of a poem: if we say they offer us an enriched, enhanced, simplified representation of reality, we must remember that the representation is offered to the intellect, our thinking, concentrating, reacting intelligence, not to our eyes.

* * *

Take this passage from Henry James's *The Wings of the Dove*. Milly, the doomed heiress who knows she is doomed, comes out from her consultation with the great London doctor, having been told, in effect, to make the most of life while she can. Her impulse, until she can come to terms with what the future can now hold for her, is to take a long walk through the streets of London; to bury herself in the anonymous London crowd; to avoid, until she has sorted out her thoughts, all friends and acquaintances; to postpone explanations until she has an explanation ready:

> She had gone out with these last words so in her ears that when once she was well away — back this time in the great square alone — it was as if some instant application of them had opened out there before her. . . . No one in the world could have sufficiently entered into her state; no tie would have been close enough to enable a companion to walk beside her without some disparity. She literally felt, in this first flush, that her only company must be the human race at large, present all round her, but inspiringly impersonal, and that her only field must be, then and there, the grey immensity of London. Grey immensity had somehow of a sudden become her element; grey immensity was what her distinguished friend had, for the moment, furnished her world with and what the question of 'living', as he put it to her, living by option, by volition, inevitably took on for its immediate face. . . . The beauty of the bloom had gone from the small old sense of safety — that was distinct: she had left it behind her there for ever. But the beauty of the idea of a great adventure, a big dim experiment or struggle in which she might more responsibly than ever take a hand, had been offered her instead. . . .
> (Henry James, *The Wings of the Dove*, Book 5, Chapter IV)

If Milly had really existed, her thoughts would have remained unstructured, unarticulated, below the threshold of formulated expression; if she had that night attempted to sort out her thoughts in a letter or diary, her formulation might have been something like the short summary I have given. In real life, it is easy to imagine her formulation having interest and a practical purpose. The thoughts of a non-existent person can have no documentary value. James, while ostensibly reporting Milly's thoughts, offers us an imaginative, conspicuously structured representation of them which takes us away from mere psychological probability ('yes, it would have been like that'), without of course neglecting the need to prompt that reaction, to a purely literary experience.

* * *

To protest that a painting is misleading is to fall into the trap of assuming the artist's intention was to record the way a particular person looked. To complain that the painting tells us less about the human being it represents than a police photograph (taken according to conventions designed to secure accurate, 'objective' representation — as neutral a perspective as possible) would be silly. The fact that the police photograph is taken according to these conventions limits what it tells us. The artist's portrait, if the artist is successful, will tell us more, though it may take us time to come to terms with what it has to tell us. When their friends protested that Picasso's portrait of Gertrude Stein did not look like her, his reply, we are told, was 'It will!'

To read Proust, Dickens, Shakespeare, Virgil, Henry James to find out 'what happened' is as limiting a deconstruction as to look at Van Gogh's 'Man with one Ear' to discover what Van Gogh looked like. To take Conrad's description of the Thames at sunset as a piece of fine writing (or poetic prose) is the equivalent of admiring the texture of the paint in a portrait, and not seeing that the paint captures and expresses the artist's interpretation of the personality portrayed.

VII
THE SELF-SUFFICIENCY OF
FICTIONAL CHARACTERS

Fiction differs from history in an important respect: we can call it the self-sufficiency of a fictional narrative — its curious property of self-confirmation; its capacity to make us believe in the reality of characters who do not exist.

A history of the period of Julius Cæsar, of Napoleon or of Hitler is designed to make sense of the available facts: the text is the author's interpretation of what happened and why; the sort of person Cæsar, Napoleon, Hitler was. We accept his interpretation in so far as it squares with the facts; its confirmation lies outside itself; these things occurred, these people existed. An interpretation, based on historical fact, of the personality of Julius Cæsar is a worthwhile intellectual possession: Cæsar was part of an important historical process; this is knowledge of the real world. A novel in which Julius Cæsar, Napoleon or Hitler appeared as a major character would have to work differently: the novelist's Cæsar need only be historically plausible; we'd not be greatly concerned with detailed historical accuracy. We'd apply instead the test of self-sufficiency, or self-confirmation: does the novelist's Cæsar convince, does his story possess the quality of essential truth? Fiction, as Aristotle said, is more 'philosophical': history is concerned with what happened, fiction is concerned with our understanding of the human condition.

* * *

About Cæsar, Napoleon, Hitler, the reader knows something before he starts. The character who actually existed is, however, the exception in fiction. In Aristotle's day, poets took their characters from myth: modern writers of fiction prefer to invent their own. About Emma Bovary, or Margaret Drabble's Liz Headleand, we know only what Flaubert or Drabble tells us: both ride along in our minds upon such ideas as we have about mid-nineteenth century provincial France or Margaret Thatcher's Britain. That world 'comes to life' in the pages of *Madame Bovary* or *The Radiant Way*; it is, in both cases, an important component of the field of significance of the novel; but what we are offered is not so much knowledge of the real world as a selective representation, vivid but incomplete, of a world it doesn't occur to us to picture to ourselves with any completeness. The extent to which Emma or Liz Headleand comes to life is strictly limited: there are all sorts of things we shall never know about them because the text does not tell us, either by explicit statement or by clear hint to the responsive reader; outside the text, they have no existence. What we are told, or can guess, may amount to as much as we know about people in real life: in real life we guess the rest. Many people are therefore tempted to guess the rest about the characters in a novel. But in real life there is a real person to be guessed about, the possibility exists of finding out more: about the characters in a novel there is no more to find out; however individual, memorable, convincing they seem, these people do not exist. We are caught up in a literary experience, one aspect of which is building a coherent reaction to an author's characters from what we are told or can fit together from hints supplied. There need be no external facts with which the author's characters must square.

The test we apply is paradoxical; we expect a well-drawn character in fiction to be distinctive, intriguing, not just like everybody else; but at the same time we expect the character to have the ring of truth, to be like people in real life after all. I'm not talking about the way the great characters of fiction linger on in our minds, as a melody can linger on, obsessively, out of its musical context; I am talking about the nature of the literary experience, not its after-effects. Nor shall I argue that the memorable characters in fiction tend to be types of more or less universal validity: James's Prince, the type of the sophisticated Italian nobleman; Graham Greene's quiet American, a type widely believed to be common in American society and characteristic of it; though that is true, too. Indeed, intuitive creation of this kind seems to me of a higher grade of value and importance than the objective data of the social sciences. It is, as Aristotle said, more philosophical. Much is made of the point by critics seeking to construct a case for literature in the modern world. But though, no doubt, this is part of the literary experience, it isn't the most important part. What is peculiarly characteristic of the literary experience is the property a literary text possesses, while the string of words is coming to life, to make us feel that the dross has been cleansed from our minds; that what we have read has made us see life with a new clarity; that our insight has been sharpened, our understanding of our human condition subjected to a significant renewal. A modern psychologist might call this literary shock. Aristotle called it *catharsis*.

* * *

Mr Podsnap was well to do, and stood very high in Mr Podsnap's opinion. Beginning with a good inheritance, he had married a good inheritance, and had thriven exceedingly in the Marine Insurance way, and was quite satisfied. He never could make out why everybody was not quite satisfied, and he felt conscious that he set a brilliant social example in being particularly well satisfied with most things, and, above all other things, with himself.

Thus happily acquainted with his own merit and importance, Mr Podsnap settled that whatever he put behind him he put out of existence. There was a dignified conclusiveness — not to add a grand convenience — in this way of getting rid of disagreeables, which had done much towards establishing Mr Podsnap in his lofty place in Mr Podsnap's satisfaction. 'I don't want to know about it; I don't choose to discuss it; I don't admit it!' Mr Podsnap had even acquired a peculiar flourish of his right arm in often clearing the world of its most difficult problems, by sweeping them behind him (and consequently sheer away) with those words and a flushed face. For they affronted him.

Mr Podsnap's world was not a very large world, morally; no, nor even geographically; seeing that although his business was sustained upon commerce with other countries, he considered other countries, with that important reservation, a mistake, and of their manners and customs would conclusively observe, 'Not English!' when, PRESTO! with a flourish of the arm, and a flush of the face, they were swept away. Elsewise, the world got up at eight, shaved close at a quarter-past, breakfasted at nine, went to the City at ten, came home at half-past five, and dined at seven.

(Dickens, *Our Mutual Friend*, Book I, Chapter 11)

The older storytellers, whether their form was tragedy or comedy, invented characters larger than life: their heroes are more heroic, their comic characters more absurd; the limitations of their form left them little choice; but by exploiting those limitations, they were able to represent essential truth.

Tragedy (in the grand, traditional sense) isn't something that happens to ordinary people: the tragic hero or heroine is exposed to anguishes and disasters from which ordinary people are protected by common sense; the essence of tragic *catharsis* is something akin to 'there but for the grace of God go I'. Comedy also simplifies, but it is the simplification of caricature, the technique of the political cartoon. Older storytellers, whatever form they adopted, looked for one or two essential traits in the characters they sought to create. Boccaccio's Fra Alberto, Defoe's Moll Flanders, Dickens's Mr Podsnap aren't the sort of person you might meet any day in the street. If not quite types in the sense that Plautus' boastful soldier (the *miles gloriosus*) or Molière's hypochondriac is a type, only superficially individual, always working essentially in the same way, they tend to be what E. M. Forster called 'flat' (as opposed to 'rounded') characters: truth is simplified and intensified. We accept the caricature, are left to supply (or to neglect) the rest. It works because the onward thrust of the narrative sweeps us along.

What makes most eighteenth- and nineteenth-century novels so long by our standards is the wealth of incident. We don't get much further with Fielding's characters; we don't really get much further, usually, with Dickens's. Contrast Flaubert's discreet, sympathetic portrayal of Emma in *Madame Bovary*: what we are asked to accept isn't a caricature, but a representation, selective but always wholly convincing, of a fully developed human being, about whose most secret thoughts Flaubert is fully informed — possesses knowledge denied the participants in the narrative. We are caught up in the sideways expansion of Flaubert's moral and artistic vision. There is still a plot, of course. But where we read Boccaccio's tale or Defoe's novel to enjoy hearing what happens to Fra Alberto and Moll Flanders, the situations in which they find themselves and their reactions to those situations, Flaubert offers us a much more sophisticated experience. Fra Alberto or Moll Flanders is reality simplified, two-dimensional truth. Emma is multi-dimensional truth, selectively presented: the trivia eliminated, the essentials vividly depicted:

> . . . The memory of Léon now became the central point of her anguish: it burned brighter than a fire left behind in the snow by travellers across some Russian steppe, throwing

out every now and then a shower of sparks. Emma would rush forward, press herself against it, stir carefully these soon dead embers, hunt all around her for something to bring them to life again — her most distant recollections along with the most recent incidents; her feelings, real or imaginary; her waning desire for sensual pleasure; her plans for happiness, which crackled as they burned, the fire fanned by the wind, like so many dead branches; her sterile virtue; her lost hopes; odds and ends from about the house; she gathered it all together, took all, pressed all into service, to take the chill from her grief.

She was still at it when the flames died down, either because the supply was exhausted, or because she had piled the fuel too high. Love was gradually extinguished by absence, regret smothered by routine, and this wan fire by which her pale sky had been tinged with a purple glow became progressively enveloped in darkness and eventually disappeared. As a way of easing her conscience, she took her feelings of revulsion from her husband as feelings of longing for her lover, her burning hatred for the warmth of affection; the wind howled around her, her passion smouldered on till only ashes were left, no help came, no sun rose in the sky: on all sides, there was the utter darkness of night, and she remained there lost in the piercing cold.

(Flaubert, Madame Bovary, Part II, Chapter 7)

VIII

I have asked you to think of a narrative text as, first and foremost, a structure of words. The reader (the competent, interested reader) is involved in a process of controlled association as the structure of words expands, so that the text is perceived in the reader's mind as surrounded by a field of significance which determines the significance of what he (or she) reads — gives it point as well as narrative interest. The interplay of the different textual components (narrative proper, dialogue, description of character or scene, discussion of motive) and the interaction of text and its constantly changing field of significance constitute the literary experience.

It sounds (doesn't it?) like something which must threaten all the time to disintegrate. What holds it together? What makes the constantly changing structure of narrative, dialogue and the rest work successfully — or fail to work successfully?

At the most easily describable level, it is a matter of the verbal texture; the feeling the reader has that the words all fit together — belong together, can be read to a discoverable rhythm which carries you along; that not a word jars accidentally, not a word is out of place.

A whole novel pitched at this level of perfection is inconceivable. The enthusiasm of critics often leads to overstatement of the degree of perfection aimed at or attainable in a long work. Ben Jonson's exclamation, on hearing Shakespeare praised for having never blotted out a line, 'Would he had blotted a thousand!' is a welcome intrusion of candour ('mine own candour') in an area where candour does not flourish.

All competent writers keep their best in reserve for when it is most needed; for when the writer's moral vision justifies a richer or a denser verbal texture. Virgil uses his divine interludes, written in a manner closer to comedy, to give his readers something to keep them moving forward through his text while they recover. The serious novelist varies the demand placed on the reader, who would otherwise be left feeling like a damp rag at the end of every chapter. But between this variation in intensity and sheer incompetence there is all the difference in the world. The unskilled writer's words don't sound right; the response they elicit lacks unity; a phrase spoils the effect aimed at; we find ourselves compelled to keep making hasty adjustments to our mental set; if we don't, we find ourselves laughing, or sneering, when we should cry; an implied appeal for our assent in a moral judgement misfires; despite our efforts to tune in, we feel we can't go along with what is said, we want to contradict, are embarrassed. Disunity of the verbal fabric, if isolated and unexpected, can jar extraordinarily; if repeated, it quickly places a text beyond redemption.

*   *   *

Success is more than a matter of harmony of the verbal structure, however: the reader must feel that the structure, as a whole, operates at an acceptable level of seriousness; or rather, at something more than an acceptable level — acceptability in literature is not enough; the reader wants expectations exceeded, transcended. I have in mind now the writer's moral vision, the view of the world which the text projects, or implies by its sideways expansion. A story in which the hero moves from lucky break to lucky break in a world viewed through rose-tinted glasses, in which toughs turn out invariably to have tender hearts, however competently written, quickly cloys, repels by its patently spurious claim to represent reality. A novel which projects no settled view of the world tumbles into inconsistency. On the other hand, a text which represents a world dominated by relentless, mindless destruction of *all* that is young and beautiful (the world, for example, of Housman's poems) likewise repels — not because Housman's moral vision of the world makes us uncomfortable, but because, when we meet it rammed home in poem after poem, we cease to take it seriously: the moral attitudes become too predictable, too easily parodied, as they have been parodied.

The test we apply is that of *essential* truth: we expect a representation of reality which hangs together, which *carries conviction*. A plot does not have to be plausible to carry conviction. A Hitchcock thriller may be wildly implausible, and yet convince while we watch it on the screen. It is really most implausible that a bunch of Australian workers should band together over Easter and on a sudden impulse, because they cannot stand his foreign ways, subject the inoffensive Jewish refugee Himmelfarb to a cruel mock-crucifixion, without consciously realizing what they are doing: and yet Patrick White's narrative in *Riders in the Chariot* carries conviction. Dickens uses caricature as the expression of his moral vision of the cruelty and vacuity of contemporary life, offset only by the immense, innocent humanity of his heroes. White's technique is different: he involves fully rounded complex characters with the ring of truth to them (they make us think of people we know, or have met) in a contrived, fantastic situation that uncovers the potential in such people for cruelty and vacuity, or for suffering or compassion:

> 'Hey, hold hard!' shouted Blue.
>
> He was not exactly protesting, but could not lose sight of the convention which demanded that cruelty, at least amongst mates, must be kept at the level of a joke.
>
> With that perhaps in mind, he broke away briefly and ran into the plating-shop. And returned with a rope, or coil of lithe cord.
>
> The others were not sure they were going to approve. Some of them felt, in fact, they could have attempted heights of tragedy, they could have made blood run redder and more copiously than ever before. However, the majority were pacified by the prospect of becoming involved in some episode that would degrade them lower than they had known yet; the heights were not for them.
>
> Blue was very active. Fixing and tying. Shouting orders. . . .
>
> The Jew had been hoisted as high as he was likely to go on the mutilated tree. The rope pulleys had been knotted to a standstill; one of Blue's accomplices had fumblingly, but finally, fastened the ankles. There he was, nobody would have said crucified, because from the beginning it had been a joke, and if some blood had run, it had dried quickly. The hands, the temples, and the side testified to that in dark clots and smears, too poor to attract the flies. If some of the spectators suffered the wounds to remain open, it was due probably to an unhealthy state of conscience, which could have been waiting since childhood to break out. For those few, the drops trembled and lived. How they longed to dip their handkerchiefs, unseen.
>
> (Patrick White, *Riders in the Chariot*, Chapter 13)

As soon as the Hitchcock film is over, the experience disintegrates because it is built upon low-grade clichés about human nature, because it communicates an insight inferior to our own; its only object is to carry conviction long enough to entertain us. Patrick White's novel operates at — and beyond — 'an acceptable level of seriousness'; we can feel that the mock-crucifixion is a symbolic statement of an insight superior to our own — superior because it digs deeper into the tensions in Australian society, because it builds upon a maturity of insight we don't possess.

It is often said we must take a text upon its own terms, not read high tragedy as social realism. There's a good deal in this. With some texts, however, the terms proposed may be unacceptable; trash can be perfectly coherent as trash, a novel written to pander to our sexual curiosity can display skill, efficiency, in attaining its chosen ends. There are issues here which I shall discuss more fully in Chapter 5. All that need be said for the moment is that competence is not enough. We should do better to say that a sensible reading of a text is one that accepts provisionally the conventions according to which it is written; any other reading is, in some degree, a misreading — we stumble against conventions not recognizing them as such, mistake their purpose. No modern story form, probably, is as dependent on wholly artificial conventions (as false to reality, if you like to put it that way) as the detective story; yet, provided the story is decently written, the conventions do not offend the practised reader of detective stories, who welcomes the implied pact with the author to accept the pseudo-realism, enhanced by the exploitations of these conventions, for the sake of the literary experience. Virgil's *Aeneid*, a novel by Patrick White, may bore the same reader because he mistakes the nature of the transaction proposed.

A novel and a sonnet, in many respects, work the same way, just as, in many respects, a Haydn quartet and a Mahler symphony work the same way. I take a novel and a sonnet because these represent extremes of the literary experience: the longest and one of the shortest. A novel, or a sonnet, sets up a hypothesis, which is first explored (turned around, looked at from various aspects), then brought to some kind of resolution: there is involved in both cases pretty much the same rough tuning of our mental set.

The mental set decides which properties of the text we react to, and how. In itself a text has no describable properties save those of whiteness of paper, size, shape and blackness of type, and so on; indeed, we have to be familiar with written texts, able to read them, in order to recognize even these as relevant properties (sharpness is desirable in type, undesirable in a portrait photograph, where softness of outline is usually preferable) or to describe them accurately. For those who can read the language it is written in, a text has structure, meaning, significance. For those who can read the particular code (in our case, the code of literature, or rather one of the codes literature employs) the text offers a literary experience.

Whether we are reading a novel or a sonnet, the forward movement of the text touches off a complex associative process as the reader proceeds through the text. The scale is different; the line of sense is different — the forward movement of the text of a true Italian sonnet is logical and argumentative; in a novel the movement of the text is narrative and episodic. Both demand of the reader a mental set responsive to the value system within which the text moves and the quality of the verbal fabric. The fine tuning of the mental set varies; in a particular case, it may take a while to get it right. We then know 'how to read' that text, as we know how to play the score of a sonata we have studied. That does not mean we have finished with it, have solved the problem and can turn elsewhere: the experience of a high-grade text is never exhausted and can never be exactly repeated.

IX
THE STORY THAT UNWINDS UPON THE STAGE

A poem is often a kind of miniature drama. The poet creates a character, and leaves that character to do the talking, taking steps only to ensure that the character is placed in some kind of appropriate setting. It is a form Browning was especially fond of. Yeats likes to plant the necessary information in a title, as in 'The Lamentation of the Old Pensioner' (see p. 45). Hardy is rather fond of making a short poem a dialogue between two characters:

> 'O 'Melia, my dear, this does everything crown!
> Who could have supposed I should meet you in Town?
> And whence such fair garments, such prosper-ity?' –
> 'O didn't you know I'd been ruined?' said she.

'You left us in tatters, without shoes or socks,
Tired of digging potatoes and spudding up docks;
And now you've gay bracelets and bright feathers three! –
'Yes: that's how we dress when we're ruined,' said she.

– 'At home in the barton you said "thee" and "thou",
And "thik oon", and "theäs oon", and "t'other"; but now
Your talking quite fits 'ee for high compa-ny!' –
'Some polish is gained with one's ruin,' said she. . . .
(Hardy, 'The Ruined Maid')

And so on, for three stanzas more, with only a 'said she' at the
end of each interchange to mark the stanza-end.

One speech, however, or even an exchange between two
speakers for half a dozen stanzas, doesn't make a play. Drama
is also a matter of action — the word *drama* means 'action'. A
play, like a novel, is a story; things have to happen; a single
situation isn't enough. The difference isn't just that a play is
more 'dramatic' — more 'spectacular', more 'theatrical'.
These are all terms which have their origin upon the stage.
Their use to describe particularly exciting or intense 'scenes'
in a novel involves a metaphor; we are no longer talking about
a scene that unwinds before our eyes upon the stage, but
about a 'scene' that exists only in the reader's imagination,
conjured up by the string of words before the reader upon the
printed page.

The difference, in short, is one of form. A novel is, first and
foremost, a structure of narrative, dominated by the speaking
voice of a narrator; where appropriate, the narrator invites us
to suppose we are hearing the actual words of the characters;
but the use of dialogue is always selective, never continuous. A
play is wholly talk — but talk before our eyes. What one
character says to another isn't reported, we hear the exchange
for ourselves. It is through what one character says to another
that the play must work.

Take the mock crucifiction of the Jew Himmelfarb by his
workmates in Patrick White's *Riders in the Chariot* quoted in the
previous section. Try rewriting it as a scene from a play.
Where White contents himself with three words of dialogue,
you would probably feel you wanted more. If you were to be
faithful to White's text you would have to do something about

those shouted orders. But what could you possibly do with the
fiercely selective focus, the almost intolerably loaded comment, built into the narrative? No doubt, you would find some
way of building some of this into your dialogue. The rest you
would have to leave to your producer, who, in his turn, can
only show what you can describe; and might not understand,
or choose to respect your intentions, supposing you tried to
build these intentions into the stage directions you added to
your script. Obviously, there are the makings of a very
powerful scene in White's narrative, but it would have to be
an entirely different script, designed to work in a completely
different way.

* * *

The fact that a play is, first and foremost, a *spectacle* can result
in more than one interesting reversal of priorities. There are
many plays in which the verbal fabric is secondary, hardly by
itself to be taken seriously.

We can compare the reversal of priorities in poems written
to be sung. Think of some of Shakespeare's songs (which,
though often printed separately in anthologies, come of course
from the plays). What I shall call in the next chapter the
'singing voice' sustains an emotional level the words could not
by themselves sustain. More interesting, from our present
point of view, are those cases which aim at something more
than an illusion of spontaneity or a passing mood captured in
its immediacy. Take German Lieder: many who enjoy the
songs of Schubert, Schumann, Brahms or Wolf have only the
vaguest idea of what the German words are about. The great
masters of the Lied tended to prefer a text which was simple
and straightforward. The text of Schubert's *Winterreise* is
dismissed by most critics as unworthy of serious consideration; yet, out of this pretentious, ridiculous, exaggerated
Romantic sentimentality, Schubert has made, by his own
musical creation, an exquisite, intensely dramatic cycle of
songs. It can't be said that any text would have done: what is
needed is a text that will provide an idea, sustain a mood —
and not get too much in the way. The complexity of the
musical structure requires a verbal structure that is little more
than a springboard. Much the same can be said of opera.

Many plays work this way. In these, what matters is the spectacle — not the confrontation of complex personalities (which is the stuff of serious drama and can sustain even seriously poetic dialogue), but the time-honoured tricks of the comedy of manners: the unexpected appearance on stage of a character everybody on stage is busy pulling to pieces; the hilarious sequence of scenes in Plautus' *The Menaechmus Brothers* built around the assumption of all on stage (except the victim of the mistake) that one brother is the other — utterly implausible, but excellent theatre. Polonius, laying down with heavy hand how to behave in polite society, undercutting by his way of talking his claim to authority on the subject. Molière's Trissotin, ridiculing (to the admiring blue-stockings seated around him) poets who insist on reading their latest verses to their friends, while busy pulling from his pocket his latest sonnet. The old tricks never fail; if the object is only popular entertainment, the text can never be too mediocre or too corny — something no serious reader would waste time with (because he cannot visualize for himself the comic effect when this text is transformed into spectacle upon the stage), any more than any serious reader would waste time reading the text of the latest popular song hit.

The popular song and the play are, naturally, extreme cases of an imbalance. But this extreme imbalance, if hardly to be found in German Lieder, is very much a resource of the serious comic dramatist. In the one case, that of German Lieder, the verbal text is often negligible, but inoffensive; in the other case, a text which in itself would be utterly contemptible can become the indispensable vehicle of comic spectacle.

* * *

In the case of German Lieder, both the verbal and the musical texts are available for those in a position to enjoy them, accessible to their private pleasure. Good comedy of manners, along with all good plays, anticipates, invites, depends on the creative imagination of the producer; even where a tradition of performance has been built up (as with the Comédie Française) the opportunity for fresh creation is always present to a degree hardly possible with song.

The typical modern poem is a different case entirely. The skill required for successful performance aloud is considerable, and attained by few readers aloud, whether poets or actors; but the skill is aimed at creating the illusion of the poet voicing his thoughts in an interior monologue or confiding them to personal friends. The rhetoric of a Shakespearean soliloquy (Hamlet's 'To be or not to be', for example) is out of place, a convention of the dramatic stage which reduces the speaker to the status of actor, forced to work within the confines of dramatic illusion; the skilled reader of verse can transcend these — not by a naturalness that sweeps convention aside, but by working to different conventions.

I speak of conventions because there is an element in all art forms of the larger than life, a preference for the stylized, the typical over the crudely individual. But the result of this stylization is a more intense presentation of essential truth. People do not talk in real life as they do in plays and poems, any more than they look in real life as they look in pictures. Even in those plays and poems which aim at presenting the effect of everyday talk, the effect is always an illusion: the everyday talk is tidied up, improved upon. The object is a representation of the human condition within a structure that detaches and intensifies reality.

* * *

A play, to pick up the key term in Aristotle's definition in the *Poetics*, is a *mimesis* of reality; it shared that property, in Aristotle's view, with other forms of artistic creation — painting as well as poetry. The usual translation of *mimesis* is 'imitation', a word which in the modern world tends to suggest a reproduction as close to the original as possible; even something counterfeit, something designed to pass for the real thing. It is unlikely Aristotle had anything of the sort in mind, however much imitation of reality in this sense was to become in modern times the ideal of producers of plays, films and television drama.

A better translation is *representation* — a presenting afresh, an invitation to take a fresh look at a situation, a moral dilemma, some aspect of the human condition the rights and wrongs of which are hard to sort out, or hard to come to terms with. A painting, a play, differ in all sorts of ways from the reality they 'represent'; by exploiting these differences, the painter or the writer of plays is able to 're-present', to present in a fresh light some essential truth. The odd thing — it is the fundamental paradox of all art — is that the differences, the ways in which painting, works of sculpture, poems, novels, plays depart from reality (those at any rate that set out to represent human beings or their problems) somehow enhance the impact of their essential truth.

* * *

The basic difference between a play and other literary forms (a narrative poem, or a novel) is, as I have said, that the story, instead of being narrated, is acted out upon a stage. It is a re-enactment of reality. A play lasts a couple of hours or so. That's a lot longer than a poem like Yeats's 'Lamentation of the Old Pensioner' or Hardy's 'The Ruined Maid', which are no more than a scrap of talk torn from a context the poet can do no more than evoke in passing. But a lot shorter than a novel. There's no time to build up that structure of narrative and description, that ironic evocation of life in war-time Sierra Leone which we find in Graham Greene's *The Heart of the Matter*, or that fascinatingly detailed picture of life in a mediaeval monastery which we find in Umberto Eco's *The Name of the Rose*. Nor is there the same need: the author's characters are there before our eyes: we hear them speak, watch their growing involvement with one another for ourselves. The author can get on with the plot, the tightening net of events which entangles the characters, precipitates the inevitable crisis.

If story-telling takes us back to the very beginnings of society, re-enactment of a story before an audience can hardly be much later. The two forms developed differently, however. They appeal to different audiences. The teller of tales, until he (or she) aims higher, is confined to the fireside, the bar-counter and the like. In an oral culture, the teller of tales is succeeded by the epic poet, the professional entertainer of aristocratic audiences in their cups, or the chance audience at a festival, where the poet is one entertainer among many. The short story, the novel have to wait for a literate culture, one in which the ability to read, fluently and for pleasure, is widespread and habitual. A play, even a tragedy, can hold the attention of a large popular audience assembled for that purpose: Athenian drama in the fifth century BC; Elizabethan drama in the sixteenth century AD. The challenge to hold, to enthral such an audience is a powerful incentive to genius: in some ways it resembles the incentive offered composers in early nineteenth-century Vienna or London with the institution of public concerts. At Athens, in Elizabethan London, the dramatists gave their audiences much more than they bargained for; their plays — the best of them — have a permanent place among the literary masterpieces of the world.

In both cases, spectacle, as we understand it, played a limited role. In Athenian tragedy, spectacle is rudimentary, however impressive, however 'dramatic', the masks worn by the characters; in Elizabethan drama, no more than a casual gesture at setting or appropriate dress seems to have been attempted. The twentieth-century German dramatist Bertolt Brecht held that elaborate sets, strenuous attempts at realism, actually interfered with the dramatic experience, and forbade them in the performance of his plays; in modern radio drama spectacle is entirely absent. A good producer can do a lot to help, a bad producer a lot of harm.

But it is the situations the text creates as it unwinds, the appeal of the text to the imaginative response of the audience, which stand at the heart of the dramatic experience. In the end, everything turns on the words the dramatist places on the lips of his characters. Drama, if you like to think of it that way, is the most primitive of the literary forms: it invites surrender to the intoxicating power of words (the more intoxicating because actually heard), the power of words to stimulate the imagination, to arouse empathy with the characters enacting that situation upon the stage. This is not to underrate the power of words in all good poetry. In drama, however, the appeal of words is simpler, even cruder: we can savour the words of a poem or a novel — look back, readjust our understanding; a good play, too, will repay us if we read it afterwards, but its initial impact must be swift and unfailing. We surrender to the poetic rhetoric of Shakespeare or Christopher Fry, the political rhetoric of Shaw even when the rhetoric is pitched at a level we should find offensive in a poem. The reason, no doubt, is that a poem works through the illusion of the speaking voice, the felt personality of the poet or the poet's chosen persona. A play works through the interplay of voices, all somewhat larger than life. There is a world of difference between sitting down to read *Hamlet* by ourselves (unless we know the play well, it will just not work that way) and hearing an enactment of it in a radio play (where there is no spectacle). A *poem* read on radio by an actor more often than not simply annoys us: we feel the actor gets in the way because his understanding of the text is inferior to ours, because the rhythm of the sense is too subtle for him to grasp. For our imagination to respond to *Hamlet* we need the actors; they may still annoy us here and there, but together they can bring to life what we alone cannot.

* * *

Greek tragedy, in addition to dialogue, has a *chorus*, which intersperses the dialogue with conventional, uncomprehending commentary — a kind of stylization (the chorus parts are in lyric verse, metrically differentiated from the dialogue) of the inability of ordinary people to comprehend the harrowing nature of disaster. Often there is a formal prologue (usually, in tragedy, delivered by an omniscient divinity) to present a brief summary of essential facts. Shakespeare has such a prologue in *Henry V*; in other plays the essential facts are woven into the opening scene — more or less perfunctorily, as in *The Merchant of Venice*; in *Macbeth* and *Hamlet*, the opening scene seems designed to give the ensuing action a kind of cosmic dimension, but serves also to present the spectator with essential information (the circumstances of the death of Hamlet's father, the war with Poland; the events which have placed Macbeth in the line of succession, thus firing the ambition of his wife). Again in Greek tragedy, it happens frequently that a messenger arrives at a crucial point to deliver a long set narrative of important events that have to be got out of the way before the play can continue, or which ancient standards of taste preferred to have happen off-stage.

In Jean Anouilh's famous reworking of Sophocles' *Antigone*, the chorus becomes a kind of worldly-wise literary critic who both foresees the action and offers us his cynical commentary upon it. Mostly, however, modern dramatists have tended to dispense with such aids to plot, in order to concentrate on the unwinding of the dialogue. The printed texts of plays designed to be read (as well as acted, or instead) often have a more or less elaborate commentary added to them disguised as stage directions. It is a concession to the reader, an admission that a play designed as a play cannot be expected to work without help when read silently by an individual reader. This commentary lacks the status accorded the marks composers add to their scores as an indication of how they want their works performed; producers feel free to disregard the dramatists' commentaries, and often do.

*   *   *

When we witness a performance on the stage or on television, or listen to a radio play, an interesting change takes place in the nature of the literary experience. With a novel or a poem (unless we are listening to somebody else reading the poem aloud), the starting point and the constant point of reference is the text, the string of words on the printed page. The novel or the poem is what *we* make of it. Unless we happen to have a copy of the play before us, it might be supposed we are wholly dependent on the producer's interpretation. But that is not the case. It isn't quite that we are reduced to making what we can of what somebody else has made of the play. The attentive spectator or listener is left some freedom to form an independent judgement. We can feel the rhythm an actor gives a passage of dialogue is 'wrong' (does not fit the character, or the situation, or either); or, on the contrary, brings out a meaning, an aspect of the character or the situation we had missed and now feel compelled to consider, or immediately accept — one that would never have occurred to us unaided.

The presence, or absence, of the visual spectacle is also intriguing to consider. On the stage or the television screen the spectacle represents before our eyes what the novelist would have to represent in words. Because it is before our eyes, it is (if the performance is any good) more challenging, more intense, but at the same time more limited. The producer has had to take decisions we, if we were reading a novel, would not have had to take. A radio play works differently: there our whole understanding of what is happening, and the people to whom it is happening, must come from the words we hear spoken. A play adapted for radio (as opposed to a play written for that medium) will often fail because we are left unprofitably confused about who is speaking, or about what is supposed to be going on. On the other hand, a skilful writer for radio can exploit the medium — by leaving unstated, for example (as might be done in a short story), where the action is to be supposed as taking place, or that an important character is black, or blind.

*   *   *

In a society such as ours today where narrative and dramatic form co-exist, are both available to the writer who has a story to tell, a differentiation of function in the use of dialogue is only natural.

In older novels, written at a time when the novel was regarded as a development of comedy, a common use of dialogue (in addition to its obvious function — to provide information, to announce developments, decisions and the like) is to build up comic character — by repetition of stock phrases, for example, which fix the character's personality, and build up a picture of his foibles, his illusions, his conditioned responses to the situations of life. Dickens is perhaps the last of the great comic novelists. Proust, though a brilliant writer of poetic description of scene and a penetrating satirist of character, is on the whole content with this representational use of dialogue: the society he depicts practised the art of conversation with such assiduity, it was enough to represent them as saying what we can easily suppose them saying. Only occasionally does the level deepen from that of wit to something that challenges or disturbs the reader — as when Swann, old and dying of cancer, at what is likely to be his last social appearance, is made to say:

Even when one has lost interest in things, it is not wholly
without importance that one once had an interest. Because
it was always for reasons which passed unperceived by
others. The memory one has of those feelings or emotions
exists, we sense, only in ourselves; it is into ourselves we
must penetrate if we are to contemplate it.

(Proust, *Sodome et Gomorrhe*, Chapter 2)

A more ambitious use of dialogue is found in the late novels
of Henry James. All pretence of realism abandoned, a conversation becomes a probing of a complex situation which the
speaker is struggling to grasp — struggling to work out what
another character means or intends; struggling to come to
terms with where he, or perhaps more often she, stands. So
fond is James of this device, he will resort to it even when there
is no indication in the narrative that the conversation actually
takes place, structuring as direct speech what in the narrative
remains unspoken — the unformulated ideas of a character,
what that character might have said, given time or in other
circumstances. Only James's extraordinarily sound ear for the
rhythms of conversational English can make some of these
long passages of unspoken dialogue tolerable. Yet in them
James is on the verge of a device several writers in the early
twentieth century will take a step further: the flow of unspoken, unstructured silent thought given the structure of an
interior monologue. James Joyce and Virginia Woolf are the
most brilliant exponents in English:

A blind stripling stood tapping the curbstone with his
slender cane. No tram in sight. Wants to cross.
– Do you want to cross? Mr Bloom asked.
The blind stripling did not answer. His wall face frowned
weakly. He moved his head uncertainly.
– You're in Dawson Street, Mr Bloom said. Molesworth
street is opposite. Do you want to cross? There's nothing in
the way.
The cane moved out trembling to the left. Mr Bloom's
eye followed its line and saw again the dyeworks' van
drawn up before Drago's. Where I saw his brilliantined

hair just when I was. Horse drooping. Driver in John Long's. Slaking his drouth.

– There's a van there, Mr Bloom said, but it's not moving. I'll see you across. Do you want to go to Molesworth street?

– Yes, the stripling answered. South Frederick street.

– Come, Mr Bloom said.

He touched the thin elbow gently: then took the limp seeing hand to guide it forward.

Say something to him. Better not do the condescending. They mistrust what you tell them. Pass a common remark:

– The rain kept off.

No answer.

Stains on his coat. Slobbers his food, I suppose. Tastes all different for him. Have to be spoonfed first. Like a child's hand his hand. Like Milly's was. Sensitive. Sizing me up I daresay from my hand. Wonder if he has a name. Van. Keep his cane clear of the horse's legs tired drudge gets his doze. That's right. Clear. Behind a bull: in front of a horse.

– Thanks, sir.

Knows I'm a man. Voice.

– Right now? First turn to the left.

The blind stripling tapped the curbstone and went on his way, drawing his cane back, feeling again.

Mr Bloom walked behind the eyeless feet, a flatcut suit of herringbone tweed. Poor young fellow! How on earth did he know that van was there? Must have felt it. See things in their foreheads perhaps. Kind of sense of volume. Weight. Would he feel it if something was removed? Feel a gap. Queer idea of Dublin he must have.

(James Joyce, *Ulysses*, p. 230)

A mixture like this of interior monologue and spoken commonplace is obviously impossible in the theatre. Joyce's exploitation of the device makes of course strenuous reading. Patrick White has evolved a modification of the device to represent the tension between the traditional taciturnity of the average Australian and the active cliché-ridden, prejudice-soaked mental life which is left unexpressed: .

'Who was that woman?' asked Mrs Colquhoun, a rich lady who had come recently to live at Sarsaparilla.

'Ah', Mrs Sugden said, and laughed, 'that was Miss Hare.'

'She appears an unusual sort of person', Mrs Colquhoun ventured to hope.

'Well', replied Mrs Sugden, 'I cannot deny that Miss Hare is *different.*'

But the postmistress would not add to that. She started poking at a dry sponge. Even at her most communicative, talking with authority of the weather, which was her subject, she favoured the objective approach.

Mrs Colquhoun was able to see for herself that Miss Hare was a small, freckled thing, whose stockings, at that moment, could have been coming down. To tell the truth, Mrs Colquhoun was somewhat put out by the post-mistress's discretion, but could not remain so indefinitely, for the War was over, and the peace had not yet set hard.

(Patrick White, *Riders in the Chariot*, opening lines)

3

The Singing and the Speaking Voice

I

The text which tells a story is the simplest case: Homer, Virgil, Shakespeare, Dickens, Patrick White, Margaret Drabble are all engaged in a transaction comparable to other transactions between human beings. Their business is to entertain us. They may give us more than we bargained for: they may have in mind to manipulate our opinions about how the world works; artistic creation may take over from the business of entertaining. But they must be careful to keep manipulation of opinion and artistic creation within the limits of a transaction acceptable to us, their readers or audience.

The author does not figure prominently in this transaction – not entirely absent, but not the centre of our attention; a background figure whose speaking voice lends perspective, style, tone to the story told. This is true even when the story is told in the first person:

> That was when I saw the Pendulum.
> The sphere, hanging from a long wire set into the ceiling of the choir, swayed back and forth with isochronal majesty.
> I knew – but anyone could have sensed it in the magic of that serene breathing – that the period was governed by the square root of the length of the wire. . . .
>
> (Umberto Eco, *Foucault's Pendulum*, opening words)

119

We do not have to wait to discover the speaker's name to know that Casaubon is not Eco, just as we know that Moll Flanders is not Defoe; we know that the speaking voice is that of an assumed persona, not that of the author in everyday life. We know because we have taken up the text with our mental set prepared for a work of fiction, alert to catch the first hints of the larger-than-life, too-good-to-be-true quality of the speaking voice which we expect from such a work. We accept Casaubon and Moll Flanders for what they are: characters in a story, creations of the writer's imagination, tailored to fit a fiction. Not the author struggling to present himself, or herself, as honestly, or as interestingly, as possible. Novels tell us little or nothing about the novelist. Dickens is as hard to imagine from what he writes as Homer or Shakespeare. About Margaret Drabble or Patrick White we may have suspicions; but speculation is unprofitable, not *our* business as readers.

In this chapter our attention turns from literature as story to literature as expression of the poet's feelings and ideas. The basis of the transaction now changes: the poet may be so wrapped up in feelings and ideas as to seem to ignore us completely; yet the poem which expresses those ideas and feelings remains a social act. The poet may set out to involve us in a battle of wits, to trick us into taking at least half seriously an argument we shouldn't, in different circumstances, take seriously for a moment. Either way, at the core of the social act we sense the living personality of the poet — posing, pretending, perhaps; but a real human being, not a character of fiction.

We are now talking about quite short poems: poems seldom more than a dozen lines or so, not thousands of lines long. They retain, usually, some of the traditional features of song-form: but they are not intended to be sung. Imagine yourself singing Gerard Manley Hopkins's sonnet 'Carrion Comfort':

> Not, I'll not, carrion comfort, Despair, not feast on thee;
> Not untwist – slack they may be – these last strands of man
> In me ór, most weary, cry *I can no more*. I can;
> Can something, hope, wish day come, not choose not to be,
> But ah, but O thou terrible, why wouldst thou rude on me

Thy wring-world right foot rock? lay a lionlimb against
      me? scan
With darksome devouring eyes my bruisèd bones? and fan,
O in turns of tempest, me heaped there; me frantic to
      avoid thee and flee?
Why? That my chaff might fly; my grain lie, sheer and clear.
Nay in all that toil, that coil, since (seems) I kissed
      the rod,
Hand rather, my heart lo! lapped strength, stole joy,
      would laugh, chéer.
Cheer whom though? The hero whose heaven-handling flung
      me, fóot tród
Me? or me that fought him? O which one? is it each one?
      That night, that year
Of now done darkness I wretch lay wrestling with (my God!)
      my God.

Hopkins is too involved, emotionally and intellectually, too
determined to compress thought into organized form, for there
to be any question of song. A well-established convention
allows the movement of the thought to take the upper hand,
the sound of the sense (as Robert Frost put it) breaking across
the beat of the metre.

   In song, it has to be the other way round: for the song to
work as a song, the sense must be subordinated to the melody;
the words of the song may be those of a poem, but, as a poem,
it would have to work differently. There is of course room for
what is usually called 'expression' in song, but the conventions governing expression are strict and limiting. To attempt
to fit the violent, tortured rhythm of Hopkins's soliloquy to the
conventions of song would be as absurd, as indecent, as if
Shakespeare's Hamlet were to sing his soliloquy, 'To be or not
to be'. With this added indecency: Hamlet's anguish is that of
a dramatic character; Hopkins's sonnet dramatizes the soul-
searching anguish of the poet himself, laying his soul bare.

   The singing and the speaking voice. I'm not going to
suggest that poems which argue with us are better than those
in which we hear, or are invited to imagine we hear, the poet
singing to us. My object in this chapter is to show how two
quite different kinds of poem work.

*   *   *

Some personal poets, sometimes, are reassuringly personal. James K. Baxter on a visit to the lab for a blood test is an easy case:

> The big mosquito
> Has filled its glass belly
> with *my* blood, a teacupful
> Reddish black and frothing. . . .

Baxter's visit to the lab ends up as sixteen lines of verse, arranged in four stanzas. Structured differently, 'Blood Test' might have become a minor incident in a novel. In the eyes of one of the participants, the nurse, what took place *is* of hardly more consequence than Mr Bloom escorting the young blind man across a Dublin street, or Mrs Colquhoun's brief exchange with the postmistress (see Chapter 2, Section IX). Here, however, it is Baxter himself who is the protagonist, and 'what happened' becomes the starting point for an exploration touched off in the poet's mind by that incident. His reactions can lay claim to an authority Mr Bloom's reactions, or Mrs Colquhoun's, cannot claim, since *they* are only characters in a fiction. And since the reactions are his reactions, the reactions of a poet, instead of leaving them ostentatiously unstructured (as in Joyce) or ironically paraphrased (as in Patrick White), the poet plays around with them, lets his imagination loose on them until they begin to fall into a shape and a rhythm that will work as a poem.

For us, the battle is merely to keep up with the poet's thoughts as they take shape (or appear to) while the poem itself takes shape (or appears to). But this urbane whimsy is Baxter relaxing, an easy, straightforward poem slipped in to reconcile the reader who finds the real Baxter disconcerting. Baxter's 'The Lion Skin' adopts the same matter-of-fact tone, but we pass now from everyday incident into the world of the poet's personal fantasy: something that never happened is explored by the poet's creative imagination while he talks about it as though it *were* an everyday incident. The struggle to keep up is correspondingly more intense:

The old man with a yellow flower on his coat
Came to my office, climbing twenty-eight steps,
With a strong smell of death about his person
From the caves of the underworld. . . .

Baxter, it turns out, has been honoured with a visit from
Baron Saturday; he welcomes him, pours him a glass of cherry
brandy, while his gaze remains fixed on that yellow flower on
the Baron's coat which 'blazed like a dark sun'.

The modern reader, more accustomed to novels than to
poems, finds poems like 'Blood Test' or 'The Lion Skin' easy
enough to adjust to. They read sufficiently like novels for the
reader to feel reassured. Each time there is a story of a kind to
latch onto.

In a novel, the story provides the mainspring which draws
us through the text. It may be the gentle, ambling progression
of Fielding's *Amelia*; it may be the elegant sequence of events
(all in themselves of little moment, though perceived by the
participants as full of excitement) which takes the reader of
Jane Austen's *Emma*, through minor complication after minor
complication, to the ultimate triple marriage by which the
conclusion of Jane Austen's urbanely witty portrayal of
middle-class manners is contrived; it may be the compulsive,
single-minded thrust of the typical Graham Greene thriller,
which provides, not merely narrative excitement, but the
particular cathartic excitement of *plot*; it may be the periodic
concession to narrative convention which holds together the
imaginative fantasy of Patrick White's *The Twyborn Affair*, or
the constant tricks played upon those conventions which make
Eco's *Foucault's Pendulum* a narrative tour de force. Whatever
the strategy adopted, the capacity of the text to arouse and
sustain the literary experience derives its energy from the
unwinding of the story.

The short personal poem works differently. It has to. You
can have a whole poem laid out on the page in front of you; to
read it is only a matter of a minute or so; you can hold the
whole poem in your mind while your eye runs down the
printed text. There is space only for a shred, a fragment, of
story: Baxter at the lab, Baxter visited by Baron Saturday.

The tension which carries us through the text doesn't come from the unwinding of a story; it is provided by the unwinding of the poet's thoughts.

* * *

Most often, poets don't chat to us like Baxter in this reassuring way about what happened to them, in fact or in fancy. They may claim to be talking to a mistress, or a friend; often they seem to be talking more to themselves than to us — trying to sort out thoughts under the pressure of emotion, to give shape to the ideas and fantasies which crowd into their minds. Or just playing with words, ideas, images, because the impulse to work out that pattern of words, ideas, images, won't let them go. The nature of the transaction and our role in it aren't easily defined. We overhear a text which seems to ignore our existence; we are reduced to the status of eavesdroppers, of pryers into other people's letters, or treated as no more than convenient listeners buttonholed by poets who (like Coleridge's ancient mariner) have something to get off their chest.

Of course, this is largely an illusion: most personal poets, if there is a sense in which in the last resort they write only for themselves, keep one eye fixed on posterity. But it is a necessary illusion; the form demands a different relationship of writer to reader. A novelist has to remain conscious all the time of an audience to be entertained, whatever else the novelist may have in mind to attempt. The short personal poem isn't subject to this requirement, and often neglects it completely, or appears to. I'm not talking about the poet's private motives or intentions; they're not our business. I'm talking about the primary assertion of the text itself; the transaction which the text proposes; the assumption it invites about the way it came into existence; the implied demand that the poem is to be read on the poet's terms, not ours; the adjustment *we* must make before we can read the text as the text itself demands.

Implied in return is an undertaking to play fair, to be honest with the reader. A novelist assumes no such responsibility. Foucault is not Eco, though Eco writes in the first person throughout. Let me quote Auden on the subject. In his foreword to *Collected Shorter Poems 1927–1957*, Auden confesses that 'some poems which I wrote and, unfortunately, published' have been rejected in the collected edition because they were dishonest. He explains what he means:

> A dishonest poem is one which expresses, no matter how well, feelings or beliefs which its author never felt or entertained. For example, I once expressed a desire for 'New styles of architecture'; but I have never liked modern architecture. I prefer *old* styles, and one must be honest even about one's prejudices. Again, and much more shamefully, I once wrote:
>
> > History to the defeated
> > may say alas but cannot help or pardon.
>
> To say this is to equate goodness with success. It would have been bad enough if I had ever held this wicked doctrine, but that I should have stated it simply because it sounded to me rhetorically effective is quite inexcusable.

Most of us will want to protest the issue is less simple, less easily decided, than Auden makes it sound. Before we do so, it is as well to realize that Auden is talking about his conscience as a poet — it offends that conscience, on re-reading poems he has written and published over a writing life of thirty years, to have sometimes argued a case he did not believe in, or stated an opinion he did not hold. Auden does not suggest that we, his readers, are entitled to apply the same test (supposing we were in a position to), or that this is really our business.

It is hard to be sure it is our business. True, we should be disturbed (rightly, I think) if we were to discover that Gerard Manley Hopkins had remained, for the rest of his life, the conscientious, caring guardian of other people's souls implied by his poem 'Felix Randal', written while he *was* a parish priest in Liverpool:

Felix Randal the farrier, O he is dead then? my duty
   all ended,
Who have watched his mould of man, big-boned and
   hardy-handsome
Pining, pining, till time when reason rambled in it
   and some
Fatal four disorders, fleshed there, all contended?

Sickness broke him. Impatient he cursed at first,
   but mended
Being anointed and all; though a heavenlier heart
   began some
Months earlier, since I had our sweet reprieve
   and ransom
Tendered to him. Ah well, God rest him all road ever
   he offended!

This seeing the sick endears them to us, us too it
   endears,
My tongue had taught thee comfort, touch had quenched
   thy tears,
Thy tears that touched my heart, child, Felix, poor
   Felix Randal;

How far from then forethought of, all thy more
   boisterous years,
When thou at the random grim forge, powerful
   amidst peers,
Didst fettle for the great grey drayhorse his bright
   and battering sandal!

Suppose (we know it wasn't that way, but suppose) that
Hopkins had never undergone the emotional and intellectual
torment which is so powerfully dramatized in 'Carrion Comfort', written just five years later; that a talent for condensed
expression of emotional conflict had got out of hand. What
would we say? What would we say of a writer of plays who
had invented such a character and written for him, as an act of
pure imaginative insight or intuition, a speech representing
such a state of torment? If a poet represents himself as madly
in love, madly jealous, tormented by unrequited passion, need

we believe him? Does the question of belief arise? What do the very personal poems of Philip Larkin tell us about the historical Philip Larkin? Clearly, Baxter does not expect us to believe that, in fact, he received Baron Saturday in his office and offered him a cherry brandy. Ah, but that is different, isn't it? The 'point' of Baxter's poem, if the matter can be put that way, is to represent Baxter, at a stage in his life when he was seeking middle-aged respectability, as, despite that, a poet still, still gifted with a lively fantasy, but more easy-going now, no longer the young rake of his early poems. It is this core of truth, we may say, which gives the poem its integrity.

This is not an issue which arises only with poems written in the first person. It arises with all poems which invite us to take them as, somehow, an expression — however ironical — of the personality of the poet (the historical human being, not a persona he has set up). We seem, instinctively, to set for such poems a standard of integrity which we do not expect from other literary forms. Can this be justified? I shall take the issue up at greater length in Chapter 5.

* * *

In the simplest form of poem, story is totally dispensed with. You have what at first glance looks like the simple outpouring of emotion. Take Autolycus's song from *The Winter's Tale*:

> When daffodils begin to peer,
>   With hey! the doxy over the dale,
> Why, then comes in the sweet o' the year;
>   For the red blood reigns in the winter's pale.
>
> The white sheet bleaching on the hedge,
>   With hey! the sweet birds, O, how they sing!
> Doth set my pugging tooth on edge;
>   For a quart of ale is a dish for a king.
>
> The lark, that tirra-lirra chants,
>   With hey! with hey! the thrush and the jay,
> Are summer songs for me and my aunts,
>   While we lie tumbling in the hay.
>
>   (Shakespeare, *The Winter's Tale*, Act IV, Scene 2)

We are a long way from Wordsworth's daffodils:

> I wandered lonely as a cloud
> That floats on high o'er vales and hills,
> When all at once I saw a crowd,
> A host, of golden daffodils. . . .

Read Autolycus's song more carefully, however. Better still, read it aloud. A pattern of rhymes, rhythms and stanzas, superimposed on the visual pattern of the text before you on the printed page, sets up a counterpoint between sound and sense that refuses to be ignored and is obviously contrived. This is song, not argument; its apparent simplicity and directness are the result of a successfully manipulated illusion. Song sounds simple: the appeal is not to the head, but to the heart; if well handled, it can be extraordinarily effective.

Some songs sound so good when you read them, you forget you are reading a text that pretends to have been written to be sung. Others depend on being sung:

> Look me over closely,
> Tell me what you see,
> The lady likes to look her best
> Before she pours the tea. . . .

On the printed page, Marlene Dietrich's song hardly impresses. Sung by Dietrich (it was written for her by Terry Gilkyson), it creates a character from the opening line, enacts a life-style and a period, instead of describing them or allowing them to emerge from a pattern of narrative: it might take a novelist pages to build up that character. But it hardly gets you anywhere; the successive stanzas merely sustain the first, prolonging the experience for your enjoyment without adding to it.

Turn from songs like these to the sort of poem that sets up an argument and the difference is apparent. Take that best known, perhaps, of all Auden's poems, 'Musée des Beaux Arts': we are asked to imagine we are in a picture gallery (the Musée des Beaux Arts in Brussels, as it happens) when an idea occurs to Auden, which develops into a witty train of argument as he puts it to us:

> About suffering they were never wrong,
> The Old Masters: how well they understood
> Its human position; how it takes place
> While someone else is eating, or opening a window, or
>   just walking dully along. . . .

The formal pattern is looser than it would have to be if the words had to fit a melody. The argument is structured into lines of varying length, the identity of the lines marked by a somewhat complicated pattern of rhymes ('wrong' rhymes with 'along', 'understood' eventually rhymes with 'wood' in line 8; line 3, as it happens, is the only line in the 21 that is left unrhymed). The rhythms are those of the thinking voice, not the voice raised in song. The appeal is no longer to the heart, but to the head. The first four lines state Auden's case. Lines 5–13 proceed to illustrate that case (without naming particular pictures) by reference to the birth and death of Christ: while the 'dreadful martyrdom' runs its course, there, in a corner of the picture, a horse scratches its behind on a tree. The last six lines clinch the case by reference to Breughel's *Icarus*: there is a ship in the picture, those on board must have seen Icarus crashing down out of the heavens when the sun melted the wax that held his wings in place, but the ship is depicted as sailing on apparently oblivious.

Poems that argue with us like this are nothing new. In English they are at least as old as the sixteenth century; they become especially common early in the seventeenth century.

Take Donne's poem 'The Triple Foole'. The argument is less relaxed than in Auden's poem — more passionately structured and at the same time more pitched at the level of wit. (The 'inward narrow crooked lanes' are probably the channels of the evaporating pans, into which sea water was run, in the production of salt.) A paradox is expressed with a compressed energy impossible in prose: Donne is a fool to be in love; to write and publish poems about himself in love is to make a second fool of himself; to have his poems performed in public by someone else is to make yet a third fool:

> I am two fooles, I know,
> For loving, and for saying so
>   In whining Poetry;
> But where's that wiseman, that would not be I,
>   If she would not deny?
> Then as th'earths inward narrow crooked lanes
> Do purge sea waters fretfull salt away,
>   I thought, if I could draw my paines,
> Through Rimes vexation, I should them allay,
> Griefe brought to numbers cannot be so fierce,
> For he tames it, that fetters it in verse.
>
>   But when I have done so,
> Some man, his art and voice to show,
>   Doth Set and sing my paine,
> And, by delighting many, frees againe
>   Griefe, which verse did restraine.
> To Love, and Griefe tribute of Verse belongs,
> But not of such as pleases when 'tis read,
>   Both are increased by such songs:
> For both their triumphs so are published,
> And I, which was two fooles, do so grow three;
> Who are a little wise, the best fooles bee.

As in Auden's poem, the case argued is one we can take
seriously. Indeed, Donne's case seems something more than a
witty argument strung together on the impulse of a moment: a
poet *can* feel humilated hearing a poem written to 'tame'
emotion by 'fettering it in verse' sung with feigned emotion by
somebody else; there are times when he *must* wonder whether
making verse out of inherently foolish thoughts and emotions
wasn't redoubling the folly.

Donne's poem is programmatic: it proclaims his support for
the swing, which began in the second half of the sixteenth
century, away from sung lyric to a more intellectual kind of
poem designed for silent reading. 'The Triple Foole' proclaims, in short, the transition from the singing to the
speaking voice. It is interesting that Donne seems to have
sensed, from the outset, the special status demanded by this
kind of poetry: the need for what Auden called honesty, an

integrity underlying the wit, strengthening the irony; a quality that could not survive performance by professionals trained in the larger rhetoric of the theatre. As is still the case today, of course.

Poems written for the speaking voice make heavy demands on their readers — their silent readers, too. Some appeal to the logical mind; many demand an imaginative response beyond the ordinary. The appeal to the logical mind is seldom wholly meant, the argument never pushed to the exclusion of all else; often what we have is more a kind of intellectual block-building — each fresh block tentatively added, as if the poet is unsure the structure will bear the load of sense now added, alert, like a tightrope walker, to make no false step. Simple statement, seriousness of tone, or their opposites — complex statement, a provocative flippancy, structured, however, so as to seem seriously meant, however flippant the tone — equally draw us into battling with the sense, give us something to hold onto and to think over. We need, if we are to take part successfully in this mental exercise, something comparable to the aptitude and training required for most forms of mental exercise. The public for poetry is about as numerous as the public for string quartets.

II
THE BEGINNINGS OF SONG

The beginnings of song lie in ritual, in the expression of the shared activities and emotions of what used to be called primitive cultures. Sea-shanties, soldiers' marching songs — all songs which regulate, or enliven, the complex routines of a rigidly disciplined group — work this way; there is little scope for the individual voice.

We find something closer to personal poetry in such things as lullabies, or this song of an Eskimo hunter to his betrothed:

My betrothed,
My beloved,

I leave you now.
Do not sorrow too much for me. . . .
                    (Quoted from C. M. Bowra, *Primitive Song*)

The songs of 'primitive' peoples, like the hymns we sing in church, express emotions which are traditional, appropriate, publicly acceptable. To look for expression of the personal emotions of the singer is idle. When Odysseus and his friends come in a deputation to Achilles in *Iliad* 9, they find him singing and accompanying himself on the lyre. What he sings isn't a love song, however, or a song expressing his own feelings about Briseis or Agamemnon: his song is of 'the famous deeds of men'. For anything we can fairly call personal poetry we have to wait until the individual develops an awareness of himself as distinct from the group, with thoughts and feelings of his own.

When that happens, song abandons its public function of expressing what the majority feels more eloquently than the majority knows how to, and becomes the expression of the poet's own personal thoughts and feelings; instead of voicing traditional, conventional, publicly acceptable sentiments, poets speak now for themselves — and only for themselves. Their subject isn't now the present activities or the past glories of the group, no longer the group communicating with its gods (in a formal hymn or prayer). Instead poets offer themselves to the group as individuals competent to express in song what others will understand as the poet's personal reaction to experience; it is their thoughts and feelings, not just their technical skill, which establish their claim upon the attention of the group.

What we have now isn't really a song at all. The poet who made it may still call it a song, because the poet still thinks of himself as working in the tradition of song. We still hear (or are invited to imagine we hear) the poet's *singing voice*. But there is involved a significant reversal of priorities: what we have now is a text in which the words count more than the melody; or to put it more precisely, in which the verbal structure is accorded priority over the musical structure by the manner of performance. The earliest personal poems were probably declaimed to music rather than sung. In the form as we know it, what we have is a written text — a text to be read; if a musical setting exists, the sung performance is a separate occasion.

The separation of text from melody seems perhaps a natural enough development, but it represents a change in the nature of the literary experience of enormous significance, comparable to that brought about by the invention of printing. So long as there are no written texts, a song is known only through performance — either performance in a ritual context, or performance out of context by an individual who knows the song from having heard it performed, and sings it as a personal expression of emotion, the remembered words lending a kind of inspired eloquence to the felt emotion; often a performance is more an improvisation, a fresh stringing together of remembered material, than a recapitulation of a fixed text. Even where there is a fixed text, the fact that the words must have been at some stage put together, worked out, is forgotten in the immediacy of performance. Songs like that depend heavily on performance: what makes Marlene Dietrich's 'Look Me Over Closely' is the personality which the song enables the singer to project; sung by another singer, the triviality of the verse would be exposed.

* * *

Poems written to be read work differently, and are designed to provide a different kind of experience. Because such poems were felt to have their origin in song, because, in some respects, they still worked like songs, they were often set to music by contemporary musicians, as Richard Lovelace's poems to Lucasta were set to music by a variety of seventeenth-century musicians — for example, 'Tell me not, sweet, I am unkind':

> Tell me not, sweet, I am unkind,
>   That from the nunnery
> Of thy chaste breast and quiet mind,
>   To war and arms I fly . . .

This still happens: Donne's *Holy Sonnets* have been set to music in the twentieth century by Benjamin Britten; poems by

A. E. Housman have been set by Vaughan Williams; poems
written in the 'thirties by George Seferis were set to music in
the 'sixties by Mikos Theodorakis. More and more, however,
since the seventeenth century, poetry and song have gone
separate ways.

Serious poems, however lyrical the expression, are today
most often written with no thought of their being sung. The
normal process of bringing a poem to life is today a private
meditation upon a written text; the process of taking in the
text, like the process of composition of the text, is deliberate,
intellectual, pondering; the thinking mind orchestrates the
emotional experience. Poems are written to work when read
this way — and, as a result, finally lose all connection with
song, though it may still suit the parties to the transaction in
some cases to pretend that the reader is reading a poem
written to be sung.

There are poems which simply demand to be sung. You can
hardly resist the impulse to sing Shakespeare's song 'It was a
lover and his lass':

> It was a lover and his lass,
>   With a hey, and a ho, and a hey nonino,
> That o'er the green corn field did pass
>   In springtime, the only pretty ring time,
> When birds do sing, hey ding a ding, ding:
> Sweet lovers love the spring.
>   (Shakespeare, Page's Song from *As You Like It*, Act V,
>   Scene 3)

'Look Me Over Closely' really *only* works as a song. Try to
read the words aloud and you have at once a sense of
something wrong; like the words of the great majority of
popular songs, they refuse to submit to the speaking voice.
Then there are poems which are undeniably singable, but the
compulsion to sing them is less strong — isn't built into the
text. You can easily imagine yourself singing Shakespeare's
'Fear no more the heat o' the sun' or Robert Burns's 'My
luve's like a red, red rose'; but these work equally well when
we read them as poems. At the other end of the scale there are
poems which simply refuse to be sung, or can only be sung by

doing violence to them (ignoring the movement of the thought, ignoring the thought itself). To sing Donne's 'I am two fooles, I know' is to make nonsense of it. You *can't* imagine yourself singing Hopkins's 'Carrion Comfort' or Auden's 'About suffering they were never wrong'.

In Auden's poem or Donne's the transformation of song into poem is complete: the text demands the speaking, not the singing, voice. The organization of the sense has taken on a new complexity. The spontaneous lyric voice has been replaced by the more tentative voice of the poet sorting out his ideas and giving them the structure of a more elaborate, more deliberate syntax. The rhythms now are not those imposed by the melody, but what Edward Thomas called 'the patterns of stress and pause which reflect a mind actually engaged in the act of thinking, rather than offering concluded thoughts'. What makes the poem work now is no longer the poet's success in creating the illusion of a surrender to emotion; the energy needed to keep the poem going is generated by a challenging complexity in the line of statement, by the field of significance which the text spins around itself as it proceeds.

III
EPIGRAM AND THE TRADITION OF WIT

The simplicity and spontaneity of song are also its chief limitation. Song preserves archaic patterns of speech. The unit most often is the four- or six-line stanza. There is no continuous onward movement of the sense to draw us through the text from one stanza to the next. The commonest structuring device is repetition; repetition, stanza by stanza, of the melody if the poem is sung; repetition of a pattern of rhymes from stanza to stanza; repetition of a key phrase at the end of each stanza. There are songs where you could scramble the order of the stanzas; or leave stanzas out, and you couldn't tell anything was missing. The obvious strategies are theme and variation, and that particular version of theme and variation which is rounded off by a key modulation in the final stanza; or the different stanzas of a poem may adopt different tempi, or different levels of emotional intensity, like the movements of

a symphony or sonata. The line of sense follows a musical
logic, so that we naturally resort to musical terms to describe
it. In Wordsworth's 'She dwelt among the untrodden ways',
for example, the third stanza repeats the pattern of the
previous two, but, as the line of statement moves into a more
personal field of significance, there is a modulation into a
more plangent key:

> She dwelt among the untrodden ways
>   Beside the springs of Dove.
> A Maid whom there were none to praise
>   And very few to love;
>
> A violet by a mossy stone
>   Half hidden from the eye!
> – Fair as a star, when only one
>   Is shining in the sky.
>
> She lived unknown, and few could know
>   When Lucy ceased to be!
> But she is in her grave, and, oh,
>   The difference to me!

* * *

So long as the text before us can be read as simple, spontaneous expression of personal feeling, theme and variation is a
perfectly adequate structure. When it's a matter of thought
more than feeling, to have no indication built into the
structure of the poem of how it hangs together will hardly do.
Poems like Blake's 'Tyger' acquire a kind of oracular authority by their very obscurity. But, usually, when thought takes
over from feeling, poets prefer a chane of strategy. Let's go
back a moment to 'It was a lover and his lass':

> It was a lover and his lass,
>   With a hey, and a ho, and a hey nonino,
> That o'er the green corn field did pass,
>   In springtime, the only pretty ring-time,
> When birds do sing, hey ding a ding, ding:
> Sweet lovers love the spring.

Now compare this:

> When I do count the clock that tells the time,
> And see the brave day sunk in hideous night;
> When I behold the violet past prime,
> And sable curls, all silvered o'er with white;
> When lofty trees I see barren of leaves,
> Which erst from heat did canopy the herd,
> And summer's green all girded up in sheaves,
> Borne on the bier with white and bristly beard,
> Then of thy beauty do I question make,
> That thou among the wastes of time must go,
> Since sweets and beauties do themselves forsake
> And die as fast as they see others grow;
> And nothing 'gainst time's scythe can make defence
> Save breed, to brave him when he takes thee hence.
>
>   (Shakespeare, Sonnet 12)

Shakespeare wrote both these texts. The two work, however, in completely different ways: their structure is different, and, therefore, their mood, their tone, the relationship between poet and audience. The complicated syntax of the sonnet (a single sentence, unwinding over fourteen lines) puts song out of the question. The poet is talking to us, laying out an argument; structure based on syntax takes the place of structure based on metre — a single long stanza, instead of a series of short, syntactically independent stanzas. For all the show of logic, the argument is, of course, a poetic argument, ingenious rather than clear, aimed at winning from us something more complicated than simple assent; wit, word-play, intellectual challenge take the place of lyric spontaneity. But however witty the argument, the argument remains none the less an argument. The stages in it are indicated by the three 'when's' at the beginning of lines 1, 3 and 5: each 'when' clause consists of two parts (connected by 'and'); the first and second 'when' clauses each occupy two lines, the third spills over into four lines, to emphasize the climax of the octet — it is the rhetorical trick (of which we have seen several examples already) of the increasing triad, or tricolon crescendo; a pattern of rhymes (a, b, a, b, c, d, c, d) binds the eight lines

together. 'Then' at the beginning of line 9 marks the beginning of the sestet and the process of drawing conclusions from
the premises stated. From the first word to the last the
argument is patiently, logically conducted: any change in the
order of the lines would spoil it.

* * *

Shakespeare's sonnets are written in the tradition of Petrarch
and the Italian Renaissance. The credit, that is to say, is
Petrarch's (or seems to be) for popularizing the metrical form.
The short personal poem dominated by the poet's speaking
voice is much older, however. To find where it began we have
to go back to Roman times. Take this poem, by the Roman
poet Horace. The scene is set in the opening five lines: a boy in
love for the first time making love to a woman older, more
experienced than himself; the remainder of the poem explores
that situation by means of a metaphor, in which the boy
becomes a sailor putting to sea for the first time on a calm
sunlit sea, with no thought of the storms that lie ahead;
Horace is the old sailor, who has survived at least one
shipwreck and knows what the sea is like:

> What slip of a boy amid a profusion of roses,
> scent-drenched, gleaming, importunes you, Pyrrha,
> in this attractive grotto? For whom do you
> bind back your blond hair,
>
> all chic simplicity? O dear, what wailings about
> promises and gods who let men down when he gazes
> shocked on a sea rough and storm-black,
> innocently presuming.
>
> because your golden self is now at his disposal,
> he can hope to keep you ever his, ever lovable –
> unaware that calm airs cannot
> be trusted. What miseries await
>
> the wretches your splendour unassailed allures! Me? –
> a votive plaque on holy wall declares I've hung
> my sopping garments up to the mighty
> sea-divinity.

(Horace, Odes 1, 5)

Horace's poem is, in several obvious ways, very different from 'When I do count the clock that tells the time'. Like the rest of Horace's Odes, the Pyrrha Ode claims a formal allegiance to the ancient Greek of sung poetry; the metres used are those used by Sappho and Alcæus and their successors; but the syntax sprawls across the stanza-ends, asserting the primacy of sense over metre in a new rhythm — the rhythm of the thinking mind. Where Shakespeare's sonnet builds up a structure of logical argument, Horace's Ode represents the unwinding of the poet's thoughts in a scene. The line of argument of Shakespeare's sonnet expands into a string of images; Horace's Ode builds up a single sustained metaphor. In one important respect, however, the two texts are alike: in both we hear the poet's speaking voice; despite the lyric form, nobody in his (or her) right mind could suppose Horace's poem written to be sung; the measured, complicated syntax exploits the potentialities of the Latin language of Horace's day, represents the reorganization in verse of the complex thought patterns of a highly sophisticated mind; both poems are equally remote from the timeless spontaneity of song.

Horace's Odes represent the fusion of two traditions till then unconnected. A form whose metrical structure authorizes the lyric intensity, the imaginative richness of the singing voice, is restructured syntactically to express the more complicated rhythms of the poet's speaking voice. Song expresses emotion; the more deliberate rhythms of the speaking voice permit the expression of the poet's personality (or that of his chosen persona). A new way of writing poems comes into existence which will last for two thousand years. It's a bold claim to make: to substantiate it, I must go back beyond Horace and say something about epigram. For it is from epigram that the tradition of the poet's speaking voice derives.

*   *   *

The original function of epigram was practical: to organize succinctly the essential facts about the life of a man or woman, so that they could be cut on stone. Take the famous epigram composed by Simonides for the grave of the three hundred Spartan soldiers ordered to hold the pass at Thermopylæ at all costs against the Persian invader:

Tell them in Lacedæmon, passer-by,
That here obedient to their word we lie.

Spartan soldiers were brave; Spartan soldiers obeyed orders,
did not indulge in recrimination; Simonides' epigram captures
a moment in history and an attitude to it. The tone of
detachment, of control maintained against the pressure of
emotion, is enhanced by the precise, measured syntax.

Hundreds, if not thousands, of such epigrams have come
down to us from classical antiquity; thousands more have
been preserved in which the epigrammatical form has been
chosen as a literary device, in order to recall the conventions
of grave-epigram, but with no thought that they would be
carved on stone.

Epigrams are even shorter than lyrics, and more compact.
Like narrative poetry, they adopt the speaking voice; but
where the convention of narrative poetry is that the poet
surrenders to the inspiring Muse, epigram represents the
shaping intellect of the poet. The sideways expansion of the
text is dynamic, compulsive, often exploding at the climax. In
the space of a few lines, rebellious reality is brought under
intellectual control; a set of facts is detached from the mass of
detail obscuring their significance, the essential truth clearly,
dispassionately stated.

The original function of the form, to provide verses for a
tombstone, was soon left behind. Poets quickly realized the
possibilities of epigram. Take these lines from Catullus:

By your fault, Lesbia, is my mind depraved,
by devotion to you utterly destroyed.
Should you become now faultless, I could not wish you well,
nor end desire, whatever you became.

(Catullus, Poem 75)

A form which originally was public and impersonal comes to
express an involvement as intense as that of song. Epigram
permitted trenchant comment on the human comedy; it
permitted also an entirely new kind of love poem — compact,
hard-hitting, lucid, simple statement of complex emotion.

Take these lines:

> Others may write of you, or you may be unknown:
> let him praise who sows seed in barren ground.
> You and your gifts, remember, one black day
> will all be put to bed and sent away.
> The passer-by, regardless your bones, won't sit
> to ponder, 'Here lies a beauty and a wit.'
>
> (Propertius 2, 11)

The poet this time is Propertius. His epigram denies what epigrams written to be cut on tombstones must take for granted: that future generations will care about us when we are dead and buried. The tone of Propertius' six-line poem to his mistress isn't the careless hedonism of Herrick's 'Gather ye rosebuds while ye may', but the concentrated sardonic realism of a Roman lover committed (as a disciple of the materialist Lucretius) to the belief that death means the end of everything.

We're not talking now about epigrams written to be carved on stone: we're talking about poems that only pretend to be epigrams. So long as you've to pay the stonemason for each letter, four lines is quite a lot: more than four lines is an imposition on the passer-by. Freed from the constraints of the tombstone, epigram expanded. The original compact form was never completely discarded: to say something complicated well in four lines, six lines, eight lines even, constituted a challenge. We still find poets writing epigrams today; their effectiveness derives from the reader's recognition that a poem this length is something special. But as poets came to realize the possibilities of the form, they allowed themselves more elbow room; the witty argumentative manner remained, but the expression of it expanded into a full-length poem.

The typical Propertian poem is twenty to thirty lines long. Here is an example. In it, Propertius argues that the conventional picture of Cupid (the winged child-god armed with bow and arrow), though in general an accurate symbol of love, is not appropriate to Propertius (the division into stanzas and sections is mine):

I

Whoever first love as a child portrayed,
think you not he had a cunning hand?
He first saw how lovers senseless live,
by trivial dealing profitless distraught.

Pertinent, too, the windy wings he added then,
devising a god that flits within man's heart.
(Plainly conflicting ways the eddy tosses us;
ours is a breeze whose set does not abide.)

Likewise just the barbed tip that arms his hand,
the Cretan quiver from each shoulder hanging.
(Against foe that unseen strikes no staying safe:
none whom he hits makes off unmaimed.)

II

In me the boyish guise, the pointed arrow holds,
but those wings of his love's lost somehow:
from my heart he never flies away; in my
veins I feel love's unrelenting war.

III

Why dwell in dried-out bones? What pleasure there?
Have you no shame? Aim your shafts another place –
against the unafflicted the poison better turned;
not me but my wasted shadow they assail.

That destroyed, who will be your singer then?
(My frivolous Muse has brought you much renown.)
And who'll my black-eyed mistress sing, head and toe,
when she walks, how her steps do melting go?

                                    (Propertius, 2, 12)

Instead of summing up a situation for all time, Propertius can argue with his readers. Not in order to convince them (to convince is the business of prose), but, more often, to outwit them, to trick them into going along with an argument they can see distorted by emotion; or an argument their common sense struggles to reject; an argument that, but for the elegance with which it is presented, they'd not take seriously.

* * *

The Italian sonnet is the crowning glory of this tradition: in the sonnets of Petrarch we hear the passionate lover presenting his case elegantly, wittily, imaginatively, and yet structuring his argument according to the most stringent rules of form. In Renaissance Italy, in sixteenth-century France and in Elizabethan England, the popularity of the sonnet was immense. Shakespeare's sonnets come right at the end of this period (they were written, probably, in the 1590s) and represent in many ways the most perfect exploitation of the form in English. And then in seventeenth-century England, the sonnet suddenly loses its popularity, and never regains it; it survives as one possible form, usually for a poem marked by seriousness of tone, rather than by the ingenious expression of wit. The mood of the seventeenth century was to go back to the classical Roman models: it was a gesture of emancipation, perhaps, from Catholic Italy, a return to the true sources. For a short compact poem that developed a witty argument, especially an argument about love, poets now took as their models the epigrams of the Roman poets Catullus and Martial, the elegies of Propertius and Ovid. The most interesting case is Horace: he provided the model for an entirely new kind of poem: a poem whose rhythms suggest (by comparison with those of prose) the simplicity and directness of song, and yet remain close to the natural rhythms of conversation; whose imaginative richness and spontaneity likewise claim allegiance to the tradition of song, and yet proclaim the intellectual control of epigram. The result is a poem the very structure of which is paradoxical: a lyric poem dominated by the poet's speaking voice. The great seventeenth-century successor of Horace is Donne: in his hands, poetry develops a more flexible and at the same time more demanding structure than the sonnet could ever permit — more flexible in its metre, more flexible in its rhythms.

It is really only in the present century that this kind of poetry has come into its own. The typical twentieth-century personal poem, though in origin a revival (after two centuries of neglect) of the tradition of Donne and his school, goes well beyond anything Donne ever did with the form. Poets today, though few are aware of the fact, are more the successors of Horace than they are of Donne. In this kind of poem, however fanciful the theme, the poet is at the centre, coolly, rationally

resisting the intoxication of the imagery, disarming our pro-
tests at the paradoxical or the fantastic by a systematically
orchestrated display of wit, challenging us to follow a train of
thought, offering us in return something we can accept as an
insight into the human condition. Such poems provide more
than a flexing of our mental muscles while we struggle to
contain the poet's paradox within acceptable limits of distance.

Early in the seventeenth century, poetry loses its connection
with song: song (song in the true sense — songs written to be
sung) and poetry (poetry written to be read) go different ways.
Poets may still call the poems they write songs: some of the
characteristics of song remain — for example, the readiness
with which the line of statement expands into vivid imagery;
but from now on the head controls the heart — as it had done
in Horace's Odes, as it had done in the sonnet. Donne and his
contemporaries offer, as proof of seriousness (poetic seriousness, for the argument they advance is often fanciful, ingenious, even absurd), a new toughness in the style of thinking. A
highly mannered speaking voice replaces the singing voice. It
imposes a rhythm incompatible with the rhythm of song;
people read these poems, hear them read; don't sing them,
don't hear them sung. Though in 'The Triple Foole' Donne
speaks of his poems being sung, Donne wrote more and more
to be read and re-read, read over and over again; to intrigue
and puzzle a new audience of university wits, or a new more
strenuously intellectual class of clerics whose wits had been
sharpened by religious controversy. These are the people who
bought and read books. They made possible a kind of poetry
that had left song behind.

It is one of the most decisive moments in the history of
English poetry: from the seventeenth century onwards, song is
for popular consumption only; poetry is for an élite of readers.
The dramatic illusion, the enactment before our eyes of an
emotional state, which is fundamental to song, is often
dispensed with; poetry becomes a subsequent reorganization
of feeling — a process by which the head sorts out the
reactions of the heart; it is the process Wordsworth had in
mind when he spoke of poetry as 'emotion recollected in
tranquillity'.

In the late eighteenth century, an attempt is made, in Germany rather than England, to bring poetry and song together again in a kind of shotgun marriage: the German Lied joins opera as an art form in which the sense hardly matters; the movement towards structural complexity now asserts itself in the music; the musical setting becomes the dominant partner in the marriage, riding roughshod over, for example, the structured simplicity of Goethe's lyrics. But it is a development which belongs to music rather than to literature.

The evolution of *popular* song is more continuous and more successful: popular song does not have to be the intellectual equivalent of junk food; this happens only when songs are turned out, like hot dogs, because they will sell, by people whose only reason for making them is that they are paid to make them; or when the text becomes a negligible, sentimental vehicle for a star; when, as in advertising, slickness takes the place of integrity. Popular song, though no longer thought of as belonging to literature, can fulfil, in less esoteric contexts than serious poetry, the true poetic function of presenting a reorganization of experience, sharpened by wit and irony, reinforced by rhyme, rhythm and melody; can offer something which we recognize as insight into the human condition or as social comment. Or the creation, by the singer, before our eyes of a dramatically significant personality: the German songs of Marlene Dietrich, for example; the exploitation of this genre by Bertolt Brecht; by Noel Coward, in a slicker, more superficial style; the songs of the great French popular singers, Maurice Chevalier, Edith Piaf; the songs of Mikos Theodorakis. The night club and the cabaret play a large role in this tradition: such songs often have a tough core to their sentimentality; they have the true ironic quality — 'the value system asserted (the singer's romanticism — or his cynicism) is not the value system implied'. The American and Australian tradition of the popular ballad is hardly in the same class: it has sentimentalized and trivialized political comment by locking onto fashionable issues and attitudes. Some of Tom Lehrer's political songs are exceptions: where other singers deal in cliché (telling us only what their audience likes to hear), Tom Lehrer is out to manipulate our opinions.

IV
THE STARTING POINT IN REALITY

Donne's best poems strike us as so modern in their delicately maintained balance between the singing and the speaking voice, we are apt to suppose that the new form (new, that is, to English verse, for it had been invented by Horace about 30 BC), once it had been hit upon, lived happily ever after. That is not what happened.

The eighteenth century found Donne and his contemporaries too ingenious for an age that worshipped civilized politeness; good manners demand clarity; the unit of wit for the eighteenth century was the well turned couplet in which the point was verbal or rhetorical, not intellectual. Poetry written in the conviction that wit can expand and sustain the lyric impulse, not contradict it, ceased to be written. The dominant note of nineteenth-century poetry is emotional incitement. It is only in the twentieth century that the poetry of Donne and the 'metaphysical' poets of the seventeenth century has been rediscovered. Drastic social change has meant changed intellectual affinities: in a time when all is put in question, the poem which presents the reader with an intellectual argument is once again in fashion. The First World War killed the Romantic in us. Poets became ironic, some (D. H. Lawrence, Siegfried Sassoon) even sardonic. We expect of poetry in the modern world a balanced, witty detachment. Confronted with a poem, we sense a challenge; we read alert to catch the inflections of the poet's speaking voice, the overtones of irony and reservation, the echoes (often gently mocking) of contemporary speech; it seems to us the right tone of voice for a poet to assume in a runaway world. We read no less alert to follow the poet when he leaps into imaginative expansion of the line of thought. For the lyric manner is never wholly discarded; sometimes (e.g. by Yeats) it is even flaunted: it adds to the speaking voice an imaginative spontaneity and compression of thought, a liveliness of rhythm which gives that voice a character of its own distinct from argument in prose. 'Argument lyrically expressed' might serve as a description of much modern poetry.

* * *

To leave the matter there, however, is to leave out of account something important. Go back a moment to Auden's 'Musée des Beaux Arts'. A line of argument occurs to the poet:

> About suffering they were never wrong,
> The Old Masters . . .

The rest of the poem develops that argument. The title of the poem suggests where the train of thought started, but there is no hint in the poem itself of when or where the poem began to take shape. Fleur Adcock's 'Tigers' is a cool appraisal of the old cliché that lovers fight like tigers:

> We do not, in fact, fight like tigers.
> Look, the cubs are only playing: you
> Would think their teeth made of rubber, and
> Their pretty claws. We hurt. We draw blood. . . .

It's the same with Shakespeare's 'When I do count the clock that tells the time', the same with Donne's 'I am two fooles, I know'. There are countless poems that work like this. Something happened in the poet's life which set his poem going: he doesn't have to tell us what it was.

Often, however, he does: the result is a different kind of poem. Look again at Baxter's 'Blood Test'.

> The big mosquito
> Has filled its glass belly
> With *my* blood, a teacupful
> Reddish black and frothing . . .

In Baxter's poem there is a situation to tune into: Baxter went to the lab for a blood test; his poem represents his reactions to that experience. The poem is a drama in miniature, in which experience is reacted to with all the immediacy of something happening as the poet speaks. 'The Lion Skin' sets out in the same way from a described situation — imaginary this time, and therefore more explicitly described:

> The old man with a yellow flower on his coat
> Came to my office, climbing twenty-eight steps,

With a strong smell of death about his person
From the caves of the underworld.

The short personal poem which has built into it an indication of when and where the thing happened that set the poem
going isn't new either. Probably, in the infancy of personal
poetry, there was always a starting point in reality. The
Roman personal poets tended to cling to occasions where the
use of verse was justified by tradition: deaths, birthdays, a
friend to be welcomed home, an enemy to be ridiculed. In
Horace's Pyrrha Ode, the starting point is a scene at a party,
perhaps, sketched in with a few rapid strokes in the opening
lines. In another ode, the starting point is a tree on Horace's
estate which fell and nearly brained him; a train of thought is
set off which ends with Horace imagining himself in Hell
listening to Sappho and Alcæus as they declaim their poetry to
an audience of the dead:

Evil the day he planted you
(Whoever the man), sacrilegious the hand
That nurtured you, tree that was to bring disaster
To future generations, disgrace upon our town.

He cracked his father's neck, I can well
Believe, splashed household shrine with blood
Of guest at dead of night, dealt in
Middle-eastern poisons, practised every crime

One could imagine, that scoundrel who
Set you upon my land, one day to crash,
You lump accursed of wood, down on
Your master's undeserving head.

A man's never on his guard enough against
The perils of each hour. The sailor from Bithynia
Looks terror-struck upon the Bosporus,
Not supposing death from other quarter.

The soldier fears the fleeing archer's Parthian
Shot; the Parthian, in his turn, incarceration
In Italian gaol. But death has struck and will
Strike ever down from where we least expect.

How close I came to seeing wan Proserpine's
Royal estates, Judge Aeacus on the bench,
The righteous in their exclusive homes,
Aeolian Sappho, plaintive strings sadly

Complaining Lesbian girls had played her false!
While you, Alcaeus, golden plectrum drawing fuller tones,
Recount all that at sea, all, exiled in distant
Parts, all that in battle you endured!

Each of you exacts respectful silence from
The listening shades, but it is the songs
Of war and tyrants driven out that hold
The dense-packed crowd enthralled.

What wonder if hundred-headed Cerberus,
By such strains beguiled, lets black
Ears droop; if snakes relax
Their grip on Furies' tresses?

Prometheus himself and Tantalus
Forget their toil, so sweet the sound;
Hunter Orion loses interest in pursuit
Of lion and the timorous lynx.

(Horace, Odes 2, 13)

In a short personal poem there is no space for sustained
narrative, only limited space for detailed description. All the
poet can do is conjure up a scene in which to locate the train of
thought running through his mind. He can then proceed to
argue with us in the strict tradition of epigram. Or his poem
can record the unwinding of his thoughts in that scene: the
unity, in that case, is psychological, not logical; the poem
represents what the poet saw, how he reacted to what he saw.

V

TWENTIETH-CENTURY TRENDS

The oldest, simplest poetic forms last remarkably well. Poets
still write poems which purport to be songs, still write sonnets,
still write epigrams. It's true twentieth-century volumes of

poetry contain few songs you'd really want to sing. Twentieth-century poems whose simple directness at first glance suggests song, when we read them aloud, demand usually to be read according to the rhythms of the speaking, not the singing, voice. Poetry and song (song in the strict sense, texts written to be sung) have parted company, it seems, for good. As for poems written in the tradition of epigram — well, there are still poets who present their argument as simply, as starkly as possible. My impression is, however, that most poets today prefer to locate their train of thought in some kind of briefly evoked dramatic context.

* * *

Here are two poems about death. The first is by Yeats:

> Nor dread nor hope attend
> A dying animal;
> A man awaits his end
> Dreading and hoping all;
> Many times he died,
> Many times rose again.
> A great man in his pride
> Confronting murderous men
> Casts derision upon
> Supersession of breath;
> He knows death to the bone —
> Man has created death.
>
> (Yeats, 'Death')

Yeats's poem has all the starkness, the universality of argument. In the second, by John Crowe Ransom, a complex situation is evoked — a fashionable Southern funeral, viewed by an ironic observer:

> The little cousin is dead, by foul subtraction:
> A green bough from Virginia's aged tree,
> And none of the county kin like the transaction.
> Nor some of the world of outer dark, like me.

A boy not beautiful, nor good, nor clever,
A black cloud full of storms too hot for keeping,
A sword beneath his mother's heart — yet never
Woman bewept her babe as this is weeping.

A pig with a pasty face, so I had said,
Squealing for cookies, kinned by poor pretense
With a noble house. But the little man quite dead,
I see the forbears' antique lineaments.

The elder men have strode by the box of death
To the wide flag porch, and muttering low send round
The bruit of the day. O friendly waste of breath!
Their hearts are hurt with a deep dynastic wound.

He was pale and little, the foolish neighbors say;
The first-fruits, saith the Preacher, the Lord hath taken;
But this was the old tree's late branch wrenched away,
Grieving the sapless limbs, the shorn and shaken.

                    (John Crowe Ransom, 'Dead Boy')

Both poems were written in the late 'twenties, within a few years of one another. 'Nor dread nor hope attend' succeeds by its savage directness. 'Dead Boy' has a starting point in reality; the poem is a commentary on the scene at a funeral, a commentary charged with personal involvement; we feel the speaker struggling unsuccessfully to attain objectivity; yet the status of the speaker never becomes clear — in what sense does he belong to 'the world of outer dark'? Is he beyond the social pale, an old family slave? Is he the black sheep of the family, back for the funeral but shunned by his own kin? Or is he dead himself?

* * *

The forms of personal poetry don't wear out any more than the poems — the good ones — written in those forms. But there are fashions. Ransom's 'Dead Boy' is very much a twentieth-century poem. Turn a moment to Keats's 'Ode to a Nightingale' and you'll see what I mean:

My heart aches, and a drowsy numbness pains
  My sense, as though of hemlock I had drunk,
Or emptied some dull opiate to the drains
  One minute past, and Lethe-wards had sunk . . .

Keats's Odes are of course very carefully organized poetic structures. The feelings expressed are neither unpremeditated nor the simple outpouring of despair:

O, for a draught of vintage! that hath been
  Cooled a long age in the deep-delvéd earth,
Tasting of Flora and the country green,
  Dance, and Provençal song, and sunburnt mirth!
O for a beaker full of the warm South,
  Full of the true, the blushful Hippocrene,
    With beaded bubbles winking at the brim,
      And purple-stainéd mouth;
That I might drink, and leave the world unseen,
  And with thee fade away into the forest dim . . .

The intellect is at work here too: emotion is kept under control, pent up, in order to give it complex, reflecting expression. But the head is wholly at the service of the heart; in poetry where the heart comes first, where what matters most is the intensity of pent-up emotion, there is no place for irony or detachment.

Most poets since the First World War put it the other way round: the heart, for them, is at the service of the head. 'Poetry is not a turning loose of emotion,' wrote Eliot in 'Tradition and the individual talent', 'but an escape from emotion . . .'. Poetry for Eliot was something more than emotion structured as verse; in the making of a poem, there had to take place a kind of chemical process, a refinement of crudely personal emotion into poetical complex statement; in the course of that process were generated what Eliot called *feelings*, the reactions of the thinking, sensitive, well-stocked mind of the poet; to express these adequately was a matter of skill, wide reading, a particular kind of sensibility; it was feelings, adequately expressed, which made a poem.

Ransom's 'Dead Boy' shows Eliot's preaching put into practice. Where Keats begins on a plangent note, in a mood of complete surrender to intense melancholy:

> My heart aches, and a drowsy numbness pains
>   My sense, as though of hemlock I had drunk,
> Or emptied some dull opiate to the drains . . .

Ransom is dry, matter-of-fact, fastidious, his reactions to the scene evoked controlled by a sensitive irony — the note struck in the opening line by the unexpected word 'subtraction':

> The little cousin is dead, by foul subtraction:
> A green bough from Virginia's aged tree,
> And none of the county kin like the transaction . . .

It was the intention of Eliot's blandly argued manifesto to drive the last nails in the coffin of Romanticism. He set out to define in precise terms a new way of thinking about what goes on in the making of a poem. Poets whose poetry in other respects was very different from Eliot's could feel they were with Eliot in the general revolt against Romanticism: what their poetry had in common was a regained ascendency of head over heart.

The manifesto succeeded because it came at the right time. Eliot did not originate the swing away from Romanticism, though he had a good deal to do with the introduction to England of a new twentieth-century sensibility which was European rather than English. Already well before the war, Rainer Maria Rilke was writing the kind of short poem that expressed the poet's exquisitely tuned, imaginative reaction to everyday incidents of urban social life (the milieu the eighteenth-century version of which the Romantics had rejected, in favour of a more or less pseudo-realistic pastoralism). Take Rilke's poem (written in 1906) on the girl who is going blind, observed at a party. Note especially the rhythm: in stanza 1, staccato; in stanza 2, gathering momentum as the group breaks up; in stanza 3, slowing down to concentrate on those bright, near-blind eyes; in stanza 4, a more deliberate rhythm at first, building up to the final 'fly':

She sat just like the others there at tea.
I had at most a feeling that she didn't
Pick up her cup quite as the others did.
Once, she smiled. It almost hurt to see.

And when finally all got up and talked,
And slowly, and as chance had it, made
Their way through the various rooms, talking and laughing,
My gaze fell on her. She walked behind the rest,

Withdrawn, apart, like one who soon
Must sing before a crowd of people.
On her bright eyes, with pleasure filled,
Light played from without, as on a pool.

She followed slowly, had to take her time, as if
There were some obstacle she had still to climb;
And yet, as if, when she had surmounted it,
She would no longer walk, but fly.

> (Rainer Maria Rilke, 'Die Erblindende')

Contrast with Rilke's poem Wordsworth's 'The Solitary Reaper':

Behold her, single in the field,
Yon solitary Highland Lass!
Reaping and singing by herself;
Stop here, or gently pass!
Alone she cuts and binds the grain,
And sings a melancholy strain;
O listen! for the Vale profound
Is overflowing with the sound.

No Nightingale did ever chaunt
More welcome notes to weary bands
Of travellers in some shady haunt,
Among Arabian sands;
A voice so thrilling ne'er was heard
In springtime from the Cuckoo bird,
Breaking the silence of the seas
Among the farthest Hebrides.

Will no one tell me what she sings? —
Perhaps the plaintive numbers flow
For old, unhappy, far-off things,
And battles long ago;
Or is it some more humble lay,
Familiar matter of today?
Some natural sorrow, loss, or pain,
That has been, and may be again?

Whate'er the theme, the Maiden sang
As if her song could have no ending;
I saw her singing at her work,
And o'er the sickle bending —
I listened, motionless and still,
And, as I mounted up the hill,
The music in my heart I bore,
Long after it was heard no more.

Readers whose poetic taste has been shaped by twentieth-century poetry written in the tradition of Rilke and Eliot are apt to be made uncomfortable by the undisguised emotional incitement of Wordsworth's poem. They are inclined to feel the same way about Keats: they have come to expect more restraint, more detachment in the expression of the poet's reaction to experience. In return for the sharper focusing of our attention, twentieth-century poetry offers us an evaluation, more precise, more sensitive, than we could make ourselves, of the world of our own experience. More of us, after all, have seen a blind girl struggling to cope with modern social life than have seen a girl all by herself in a wheat field singing as she reaps; more of us can react strongly to the poet's deliberately expressed insight into that situation than can feel strongly about Keats deep in the grip of melancholy. Rilke's poem communicates a way of reacting to what *we* might have seen but been no more than casually moved by. A girl who is going blind seen at a party, if not an everyday occurrence, belongs to the everyday world of our contemporary experience; the Romantic pastoral world of 'The Solitary Reaper' or the poet sick to death with life suggests things we read about in books rather than things we meet in real life.

Even when the setting is the countryside, the rural scene is now dealt with more crisply, less enveloped in a Romantic haze. Take this poem by Edward Thomas:

Downhill I came, hungry, and yet not starved;
Cold, yet had heat within me that was proof
Against the North wind; tired, yet so that rest
Had seemed the sweetest thing under a roof.

Then at the inn I had food, fire, and rest,
Knowing how hungry, cold, and tired was I.
All of the night was quite barred out except
An owl's most melancholy cry

Shaken out long and clear upon the hill,
No merry note, nor cause of merriment,
But one telling me plain what I escaped
And others could not, that night, as in I went.

And salted was my food, and my repose,
Salted and sobered, too, by the bird's voice
Speaking for all who lay under the stars,
Soldiers and poor, unable to rejoice.
                                   (Edward Thomas, 'The Owl')

Poetry in the twentieth century doesn't ask us to accept that the poet is somehow cut off from the rest of humanity by the beauty or the intensity of his emotions: its settings are the settings of the typical twentieth-century novel. Where the two forms differ is in the way they deal with experience.

What we're talking about is fashion in poetry, the need for poetry to keep in touch with life, rather than anything you could call progress. It's silly to say we would rather have Ransom's 'Dead Boy' or Rilke's 'Going Blind' or Edward Thomas's 'The Owl' than Wordsworth's 'The Solitary Reaper' or Keats's 'Ode to a Nightingale'; equally silly to say we'd prefer poets to go on writing like Wordsworth and Keats instead of writing like Ransom or Rilke or Edward Thomas. You and I may think that Philip Larkin's 'Church Going' represents a dead end:

Once I am sure there's nothing going on
I step inside, letting the door thud shut.
Another church: matting, seats, and stone,
And little books; sprawlings of flowers, cut
For Sunday, brownish now; some brass and stuff
Up at the holy end; the small neat organ;
And a tense, musty, unignorable silence,
Brewed God knows how long. Hatless, I take off
My cycle-clips in awkward reverence . . .

I confess Larkin's pale, troubled agnosticism seems a poor
thing to me (as poetry) compared with the violent, anguished
rigour of Gerard Manley Hopkins's sonnet:

Not, I'll not, carrion comfort, Despair, not feast on thee;
Not untwist — slack they may be — these last strands of
 man
In me ór, most weary, cry *I can no more.* I can . . .
                    (Gerard Manley Hopkins, 'Carrion Comfort')

But my preference for Hopkins over Larkin is, I like to think,
more a judgement of the stature of the two poems than an
opinion about how poems should be written. I think we have
to accept, too, that the embarrassed incomprehension of a
sincere modern intellectual in the presence of the monuments
of his own cultural past is as legitimate a subject for poetry as
Hopkins's tortured Christianity. Fashion comes into it all the
same: Hopkins's sonnet deals directly with its subject; Larkin's much longer poem reflects, like Ransom's 'Dead Boy',
our modern feeling that the poet's evaluation of experience
should be suggested, built up by situation, rather than plainly
asserted. Larkin's poem creates the illusion of thought and
feeling at a stage where they are still unformulated.

The fact is poets offer a different kind of competence from
that possessed by those who discuss ideas; they make a
different claim upon our time. To turn our backs on reality is
not our only object when we take up a poem or a novel. If
literature is sometimes a kind of escapism from an otherwise
intolerable reality, it is also a way of coming to terms with
reality.

* * *

The statements we find in a poem are, most often, privileged statements, not to be submitted to a simple test of true or false. 'The poet affirmeth nothing,' said Sir Philip Sidney four hundred years ago. What, then, is the role of the statements we find in a poem?

The question isn't one to which simple answers are possible. Romantic critics liked to think of poems as inspired creations, possessing the capacity to hold their readers enthralled by a kind of verbal magic. Coleridge's 'Kubla Khan' is probably the best-known major Romantic poem for which this theory works:

> In Xanadu did Kubla Khan
> A stately pleasure dome decree:
> Where Alph, the sacred river, ran
> Through caverns measureless to man
>   Down to a sunless sea.
> So twice five miles of fertile ground
> With walls and towers were girdled round:
> And there were gardens bright with sinuous rills,
> Where blossomed many an incense-bearing tree;
> And here were forests ancient as the hills,
> Enfolding sunny spots of greenery . . .

There are many famous Romantic poems which depend for their success upon the reader's surrender to the spell of words. Such poems still have meaning: we need meaning to draw us through the text; a meaningless text arouses no more than idle curiosity; but meaning is reduced to the role of a structuring device — something to latch onto while the poet casts his spell.

A salutary effect of twentieth-century criticism has been to lead us back to respect for meaning; to get us used again, when we read a poem, to looking for a meaning to hold onto as we read, however hard it may be to express the significance of what is said in clear words of our own. To insist on the primacy of meaning is perhaps the greatest achievement of the Cambridge English school. Its influence has been world-wide: just at the moment when the fashion in poetry was changing, a critical approach unexpectedly offered itself able to cope with the new poetry being written in the twentieth century. Poets were returning to seventeenth-century models, above all Donne. Poems in which the head had regained ascendancy over the heart. The new critical approach provided a technique for dealing with poets like Eliot or Wallace Stevens; it encouraged the experiments with complex, obscure sense of poets like William Empson.

Fifty years later, the way poets write and the way critics talk about their poems have changed considerably. We still get further with almost *any* poem if we come to it determined to do battle with the words instead of simply surrendering to their spell. Meaning isn't everything, but meaning of some kind there must be. Meaning in a poem is the equivalent of narrative in a novel: it is meaning organized into statement that draws us through the text; it is our attention to meaning which creates the energy needed to touch off the literary experience. Even a nonsense poem depends on an illusion of meaning: words are structured according to the normal rules of grammar into statements which are in fact devoid of meaning; some of the words may be made-up words; but because the statements are heavily loaded with impressive-sounding resonant words (existent or non-existent), a kind of fuzz of significance is generated around the line of statement. The non-poems of Ern Malley, devised to make fools of the readers of *Angry Penguins* by tricking them into believing they were real poems, work like this:

> I had often, cowled in the slumberous heavy air,
> Closed my inanimate lids to find it real . . .
> ('Dürer: Innsbruck, 1495')

Hoaxes apart, there are poems, widely accepted as good poems, whose status as statement about reality seems at first almost equally negligible. The poems of Mallarmé and the French Symbolists, for example; much of the poetry of Dylan Thomas (immediate butt of the perpetrators of the Ern Malley hoax); much of Eliot's *Four Quartets*. Take Mallarmé's famous 'Sonnet en i majeur' (so called because the last syllable in each line contained the vowel 'i'):

The virgin, the vivacious and the beauteous today,
Will it tear with a drunken stroke of its wing
This hard forgotten lake haunted beneath the frost
By a transparent glacier of flights that never were?
A swan of former times remembers it is he
Who, magnificent, but without hope, surrenders
For failing to have sung of the land wherein to live
When winter's sterile boredom has begun to shine.
His long neck will shake off this white despair
Inflicted by space on the bird who denied its power,
But not the awful grasp of earth pinning down his plumes.
A ghost, to this place by his pure brightness condemned,
He falls motionless in the chill dream of contempt
Which, in his useless exile, clothes the swan.

Such poems (like nonsense verse) depend in part (and often it's a large part) on the resonances, melodic and semantic, of the words and structures used. They are something more, however, than resonating nonsense. Like the Ern Malley poems, they make statements which can be translated: unlike the Ern Malley poems, the statements are connected, though the connections may not be obvious; we can work our way through Mallarmé's sonnet, responding to something more than the incitement of the resonating text. Nothing in music is really comparable to the verbal intoxication of lines like these: the phrases don't just echo in the memory, summon up echoes of other phrases from other poets; the words which compose the phrases have meanings of their own — complex, conflicting meanings, arranged in a hierarchy of prominence by the verbal structure which reinforces some of those meanings and mutes others without wholly eliminating them.

The effect such poems have upon the sensitive reader is too powerful for them to be dismissed as mere tricks or passing fads. It is something more than a fuzz of significance. One proof is that the effect is more powerful when we read a text like this with persistent, responsive attention instead of surrendering to the incantation. If such texts necessarily possess the capacity to generate widely divergent processes of association (since so much depends on the reader), this does not mean that they can mean anything we like: we have to keep coming back to the text and let it create for us afresh the experience of reading it by surrendering afresh to the meaning built into it. Poems like these represent in extreme form a paradoxical feature of all poetry, certainly all poetry so compressed or so complex that the resonances of key words take over from the line of sense. That such poetry is more than a deliberate mystification is clear. It is too widely practised for that. On the contrary, if poetry has a future, it may lie here.

* * *

A typical good poem of the 1980s, to tie together some of the points discussed in this section:

The Condition

Sun on our backs, we leaned on the wooden rail
and peered at the stream threading its beads of light
among the wavering stones; then we saw them, small
and resolute, two fluttering brown trout,
steady in the water, yet swimming manfully;
'If they go with the current they suffocate', you said,
'a quick dash is sometimes possible, but only
by holding their breath, so to speak . . .' Their need
is to engage the opposing current, to hold,
confront, defy, to judge exactly the weight
thrown each moment against their shoulders, their filled
and quivering gills. It's to know the force of the fight.
But I thought how they must sometimes long to turn and leap
uncaring into that swift and fatal sleep!
(Lauris Edmond, from Catching It, 1983)

Fourteen lines, a kind of sonnet; the line-ends marked by assonance rather than rhyme until the final couplet and its monstrous implausibility:

> . . . how they must sometimes long to turn and leap
> uncaring into that swift and fatal sleep!

In our rational, everyday minds we *know* it is wholly implausible that trout should have such thoughts and emotions;

might be tempted to give up the struggle and go with the current. In Lauris Edmond's poem, this is a poet's imaginative rounding off of an interior monologue, not something the poet puts forward as true, or worth serious consideration by our rational, everyday minds.

Lines 1–5 sketch in a scene: the wooden rail, the stream, the trout 'swimming manfully'; 'manfully' is the first hint of an ironic loading (remember the speaking voice is a woman's voice), a hint that picks up the title of the poem. The 'condition' meant is, no doubt, the condition that governs the existence of the trout; but there are surely overtones as well of what we got used in the 80s to calling the 'human condition', after the title of André Malraux's famous novel of the 30s (*La condition humaine*), taken over as the title of a popular philosophical study by Hannah Arendt (*The Human Condition*, 1958). Two couples in the scene: two trout, struggling against the current; two human observers, no more than a hint of a relationship between them; no more than a hint that for one of the observers the struggling trout are a symbol of her own struggle against the current. He (the speaking voice implies a he, I think) is the talker, the practised expositor — the dots after *speak* in line 8 tell us the lecture did not stop at the point where Edmond shifts attention to herself. She is the listener. The brisk lecture-room style of the words in inverted commas, the apologetic 'so to speak' which scrupulously excuses the very humble imaginative flight of 'by holding their breath', give way to an interior monologue that is vividly imaginative. It forms (expanded by the two-word anticipation in the previous line) the sestet of this near-sonnet:

> Their need
> is to engage the opposing current, to hold,
> confront, defy, to judge exactly the weight
> thrown each moment against their shoulders, their filled
> and quivering gills. It's to know the force of the fight.

The rhetorical structure is, once again, the expanding triad of parallel clauses (a *tricolon crescendo*) which we saw in Lawrence's near-sonnet 'Moonrise' (page 4): 'to engage . . . '; 'to hold, confront, defy'; 'to judge exactly . . . '. And then, in a separate sentence, 'It's to know the force of the fight'. The strong, confident rhythm ostensibly signals only approval. But the metaphors which reinterpret the instinctive behaviour pattern of the trout in human terms, as if trout had a conscious human will, carry an increasingly heavy ironic loading. The final rhyming couplet (which in the traditional sonnet spells out the moral), instead of crowning the argument, seems to sweep it away, to prick the bubble in a surge of personal reaction:

> But I thought how they must sometimes long to turn and leap
> uncaring into that swift and fatal sleep!

For the trout, to turn and leap is literally death. What about the human swimmer against the current? Does the break with convention mean only social suicide, relegation to the status of a drop-out? Or does it mean that most final of all breaks with convention (however tempting for those who take it), actual suicide?

VI

The case I have tried to sketch out in this chapter is that the balance which was secured in Roman poetry (the poetry of Horace and Propertius) between the tradition of song and the tradition of epigram was recovered again in English poetry in the seventeenth century, then lost again, to be recovered once more in the present century, first in French and German, then in English. In other periods we see emotion unrestrained by wit or wit unenlivened by imaginative sensibility: it is really only in these three periods that the conflicting elements come together in stable, effective combination.

To some extent, my object has been to outline a conjectural history of the short personal poem, in which song and epigram, the singing and the speaking voice, are seen as the two fundamental components. As always, I am less interested in what poems are made out of than in what they are made into. My object has been to show more clearly how what they are made into works.

The history of the novel is rather like the history of the motorcar: model after model is taken out of production, the new model superseding the old as the right way to do things; the result is increasing complexity of structure within an essentially unchanging form — the form being limited, after all, by function. We, the public, may like vintage cars or vintage novels, but we have to accept that they aren't made that way any more.

Poems last better than novels: change here, most often, is a matter of change of emphasis in the components of a composite tradition; the old ways of doing things not only continue to work, but keep coming back into fashion in different intellectual contexts. The appropriate image, where poems are concerned, is the swinging pendulum, not the series of cars, each model an improvement on its predecessor, from Ford's Model T to the latest version that rolls off the production line.

All poems are in some degree a battle of wits between writer and reader. We read the text expecting it to make sense. But even in the most straightforward poems it is a sense that we, the readers, have to construct: poets haven't time to dot i's and cross t's. In a short personal poem we may find ourselves involved from the outset in building a consistency out of a series of statements that seem not to hang together, or to challenge common sense.

To show that one poem conforms more than another to the general practice of poets is no proof that the first poem is better than the second. Critics tend to talk as though there were rules; as though criticism were a normative, not a descriptive, procedure. The temptation to be smart is very great; the need to be humble in the presence of experimenting genius not always remembered. The fact of the matter is, good poems can be written to all sorts of models; there are no rules for success, however much critics would like it to be otherwise.

A poem is an artistic structure, not a cypher to be cracked; reading poems is a different process from shelling peas; it isn't a matter of ripping the text open, tearing out the intellectual nourishment, and then throwing away the verbal husk. We have to do the best we can to hold the verbal structure in our minds while we react both to the line of statement and the sideways expansion of the text. Often that's hard work.

Reading poetry isn't for people who take their pleasures lightly; it is like being admitted to an experimental laboratory, where poets are trying to find new ways of using language to express their thoughts about, and their reactions to, life. For if, in poetry, the old fashions keep coming back, the poems which result (the good ones at any rate) are always new, in some way unlike all previous poems. That's in part of course what makes reading poetry exciting.

4

The Poetic and the Prosaic Mind

I

I have concentrated on two forms of literary text: the novel and the short personal poem. The two represent opposite poles of the literary experience: in one case, a text so short you can hold the whole of it in your mind as you read it; in the other, the less intense, usually less intellectually challenging, experience of reading a novel. You can read a poem half a dozen times in a few minutes, may puzzle over it for half an hour; only the most strenuous of novel readers read a whole novel at a single stretch; mostly, it's a matter of days rather than hours.

Because even serious readers tend to read more novels than poems and because novels are written in prose, the temptation is to think of prose as the normal form of literary expression, and of poetry as something special; a survival from the past, still hanging on, still not quite dead. The novel is now *the* international literary form: English translations of novels written in French, German, Spanish, Czech confront us in the bookshops and the review pages of periodicals, often within a year of their original publication; any list you or I might care to make, or solicit from friends, of the ten best novels of the 1980s would very likely include novels written in half a dozen languages by writers spread around the world. The audience for poems is minute by comparison and doesn't easily cross national or linguistic frontiers.

166

It wasn't always that way. The novel is an upstart. Prose fiction was rare in antiquity; the exception, not the rule. Prose was for every day. If you had a story to tell, you told it in verse, even if the subject of your story was the everyday world and the foibles of those around you; ancient comedy, like ancient tragedy, was always in verse. All the great European literatures — Greek, Roman, English, French — start with verse. Even Italian isn't really an exception: true, Boccaccio's *Decameron*, the earliest masterpiece of imaginative writing in prose in the modern world, springs fully mature out of the late Middle Ages; but the *Decameron* is still half a century later than Dante's *Divina Commedia*. And the *Decameron* is, after all, only a string of tales. The novel, large-scale fiction with a plot (or, in our day, fiction struggling to free itself from plot) goes back not much more than 250 years.

On semi-technical subjects prose gets off to an earlier start: the Latin models were more easily imitated. Even so, many who wrote on such subjects continued to prefer to write in Latin until Elizabethan times, or later. Sir Thomas More wrote his *Utopia* in Latin (1510; it was translated into French in 1530, into English in 1531). Francis Bacon wrote mainly in Latin — his English *Essays* were the exception. The best original prose in English to come down to us from Elizabethan times is that of the theologian Richard Hooker.

Imaginative prose in English begins timidly. Boccaccio's sinewy, perfectly disciplined syntax was an adaptation to the vernacular of the syntax of classical Latin, an expression of a fresh vision of the world in a language structurally little altered. The architectural subtleties of the Latin sentence were less easily adapted to a non-Latin language. It took a long time for English prose to devise rhythms and syntactical patterns of its own. We have no Rabelais, no Cervantes. Even in verse, the structural complexity and the intellectual sophistication Latin permitted weren't easily matched in English. Chaucer is shrewd; his verse can imply admirably nuances he could not easily have expressed in as many words. But his narrative structures are simple, almost naive; they suggest a civilized sensibility, one that is humorous and humane; they do not bear the imprint of the structuring intellect. It is left to metre and rhythm (the rhythm of the line rather than the rhythm of the sentence) to compensate for the deficiencies of syntax.

English literary prose wins a foothold first in the theatre: John Lyly was the first to write plays in prose (in the 1580s and 90s); Shakespeare used both prose and verse. The native English tradition of simple narrative prose is a good deal earlier: it extends from Malory (*Morte d'Arthur*, 1485 — more than a century after Boccaccio) through to the Elizabethan translations of Greek and Roman classics (North's *Plutarch*, 1579; Philemon Holland's *Livy*, 1600) and of the Bible; what all these have in common (especially the first English translations of the Bible) is a modest but efficient instrument whose simple dignity exploits its limitations without overcoming them; it cannot sustain the complex superstructure of elegantly stated qualification and reservation which Boccaccio could manipulate with ease. Holland, with Livy's complex Latin sentences before him, has to sacrifice speed for syntactical amplitude. Here he is on the sack of Rome by the Gauls:

> The Gaules, both for that now they had rested from fight a whole night, and so their choler was somewhat cooled, and also because they had not in any place fought a bloudie and dangerous battell with them, nor even at that time wan the cittie by any assault or force, entered the morrow after into the cittie, without anger and heat of furious rage, by the gate Collina, standing wide open, and so passed forward to the common place of assemblies, casting their eies about them towards the temples of the gods, and to the castle, which onlie presented some shew of warre. And there leaving a sufficient guard, least happily from the castle and Capitoll they should be violently assaulted, after they were once assunder parted, they fell to ransacke and rifle. . . .
>
> (Livy, *History of Rome*, Book 5, Chapter 41)

II

It is easy to see why verse came first. Common sense tells us that, when human beings first acquired the power of speech (when they began to communicate by means of something more than grunt and groan), they must have spoken a kind of crude prose. To make what they said memorable, it had to be given perceptible structure, an air of rightness and finality. This for long only verse could supply. The urge to communicate wasn't enough; what verse could provide and prose could not was a consciousness of form. Form dictated rules which could be learnt, rules of a different kind from the rules of grammar. The rules of form aren't aimed at securing meaning but at transforming statement into something permanent, something that conveys more than it says in so many words, *more than is easily pinned down.* The result is a structure which has shape; striking, pleasurable shape; the verbal construct is exciting, worth remembering. It produces in us a feeling of finality; something got just right, not to be tinkered with.

For a long time in English (as in the beginnings of Greek and Latin literature), metre was indispensable to this illusion of finality: metre locked the words together, made them permanent, made them memorable, created the illusion of a magical transformation of speech into what the Greeks called *poiema*; something created, a verbal structure put together by a craftsman.

The less rigid artistic principles which came to govern creation in prose took longer to evolve. The larger structures of qualification, of subordination of minor statement to principal statement, require an organization of thought before they can become an organization of words. Today, all that is behind us: we have long passed the point, in short, where prose is the more limited medium. A paragraph from Virginia Woolf can claim a status as a structure of thought comparable to a poem:

> She would have been, in the first place, dark like Lady Bexborough, with a skin of crumpled leather and beautiful eyes. She would have been, like Lady Bexborough, slow and stately; rather large; interested in politics like a man; with a country house; very dignified, very sincere. Instead of which she had a narrow pea-stick figure; a ridiculous little face, beaked like a bird's. That she held herself well was true; and had nice hands and feet; and dressed well, considering that she spent little. But often now this body

she wore (she stopped to look at a Dutch picture), this body, with all its capacities, seemed nothing — nothing at all. She had the oddest sense of being herself invisible; unseen, unknown; there being no more marrying, no more having of children now, but only this astonishing and rather solemn progress with the rest of them, up Bond Street, this being Mrs Dalloway; not even Clarissa any more; this being Mrs Richard Dalloway.

(Virgina Woolf, *Mrs Dalloway*, Chapter 1)

Virginia Woolf's prose lacks the formal organization of verse, but it has its own, individual, tightly cohering organization. A paragraph of *Mrs Dalloway* can be as perfectly structured as a sonnet.

Or take Henry James's description of the dinner party at which Milly is launched upon London society. The conspicuously elaborate syntax, instead of holding things up, establishes just the flamboyant rhythm the occasion requires. But note too the undertone of pathos that runs quietly through this tour de force of narrative irony: this is the passage in which the image of Milly as the dove is planted for the first time:

Nothing was so odd as that she should have to recognize so quickly in each of these glimpses of an instant the various signs of a relation; and this anomaly itself, had she had more time to give to it, might well, might almost terribly have suggested to her that her doom was to live fast. It was queerly a question of the short run and the consciousness proportionately crowded.

These were immense excursions for the spirit of a young person at Mrs Lowder's mere dinner-party; but what was so significant and so admonitory as the fact of their being possible? What could they have been but just a part, already, of the crowded consciousness? And it was just a part, likewise, that while plates were changed and dishes presented and periods in the banquet marked; while appearances insisted and phenomena multiplied and words reached her from here and there like plashes of a slow thick tide; while Mrs Lowder grew somehow more stout and more instituted and Susie, at her distance and in comparison, more thinly improvised and more different — different, that is, from every one and everything: it was just a part that while this process went forward our young lady alighted, came back, taking up her destiny again as if she had been able by a wave or two of her wings to place herself briefly in sight of an alternative to it. Whatever it was it had showed in this brief interval as better than the alternative. . . .

(Henry James, *The Wings of the Dove*, Book 4, Chapter 1)

With prose like this, one is tempted to say, who needs verse? The question deserves to be taken seriously. It will be the object of this chapter to provide an answer.

III
THE DEVELOPMENT OF LITERARY PROSE

Until a culture can develop a degree of organization of thought that can enable the building of verbal structures in prose comparable to the lines and stanzas of a poem, prose can serve only as a conveniently flexible, unobtrusive way of stringing together matter important in itself, as fact or fiction. We do not have to be a Flaubert to tell a good tale. The graceful simplicity of Malory's narrative prose matches the fairytale mood, lending the tale a naive seriousness:

Then the King got his spear in both his hands, and ran toward Sir Mordred, crying and saying, 'Traitor, now is thy death-day come!'
And when Sir Mordred saw King Arthur he ran unto him with his sword drawn in his hand, and there King Arthur smote Sir Mordred under the shield with a foin of his spear, throughout the body more than a fathom. And when Sir Mordred felt that he had his death's wound, he thrust himself with the might that he had up to the burr of King Arthur's spear, and right so he smote his father, King Arthur, with his sword held in both his hands, upon the side of the head, that the sword pierced the helmet and the

táy of the brain. And therewith Mordred dashed down stark dead to the earth.

And noble King Arthur fell in a swoon to the earth, and there he swooned oftentimes, and Sir Lucan the Butler and Sir Bedivere the Bold ofttimes hove him up. And so weakly betwixt them they led him to a little chapel not far from the sea.

(Malory, *Morte d'Arthur*)

But set alongside Malory's simple, graceful narrative Homer's story of the death of Hector. Homer's syntax likewise displays an archaic simplicity. But even in a translation you can hear the stylized resonances of a complex literary language in which the traditional formulae for describing the ritual of hand-to-hand fight to the death are incorporated in a structure of sharply imagined detail and elaborate simile; can feel the contrast between the formal elegance of the verse and the awful bloodthirsty anger of Achilles as he strikes down the man who had killed his best friend:

So he spoke, and drew his sharp-edged sword,
That great, strong sword that hung at his side,
And, raising himself up, he swooped like the eagle
That flies on high, then hurtles groundwards through
Dark clouds to seize a tender lamb or cowering hare:
So swooped Hector brandishing his sharp sword.
Achilles rushed at him, his heart filled with savage
Rage, protecting his chest with his finely wrought
Shield, and he tossed his bright four-horned helmet,
And the beautiful golden plumes that
Hephaestus had set about the crest of it waved.
Just as the evening star shines out among the other stars
In the darkness of night, the most beautiful in the sky,
So flashed forth the keen spear that Achilles
Shook in his right hand, intending evil for great Hector,
Searching for the best point to strike Hector's fair flesh,
Everywhere protected by the fine bronze armour that Hector
Had stripped from the corpse of Patroclus when he slew him.
An opening showed where collar-bones part neck from

Shoulders at the gullet, the swiftest point to take
A man's life: here Achilles let drive with his spear.
And clean through the soft neck the spear joint sank,
But the heavy bronze did not sever the windpipe, so that
Hector could still speak and address words to his foe.
He fell in the dust, and great Achilles exulted over him:
'Hector, you said, I expect, as you killed Patroclus,
That you would be safe, had no thought of me, for I
Was not there. Fool, I was left to wait at the
Hollow ships; I, a mightier foe, now take his place,
I who have loosed your knees. The dogs and birds will tear
At your body as it lies disgraced, while Patroclus
Will be buried by his fellow Achaeans.'
Hector of the flashing helm answered him with draining
        strength:
'I beg you by your life, your knees, your parents,
Let not the dogs devour me beside your Achaean ships.
Take your fill of bronze and gold. My father and my
Mother the Queen will give you all of it, but let my body
Be sent home, so that the wives of the Trojans
Can present me with my meed of fire.'
Glaring at him, swift-footed Achilles replied:
'Implore me not, dog, by knees or parents.
If only I had the strength and the stoutness of heart
To carve and eat your flesh raw, such things you have done,
There is not man alive would call the dogs from your
        head —
Not if they came with ten-fold or twenty-fold
The ransom, promised yet more still;
Not though Priam son of Dardanus should bid them pay
Your weight in gold: not even so shall your mother
The Queen who bore you place you on your funeral bier.
Instead the dogs and the birds shall feed their fill.'
Hector of the flashing helm, dying now, replied:
'Believe me, I know you and what will be. There is no way
I could persuade you. Truly you have a heart of iron.
But take thought lest I serve to remind the gods
When the day comes that Paris and Phoebus Apollo
Shall destroy you at the Scaean gates for all your brave deeds.'
As he spoke, his end came, darkness enfolded him,

> The life in him fled and was gone to Hades,
> Bewailing fate, leaving behind manliness and youth.
> And great Achilles spoke these words to his corpse:
> 'Die. I shall accept what lies in store for me
> When it is the will of Zeus and the immortal gods.'
>
> (Homer, *Iliad 22*, 303–66)

Before prose can claim seriously to compete with verse, you have to have a culture which has learnt to assemble and organize its thoughts into complex patterns of argument or fantasy, so that structures based on syntax can challenge and delight the mind in a way comparable to the challenge and delight offered by structures the basis of whose organization is metre. Eventually, that point is reached. Prose and verse can provide alternative, equally sophisticated instruments of expression. What happens next?

What happens is that alternatives cease to be alternatives. Prose takes over some of the territory traditionally occupied by verse. The novel, not the epic poem, becomes the normal form for telling a story. In England, the take-over of fiction by prose begins modestly enough with tales like Defoe's *Moll Flanders* (published 1722). But the new form catches on and quickly takes the place of verse as the medium of sustained narrative.

The transformation of the structure of English society by the Industrial Revolution, the huge increase in population (the population of England doubled between 1780 and 1830 from eight million to sixteen million) meant an enormous extension of the reading public; for the first time that public now included a majority who seldom if ever read poetry. Similar social changes were taking place in France. By the beginning of the nineteenth century, the novel was well on its way to becoming, in both England and France, the predominant literary form; the normal, if not the only, form in which most people came in contact with the literary experience. It has stayed that way ever since.

* * *

The first English novelists thought of themselves as writing a kind of comedy of manners in narrative form: Fielding called his first novel (*Joseph Andrews*, 1742) 'a comic epic in prose'. The pretensions of the form increased with its popularity. More and more the novel came as a result to take over the role once discharged by poetry of presenting a vision of life. There results a drastic shift in the relation between literature and everyday life: the novel mirrors life with a fidelity impossible in verse; prose can permit itself a much greater degree of detail in description, report conversations that come close to real conversations since they don't have to rhyme or scan, or respect the simplifying rhetoric of verse.

As the novel increased in pretensions, it began to take over the techniques of poetry. The verbal fabric of prose narrative acquired a new density; novelists used images and recurring symbols as a way of suggesting a seriousness, a deeper significance underlying the events narrated. The distinction which classical antiquity had maintained (apart from occasional tours de force or parodies, such as Lucian's *Journey to the Moon*) between prose as the medium for fact and verse as the medium for fiction is thus destroyed. It becomes necessary to re-make the distinction within prose. Instead of the polarity which had traditionally existed between verse and prose, there now develops a polarity within prose itself.

Already in the seventeenth century, well before the rise of the novel, the need had been felt for a consciously objective prose. It was felt first in religious controversy: the traditional eloquence of the pulpit was no longer acceptable. By the middle of the seventeenth century, the view became general that logical, dispassionate discussion, objectivity consciously maintained against the pull of emotion or prejudice (or even the desire to persuade) was the proper way to approach an increasing area of experience.

Those who adopt this attitude to the world are suspicious of eloquence. When it comes to serious matters, such as the truth about man and his god, or the truth about the world we live in, they feel it is their duty to be clear, dispassionate, objective; to state the facts, to argue, to demonstrate; where proof is possible, to prove; never to persuade. Here is what Thomas Sprat, one of the founders of the Royal Society, has to say about the rules the Society set itself for its discussions and communications:

And, in few words, I dare say, that of all the Studies of men, nothing may be sooner obtain'd, than this vicious abundance of *Phrase*, this trick of *Metaphors*, this volubility of *Tongue*, which makes so great a noise in the World. But I spend words in vain; for the evil is now so inveterate, that it is hard to know whom to *blame*, or where to begin to *reform*. . . . It will suffice my present purpose, to point out, what has been done by the *Royal Society*, towards the correcting of its excesses in *Natural Philosophy*; to which it is, of all others, a most profest enemy.

They have therefore been most rigorous in putting in execution, the only Remedy, that can be found for this *extravagance*: and that has been, a constant Resolution, to reject all the amplifications, digressions, and swellings of style: to return back to the primitive purity, and shortness, when men deliver'd so many *things*, almost in an equal number of *words*. They have exacted from all their members, a close, naked, natural way of speaking; positive expressions; clear senses; a native easiness: bringing all things as near the Mathematical plainness, as they can: and preferring the language of Artizans, Countrymen, and Merchants, before that of Wits, or Scholars.

(Thomas Sprat, *History of the Royal Society*, 1667)

The Royal Society received its charter in 1642; Sprat's *History* appeared in 1667, the year of publication of Milton's *Paradise Lost*. We can see here the first beginnings of what are now commonly called 'the two cultures', the scientific and the literary, and the different modes of thought they impose.

Sprat's proposal to reduce scientific description of the world to simple, clear statement stripped of metaphor was of course an impossible ideal. Our thinking about the world is deeply structured by metaphor. I don't mean the dead metaphors embedded in words whose literal meaning has been lost, until a poet revives it, to serve his purpose in a poem. I have in mind such things as the fundamental spatial metaphors 'up', 'down', 'across', 'around', etc.: 'our hopes are up', 'the stakes are down', 'let's get the idea across', 'there's no way around the fact', and their extensions ('her spirits rose', 'his heart fell'); metaphors which give shape to the world we live in. I have in mind the representation of biological or economic processes in terms which imply conscious struggle ('the fight to survive', 'the struggle against inflation'), the encouragement such phrases give to supposing there are actual battles against identifiable adversaries, and the incitement to action which that involves. Twentieth-century science has become a tissue of metaphor as a result of efforts by its practitioners to translate into visualizable, graspable terms the concepts of microbiology, astronomy or even computer-science.

This is not to say that the attempt to create for science a distinct form of discourse devoid of stylistic pretentions and rhetorical tricks aimed at persuasion in place of proof has been futile. There *are* different ways of talking about the world. The opposition is usually expressed in terms of the polarity between *objective* and *subjective* statement; a use of 'objective' (in the sense of 'avoiding statements coloured by the feelings or opinions of the writer') probably not earlier than the nineteenth century. Where Sprat formulated the problem at a rhetorical level, 'objective' places it at a psychological level.

A majority, probably, of present-day scientists see objective statement as a possible goal. Most would not be disturbed, I think, by the military metaphor which I have deliberately sustained, by way of illustration, in the opening paragraph of the next section. The temptation to treat the metaphors as metaphors is switched off by the mental set we choose as appropriate to the context. The function of metaphor in objective prose is to aid comprehension, not to draw attention to itself. There is a risk, of course, that we will be tricked into believing things have been made clear when the impossibility of making them clear has been evaded. But, given the complexity of the things modern science wants to talk about, absolute linguistic purity is unimaginable.

* * *

The challenge to literary culture was, at first, barely appreciated. It took time for the frontiers to be drawn. The area of experience claimed by non-literary prose was, to begin with, modest and limited. Changed attitudes in the eighteenth century postponed confrontation.

The mood of English eighteenth-century men of letters was to put the clock back. Polite literature set out to reconstruct a way of life on Roman models, to rebuild the intellectual structures of the Augustan age in the London of Queen Anne or George III rather than to express the poet's moral vision or to battle with imaginative expression of the ineffable. In such a culture poetry and objective prose can coexist: there is no confrontation such as that implicit in the 1660s between Milton and Sprat. The domination of literature by the novel was unforeseeable. Men of letters were preoccupied with considerations of style, the need to evoke the right Roman precedents; the emphasis was not on thought, but on urbane, civilized expression of the great commonplaces, the familiar ironies of the human condition. True, the 'proper study of mankind was man' (Pope, *Essay on Man*, Ep. 2. 2) but study meant the enlivenment of traditional morality by wit:

> Poets like painters, thus, unskill'd to trace
> The naked Nature and the living Grace,
> With Gold and Jewels cover ev'ry Part,
> And hide with Ornaments their Want of Art.
> True Wit is Nature to Advantage drest,
> What oft was Thought, but ne'er so well Exprest.
>   (Pope, *Essay on Criticism*, 293–8)

The contrast between Pope's conscious classicism, his gentlemanly concept of experience easily comprehended and needing only to be 'well Exprest' and the ideal set themselves by the founders of the Royal Society to confine themselves to 'a close, naked, natural way of speaking; positive expressions; clear senses; a native easiness' is obvious to us, but remained latent at the time because the things the leading writers of the eighteenth century wrote about and the things the members of the Royal Society reported in their communications occupied different areas of people's minds.

It is only in the nineteenth century that the polarization becomes conscious, and the role of objective prose in presenting a scientific, 'true' account of human experience is openly advanced. The world of nineteenth-century science refused to be confined, claimed more and more acceptance as *the* explanation of the world. A veritable explosion of thought pushed the philosopher and the historian to pursue precision in the expression of their ideas, to assume a spirit of scientific detachment in the pursuit of truth. The confrontation now begins. Literature is, for the first time, put on the defensive and remained on the defensive as long as the nineteenth-century positivistic and scientific ideal prevailed that only what could be proved or measured was worthy of scientific enquiry, and that *this* was the proper study of man. Until, that is, late twentieth-century doubts about the possibility of telling anything that mattered 'the way it is' undermined that ideal. And made fashionable again, in intellectual circles, 'this vicious abundance of *Phrase*, this trick of *Metaphors*, this volubility of *Tongue*' which Sprat had condemned; restored it to prestige as the only way remaining to us to cope with the human condition in a world increasingly beyond description.

* * *

Let us end with some examples of the progress, during the past three hundred years, towards a world dominated (dominated, that is, till recently) by the pursuit of objective statement of truth. First, a passage (a famous passage) from Hobbes's *Leviathan* (1651). Hobbes is unashamedly eloquent, unashamedly rhetorical:

> Whatsoever therefore is consequent to a time of war, where every man is enemy to every man; the same is consequent to the time wherein men live without other security than what their own strength and their own invention shall furnish them withal. In such condition there is no place for industry, because the fruit thereof is uncertain; and consequently no culture of the earth; no navigation, nor use of the commodities that may be imported by sea; no commodious building; no instruments of moving, and removing, such things as require much force; no knowledge of the face of the earth; no account of time; no arts; no letters; no society; and which is worst of all, continual fear, and danger of violent death; and the life of man, solitary, poor, nasty, brutish, and short.
>
> (Hobbes, *Leviathan*, Chapter XIII)

John Stuart Mill, two hundred years after Hobbes (*On Liberty*, 1859), does not deny himself eloquence, but it is a soberer eloquence:

> The object of this essay is to assert one very simple principle, as entitled to govern absolutely the dealings of society with the individual in the way of compulsion and control, whether the means used be physical force in the form of legal penalties or the moral coercion of public opinion. That principle is that the sole end for which mankind are warranted, individually or collectively, in interfering with the liberty of action of any of their number is self-protection. That the only purpose for which power can be rightfully exercised over any member of a civilised community, against his will, is to prevent harm to others. His own good, either physical or moral, is not a sufficient warrant. He cannot rightfully be compelled to do or forbear because it will be better for him to do so, because it will make him happier, because, in the opinions of others, to do so would be wise or even right. These are good reasons for remonstrating with him, or reasoning with him, or persuading him, or entreating him, but not for compelling him or visiting him with any evil in case he do otherwise. To justify that, the conduct from which it is desired to deter him must be calculated to produce evil to someone else. The only part of the conduct of anyone for which he is amenable to society is that which concerns others. In the part which merely concerns himself, his independence is, of right, absolute. Over himself, over his own body and mind, the individual is sovereign.
>
> (John Stuart Mill, *On Liberty*, Chapter 1)

Mill, like Matthew Arnold, still thinks of himself as a man of letters: by our sense today of the etiquette of objective prose, Mill's way of writing strikes us as old-fashioned — too literary for the matter in hand.

Contrast with these, as one typical mid-twentieth-century way of doing things, a passage from Karl Popper:

It should be clearly understood that there are only two main attitudes possible towards tradition. One is to accept a tradition *uncritically*, often without even being aware of it. In many cases we cannot escape this; for we often just do not realize that we are faced with a tradition. If I wear my watch on my left wrist, I need not be conscious that I am accepting a tradition. Every day we do hundreds of things under the influence of traditions of which we are unaware. But if we do not know that we are acting under the influence of a tradition, then we cannot help accepting the tradition uncritically.

The other possibility is a *critical* attitude, which may result either in acceptance or in rejection, or perhaps in a compromise. Yet we have to know of and to understand a tradition before we can criticize it, before we can say: 'We reject this tradition on rational grounds.' Now I do not think that we could ever free ourselves entirely from the bonds of tradition. The so-called freeing is really only a change from one tradition to another. But we can free ourselves from the *taboos* of a tradition; and we can do that not only by rejecting it, but also by *critically* accepting it.

(Karl R. Popper, 'Towards a Rational Theory of Tradition', 1948)

Popper's admirably lucid prose wears already a slightly dated look. It belongs to a world where (to quote Northrop Frye) 'there are definite facts to get wrong'. The last 50 years have taught us, we believe, that the old test of right or wrong is not adequate; that the total certainty of a totally coherent conceptual system is to be guarded against; that in dealing with complex realities, common sense and logic are apt to be poor guides. That though the ostensible mode of academic discourse is logical argument, what takes place is more complicated. Agreement, total instant agreement, isn't to be expected. Disagreement can make the issues clearer; a mode of dealing with them takes shape.

To accept this is uncomfortable for those who would prefer a stable world. In our runaway world of ideas as well as technology, stability is too much to expect. If there is a source of consolation for those who find the intellectual life increasingly confusing, it is that the intellectual life shows signs, for the first time in a hundred years, of hanging together. During the past hundred years, one new subject after another has come into existence; the practitioners of each have worked out their subject matter, their methods and procedures. For a time it seemed they would go off by themselves, to explore and conquer the new territory, never to be seen again. That is not what happened. The new subjects proved to have common problems, problems to which a method evolved in one seemed to offer an answer in another. We are beginning to realize the interdependence of the social sciences. To realize that the study of literature, like that of language, is a social science. The intellectual life will never be again, it seems, in the foreseeable future, the neat, tidy thing we tried to pretend to ourselves it was.

IV
THE RHYTHMS OF PROSE AND VERSE

In the last hundred years objective prose has come to occupy a proportion of our time and an area of our intellectual lives much larger than that occupied by literature. In this area, surrender to eloquence or emotional incitement is suspect. There is a sense in which science, and the magnitude and complexity of its concepts have humbled its expositors. Until our present doubts began to obsess us, we were all Aristotelians: patient, cautious exposition of theory, supported by observation carefully recorded and reported, was the keynote; the apocalyptic voice appropriate to revealed religion was felt to be out of date, not part of the etiquette of science; the literary sophistication of a Plato (or even a John Stuart Mill or a Matthew Arnold) made us uncomfortable. The 1970s and 80s have shown increasing signs of a failure of nerve: in matters affecting human beings, and the way we conduct our lives, our faith in authority, our faith in logic, even, has been shaken; even Karl Popper begins to sound out of date.

There is still no shortage of people ready to maintain that the claims of literature to present an alternative, truer version of the world are spurious; that literature has been reduced by science to the status of sophisticated entertainment. I discuss in Chapter 5 the standing of the novelist or poet as moralist. In this chapter I am concerned with the structural differences between prose and verse. By comparison with objective prose, literary prose — imaginative prose — has much in common with poetry. Poetry is still poetry, however, and imaginative prose is still prose. The two work differently. There is still a place (if not an equal place) for each.

Built into the rhythms of objective prose are easily sensed implications aimed at controlling our mental set: 'how carefully I report the matter in hand'; 'how fully I understand the complexities of this case'; 'how reasonable I am'. The writer of objective prose advances patiently and methodically; the way of putting things is more abstract, the surrender to images more reluctant and better disciplined — their object is to make the argument easier to follow, not to adorn it. Words are persisted with until the writer has said what the writer wants to say as precisely as possible, or as precisely as is appropriate. The syntax is different. But above all it is the rhythms which are different: they emphasize the writer's points, but they disdain involvement. Objective prose need not be stodgy (despite an assumption by many of its practitioners to the contrary); it need not altogether despise clarity, or those literary devices which help clarity, but it must not trick us into agreement; it must be seen to play fair. Objective prose proclaims neutrality. No doubt, those who present their case in objective prose aren't all neutral: historians, psychologists are as fond of their theories as the rest of us; but the way they write switches on a mental set which professes detachment, and we read (assuming we know how to read this kind of prose) with the corresponding mental set switched on in our minds.

Verse, literary prose proclaim involvement, even when it is an ironic involvement. The typical syntactical structures of a poem, and the rhythms which these construct, are designed to sweep the reader along, or to seduce the reader into surrender to the intoxicating power of words; to disarm disbelief, perhaps, in an obvious fiction by the very simplicity of the narrative line; to make us *feel* how passionately the poet feels what he (or she) claims to feel; how far beyond logical analysis the thoughts, the feelings, the imaginative expansions lie; or simply, how clever, how witty the poet is. The moral impact, however powerful the moral impact is in fact of what the poet says, comes later, does not lie on the surface.

Poets usually don't even pretend to be putting their case fairly, dispassionately, reasonably; their asserted truths are more often paradoxes, the conclusions we are invited to draw lurk somewhere between the lines or are held in suspension in the imagery. The subtlety of verse resides in well-calculated understatement or overstatement — a felt, but not easily measured, discrepancy between what is said and how what is said is to be understood, the pleasure for the reader often lying in attempting to measure the discrepancy.

In even the freest verse, the sense is reinforced by the formal pattern: clumsily handled, rhyme, rhythm, the phrasing of line and stanza degenerate into rhetorical, meaninglessly emphatic statement. A good example is Matthew Arnold's poem 'Epilogue to Lessing's Laocoon'. Competently handled, the formal pattern not merely supports the sense, but serves as an indicator of how what is said is to be taken, prompts the reaction the poet expects.

This is easiest to see when the formal pattern is exploited for ironic effect. Take Elizabeth Bishop's poem about Ezra Pound in the asylum ward. The basic formal pattern is provided by the nursery rhyme 'The House that Jack Built':

> This is the knife with a handle of horn,
> That killed the cock that crowed in the morn,
> That wakened the priest all shaven and shorn,
> That married the man all tattered and torn
> Unto the maiden all forlorn,
> That milked the cow with a crumpled horn
> That tossed the dog over the barn,
> That worried the cat
> That killed the rat
> That ate the malt
> That lay in the house that Jack built.

Elizabeth Bishop has transposed this simple model to the expanding logic of such jingles as 'One man went to mow'; each of the twelve stanzas is a line longer than the previous stanza. First, a one-line stanza, then a two-line stanza, and so on; the twelfth stanza has twelve lines. The expanding structure permits a rhythmical build-up rather like that of Ravel's 'Bolero'. A contrasting trick is used to build up the picture of Pound: in Stanza 2, he is simply 'the man'; Stanzas 3 to 10 add a descriptive word (Stanza 6 two words) to 'man' (Pound is, successively, 'the tragic man', 'the talkative man', 'the honored man', 'the old, brave man', 'the cranky man', and so on); in Stanza 11, he is 'the poet, the man'; in Stanza 12, 'the wretched man'. There are no rhymes in the first six stanzas; at Stanza 7 the rhyme 'ward'/'board' is introduced, and is retained in each of the succeeding stanzas, but the couplet ending with these words drops, a line at a time, until at Stanza 12 it occupies Lines 6–7, and is preceded by an increasingly complicated rhyming pattern at the beginning of successive stanzas. The resultant rhythm sustains a mood of ironic gaiety that abruptly collapses in the concluding lines of Stanza 12:

This is the house of Bedlam.

This is the man
that lies in the house of Bedlam.

This is the time
of the tragic man
that lies in the house of Bedlam.

This is a wristwatch
telling the time
of the talkative man
that lies in the house of Bedlam.

This is a sailor
wearing the watch
that tells the time
of the honored man
that lies in the house of Bedlam.

This is the roadstead all of board
reached by the sailor
wearing the watch
that tells the time
of the old, brave man
that lies in the house of Bedlam.

These are the years and the walls of the ward,
the winds and clouds of the sea of board
sailed by the sailor
wearing the watch
that tells the time
of the cranky man
that lies in the house of Bedlam.

This is a Jew in a newspaper hat
that dances weeping down the ward
over the creaking sea of board
beyond the sailor
winding his watch
that tells the time
of the cruel man
that lies in the house of Bedlam.

This is a world of books gone flat.
This is a Jew in a newspaper hat
that dances weeping down the ward
over the creaking sea of board
of the batty sailor
that winds his watch
that tells the time
of the busy man
that lies in the house of Bedlam.

This is a boy that pats the floor
to see if the world is there, is flat,
for the widowed Jew in the newspaper hat
that dances weeping down the ward
waltzing the length of a weaving board
by the silent sailor
that hears his watch

that ticks the time
of the tedious man
that lies in the house of Bedlam.

These are the years and the walls and the door
that shut on a boy that pats the floor
to feel if the world is there and flat.
This is a Jew in a newspaper hat
that dances joyfully down the ward
into the parting seas of board
past the staring sailor
that shakes his watch
that tells the time
of the poet, the man
that lies in the house of Bedlam.

This is the soldier home from the war.
These are the years and the walls and the door
that shut on a boy that pats the floor
to see if the world is round or flat.
This is a Jew in a newspaper hat
that dances carefully down the ward,
walking the plank of a coffin board
with the crazy sailor
that shows his watch
that tells the time
of the wretched man
that lies in the house of Bedlam.

> (Elizabeth Bishop, 'Visits to St Elizabeth's')

* * *

The rhythms of imaginative prose (except when a rhetorical emphasis is consciously sought) are more elusive, more tentative, less easily pinned down. The pace of the novel is more leisurely, the experience it offers less intense; the artist in prose can fill in a detail of a scene, relate in passing a minor incident, an unimportant step in a chain of events. The subtlety of narrative prose resides often in an apparent irrelevancy; the pleasure for the reader, in attempting to gather the apparent irrelevancy into the field of significance of the text; to gauge the function as symbol of what is said. But in the novel, too, rhythm is a pointer to sense, a change of rhythm an indication of a change in attitude, a sign that an adjustment is expected of us to the tuning of our mental set.

Take Patrick White's description of the official farewell of the explorer Voss; watch as you read it for the rhythmical transition in the middle of the sentence 'It was a brave sight, and suddenly also moving' from brisk, good-mannered irony in the tradition of Jane Austen to a kind of poetry in prose which is wholly Patrick White:

Colonel Featherstonhaugh did say many other things. Indeed, when a space had been cleared, he made a speech, about God, and soil, and flag, and Our Young, Illustrious Queen, as had been prepared for him. The numerous grave and appreciative persons who were surrounding the Colonel lent weight to his appropriate words. There were, for instance, at least three members of the Legislative Council, a Bishop, a Judge, officers in the Army, besides patrons of the expedition, and citizens whose wealth had begun to make them acceptable, in spite of their unfortunate past and persistent clumsiness with knife and fork. Important heads were bared, stiff necks were bent into attitudes that suggested humble attention. It was a brave sight, and suddenly also moving. For all those figures of cloth and linen, of worthy British flesh and blood, and the souls tied to them, temporarily, like tentative balloons, by the precious grace of life, might, of that sudden, have been cardboard or little wooden things, as their importance in the scene receded, and there predominated the great tongue of blue water, the brooding, indigenous trees, and sky clutching at all.

(Patrick White, *Voss*, Chapter 5)

The notion that the novel was a kind of comedy persisted long, and is still far from dead. Novelists and critics today have got away, however, from any simple antithesis of tragic and comic, as they have got away from any simple notion of the difference between poetry and prose. We have learnt to place a work less by the seriousness which it asserts than by the quality of the moral insight which it implies.

What I mean can be illustrated by turning to one of the greatest of nineteenth-century novels, Flaubert's *Madame Bovary*; it is also one of the most serious and one of the most essentially tragic. The novel is a story of the young wife of a simple, down-to-earth country doctor: brought up in a convent, her head stuffed with literary notions of romantic love, Emma Bovary finds the kind of love she seeks in adultery; but her romantic illusions cannot stand exposure to the cynical realism of her lovers, and she poisons herself as a final evasion of reality. Flaubert sets the first systematic ensnaring of his heroine against the background of a small-town agricultural show; we hear alternately the practised, tawdry, patently insincere political rhetoric of the official speakers and the practised romantic rhetoric of Emma's lover. Her surrender takes place a few days later in a conventionally romantic setting — Emma and her lover had gone riding together in a wood:

> The shadows of evening were descending: the horizontal sun, passing between the branches, dazzled her eyes. Here and there, all around her, in the leaves or on the ground, patches of light quivered, as if hummingbirds, while in flight, had scattered out their feathers. Everywhere was silence; a kind of soothing emanation seemed to come from the trees; she could feel her heart begin to beat again, her blood to flow through her flesh like a stream of milk. Then, she heard away in the distance, beyond the woods, on the hills, on the other side, an indeterminate, drawn-out cry, a voice that trailed off into nothingness, and she listened to it in silence, as it blended into the last vibrations of her tensioned nerves, like a musical chord. Rodolphe, a cigar in his teeth, was repairing with his penknife one of the two bridles which had broken.
>
> (*Madame Bovary*, Part II, Chapter 9)

Her surrender to her second lover (an ambitious law student who has long been calculating his chances) is a tawdry affair, closer to comedy than to anything that might

sustain feelings of sympathy or pity. It takes place inside a cab
as the cab rumbles endlessly around the streets of Rouen and
the surrounding district, all day long, its drawn blinds raised
only for angry instructions from an unidentified voice each
time the driver pauses for directions — 'Keep go-
ing!' . . . 'keep on!' . . . 'keep on!' . . . . The rhythm of the
narrative, jerkier now and more disjointed, emphasizes Emma's degradation:

> 'Monsieur is going where?' asked the cabby.
> 'Wherever you like!' said Léon pushing Emma into the
> vehicle. And the heavy contraption moved off.
> It went down the Rue Grand-Pont, crossed the Place des
> Arts, the Quai Napoléon, the Pont Neuf and pulled up
> before the statue of Pierre Corneille.
> 'Keep going,' said a voice from inside.
> The cab set off again, and, on reaching the Carrefour la
> Fayette, it gathered momentum on the downward slope,
> turning into the station-yard at a gallop.
> 'No, keep on!' cried the same voice.
> The cab emerged from behind the iron fence, and soon,
> reaching the main avenue, assumed a gentle trot between
> the tall elms. The cabby wiped his forehead, put his leather
> hat between his knees, and turned the cab across the side
> alleys down to the river, alongside the grass verge.
> It followed the river, along the loose cobblestones of the
> tow path, and went on for a long time in the direction of
> Oyssel, beyond the islands.
> Suddenly, it struck across Quartremares, Sotteville, the
> Grande-Chaussée, the Rue d'Elbeuf, and came to a halt for
> the third time, in front of the Botanic Gardens.
> 'Keep on!' cried the same voice more angrily than ever.
> And so, continuing as before, the cab passed through
> Saint-Sever, along the Quai des Curandiers, along the Quai
> aux Meules, across the bridge again, along the Place du
> Champ-de-Mars, behind the gardens of the hospital, where
> elderly men dressed in black were taking a walk, along a
> terrace all green with ivy. It climbed the Boulevard Bouv-
> reuil, went the full length of the Boulevard Cauchoise, right
> along Mont-Riboudet as far as the Deville rise.

It turned back; and then, with no fixed objective, it roamed around on a random course. It was sighted at Saint-Pol, at Lescure, at Mont Gargan, at Rouge-Mare and Place du Gaillard-Bois; Rue Maladrerie, Rue Dinanderie, in front of the Church of Saint-Romain, the Church of Saint-Vivien, Saint Maclou, Saint-Nicaise, — in front of the Customs House, — at La Basse-Vieille-Tour, at Les Trois-Pipes, and at the Cimetière Monumental. From time to time, the cabby, from his seat, would toss a look of despair at the wine shops. What mania for movement kept driving these people on so that they had no wish to stop was beyond his comprehension. He tried it a few times, and at once he heard angry exclamations from behind. Then he would whip up once more his two old horses which were covered in sweat, taking no notice of ruts and bumps, crashing against obstacles on one side or the other, oblivious, demoralized, almost in tears with thirst, fatigue and mounting gloom.

And on the harbour, among the carts and drays, in the streets, at the stone pillars which protected the corners, decent people opened their eyes wide at this sight so unexpected in the provinces, a cab with its blinds drawn, which kept reappearing, more tightly sealed than a barrel and tossed around like a ship at sea.

Once, at midday, out in open country, at the time of day when the sun hurled its rays with its full force at the old silvered headlamps, a naked hand emerged from beneath the small curtains of yellowed cloth and threw away some torn scraps of paper, which scattered in the wind and came down again further on, like white butterflies, on a field of crimson flowering clover.

Then, about six p.m., the cab pulled up in a small street in the Quartier Beauvoisine, and a woman alighted and went off, her veil lowered, without turning her head.

(*Madame Bovary*, Part III, Chapter 1)

The carefully orchestrated irony of the return of Emma and her lover from their ride in the woods, the boisterous comedy of the day-long cab journey are not comic relief, but an integral part of the structure of a work outstanding for its utter seriousness: the first scene, dominated by her perception of what seems to her a sympathizing world around her, captured Emma's mood of romantic exultation; the second provides an ironically externalized correlative for the frantic, hungry pursuit of passion to which frustrated appetite has reduced her. And yet Emma remains romantic enough to poison herself when her second lover like her first tires of her demands upon him. Set now alongside the cab scene, the bitter farce of the scene in which the local priest and the local pharmacist (the one a simple-minded cleric; the other a fatuous would-be intellectual) debate the existence of God while they watch over Emma's dead body:

Though a philosopher, Monsieur Homais respected the dead. Thus, it was with no feeling of resentment for poor Charles that he came back that night to keep vigil over the corpse, bringing three large books with him, and a writing pad, so that he could make notes.

Father Bournisien was already there, and two tall candles were burning beside the bed, which had been pulled out from the alcove.

The pharmacist, who found silence burdensome, was not slow to express a regret or two with respect to this 'unfortunate young woman'; and the priest replied that all that was left now was to pray for her.

'And yet,' said Homais, 'there are really only two possibilities: either she died in a state of grace (as the Church puts it), and in that case she has no need of our prayers; or else she was impenitent at the moment of decease (I think that is the ecclesiastical expression), and in that case . . .'

Bournisien cut him off, with a curt rejoinder that one had to pray just the same.

'But,' objected the pharmacist, 'since God knows all our needs, what is the point of prayer?'

'What!' said the priest, 'the point of prayer! Are you not a Christian then?'

'Pardon me,' said Homais, 'I admire Christianity. It began by freeing slaves, gave the world a moral code . . .'

'That's not the point! All the texts . . .'

'Oh! don't talk to me about texts, you've only got to read history; it's known the Jesuits falsified them.'

Charles came in, and, going over to the bed, he drew the curtains gently. Emma's head was resting on her right shoulder. The corner of her mouth, fixed in an open position, seemed like a black hole at the bottom of her face; her two thumbs had remained twisted towards the palms; a kind of white powder was scattered over her eyelids, and her eyes were beginning to disappear into a viscous pallor which looked like some thin fabric, as if spiders had spun their webs across. The sheet formed a hollow from her breasts to her knees, rising from that point to the top of her toes; and it seemed to Charles that some great, incalculable weight was pressing down upon her.

The church clock struck two. The guttural muttering of the stream could be heard flowing through the darkness, at the foot of the terrace. Father Bournisien, every so often, blew his nose loudly, and Homais' pen kept scratching on the paper.

'Come along, old friend,' he said, 'don't stay here, what you see here is a torture to you.'

As soon as Charles had left, the pharmacist and the priest began their arguments afresh.

(*Madame Bovary*, Part II, Chapter 9)

V
THE FUTURE OF POETRY

These examples, all taken from one novel, give some notion of the range of feeling, the penetration of Flaubert's moral vision, and the subtlety with which that vision is brought out by the syntactical rhythms which articulate it (in both senses of the word) within the structure of a single work. The stops and the starts of the cab ride, the variations in tempo, are the symbol of the unseen proceedings within; but no crude symbol, the unstated reference of which could be restated point by point if we chose: we get the point, we accept the implied moral evaluation, while surrendering to the fantasy for its own sake. Writing like this makes any simple distinction between comedy and tragedy irrelevant, as it makes talk of the inherent superiority of verse over prose silly.

It's no use pretending, when we come to the literature of the last hundred years, that verse can claim a prestige which must be denied prose; no use pretending prose is the humbler, more limited medium. Set alongside the magnificent, complicated, subtle prose of Flaubert a poem like Philip Larkin's 'Ambulances':

> Closed like confessionals, they thread
> Loud noons of cities, giving back
> None of the glances they absorb.
> Light glossy grey, arms on a plaque,
> They come to rest at any kerb:
> All streets in time are visited. . . .

Philip Larkin isn't an artist of the calibre of Flaubert, but he is a respectable modern poet. There would be plenty of people to agree that city children or their mothers watching a neighbour carried out on a stretcher to an ambulance, and sensing 'the solving emptiness' of death 'that lies just under all we do' is a perfectly acceptable subject for a poem and this a perfectly acceptable poem; poems no longer have to be about themes of the sort once dismissed by Dylan Thomas as 'innocence lost and wisdom catastrophically gained'. All that can be said is that verse is something special, something resorted to for special effect. The question is: What is that special effect?

* * *

Why shouldn't poets go on writing as they have always done — the same subjects, the same poetic forms? The answer seems to be that every poem written takes its place in a series or context. Is so felt by the poet who writes it. Is so perceived by those who read it. The adjustment to our mental set switched on by our sense of the past, when we read a poem written two hundred (or two thousand) years ago, enables us to accept, as a valid use of poetry, what, in the case of a poem written today, we cannot accept; for some such poems the adjustment needed is slight; for most it is considerable.

Take John Clare's poem 'Badger', written about 1835:

When midnight comes a host of dogs and men
Go out and track the badger to his den,
And put a sack within the hole, and lie
Till the old grunting badger passes by.
He comes and hears — they let the strongest loose.
The old fox hears the noise and drops the goose.
The poacher shoots and hurries from the cry,
And the old hare half wounded buzzes by.
They get a forkèd stick to bear him down
And clap the dogs and take him to the town,
And bait him all the day with many dogs,
And laugh and shout and fright the scampering hogs.
He runs along and bites all he meets:
They shout and hollo down the noisy streets.

He turns about to face the loud uproar
And drives the rebels to their very door.
The frequent stone is hurled where'er they go;
When badgers fight, then everyone's a foe.
The dogs are clapped and urged to join the fray;
The badger turns and drives them all away.
Though scarcely half as big, demure and small,
He fights with dogs for hours and beats them all.
The heavy mastiff, savage in the fray,
Lies down and licks his feet and turns away.
The bulldog knows his match and waxes cold,
The badger grins and never leaves his hold.
He drives the crowd and follows at their heels
And bites them through — the drunkard swears and reels.

The frighted women take the boys away,
The blackguard laughs and hurries on the fray.
He tries to reach the woods, an awkward race,
But sticks and cudgels quickly stop the chase.
He turns agen and drives the noisy crowd
And beats the many dogs in noises loud.
He drives away and beats them every one,
And then they loose them all and set them on.
He falls as dead and kicked by boys and men,

Then starts and grins and drives the crowd agen;
Till kicked and torn and beaten out he lies
And leaves his hold and cackles, groans, and dies.

Read with the appropriate adjustment of our mental set,
'Badger' strikes us as a good, even a moving poem, a neat,
sharply observed sequence of scenes. But today we should find
material like this more acceptable if cast as a short story, or an
article in a magazine. At the level at which Clare aims his
poem, prose can do the job better. What justifies the use of
verse in poems such as Larkin's 'Church Going' and 'Ambulances' is the exploration of the poet's reactions which is
added to the straight reporting and the straightforward
emotional excitement.

Fashion, ways of doing things, change. The maudlin sentimentality of James Stephens's 'The Snare' (written about
1915), if we were to read it as a poem written in the 1960s or
70s, would make us feel distinctly uncomfortable:

I head a sudden cry of pain!
    There is a rabbit in a snare:
Now I hear the cry again,
    But I cannot tell from where.

But I cannot tell from where
    He is calling out for aid;
Crying on the frightened air,
    Making everything afraid.

Making everything afraid,
    Wrinkling up his little face,
As he cries again for aid;
    And I cannot find the place!

And I cannot find the place
    Where his paw is in the snare:
Little one! Oh, little one!
    I am searching everywhere.

We are more at home with Philip Larkin's drier, more
starkly structured exploration of his reactions in 'Myxomato-
sis':

What trap is this? Where were its teeth concealed?
You seem to ask.
              I make a sharp reply,
Then clean my stick. . . .

* * *

Suppose we tackle the problem head-on: after something like
two hundred and fifty years of progressive invasion by prose of
territory formerly the sole preserve of verse, where do we
stand? Is the take-over to all intents and purposes complete? If
we are to be honest, must we admit that we've reached the
point where prose can do anything verse can do — and
perhaps do it better? Must we agree with A. E. Housman?

> No truth, it seems to me, is too precious, no observation too
> profound, and no sentiment too exalted to be expressed in
> prose. The utmost I could admit is that some
> ideas . . . receive from poetry an enhancement which glori-
> fies and transfigures them.
>
>   (A. E. Housman, *The Name and Nature of Poetry*, 1933)

Is the significant opposition no longer that between prose and
verse (each presenting its own, but equally valid reorganization of experience) but that between objective prose and a
kind of prose which attempts to cope imaginatively with
experience? Can imaginative prose cope *more* adequately with
the complexity of human experience than verse? Is verse
reduced to elegant trifling with words — æsthetically pleasing
but, as far as truth to the human experience is concerned, no
match for prose?

There are times when we all feel that reading poetry in a
world like ours *is* fiddling while Rome burns; that poetry is
only a vestigial survival with no longer any useful function.
Marianne Moore states the case against poetry we all, I think,
find ourselves making occasionally to ourselves and then
proceeds to answer that case:

> I, too dislike it: there are things that are important
>   beyond all this fiddle.

> Reading it, however, with a perfect contempt for it,
> one discovers in
> it after all, a place for the genuine. . . .
>
> (Marianne Moore, 'Poetry')

Marianne Moore's answer is the answer most poets today give when cornered: that poetry is a kind of laboratory or testing ground for fresh linguistic discovery; a place where exciting things go on, a way of revitalizing the language for others to use.

Is that the most we can honestly say for poetry? Or are there still things verse can do better than prose? Well, 'better' isn't easily settled. It seems to me, however, there are two things verse can still do, and do them exceedingly well: it can express feeling too heavily charged to be expressed effectively in prose; it can set in motion thought too complex to be dealt with effectively by the more analytic techniques of prose. Let's consider each of these.

First, feeling. Obviously, prose is well equipped to deal with feeling: the prose of Flaubert can cope with the most intense feelings; the prose of Virginia Woolf can cope with the most exquisite, most elusive feelings. But it must cope differently, by diffusing feeling through less compact, more intellectually disciplined structures.

In most modern poems, the emotional charge is kept under tight control. The prevailing fashion is still that of the 1930s: it calls for the drily elegant expression of a refined sensibility — civilized poet achieving a well-bred balance between private standards and the standards of a mass culture felt as wholly repugnant, however persistent the feeling that, ideologically, it is a poet's duty to stand with the masses against their corruptors. Auden was the great master of this kind of poetry:

> The sailors come ashore
> Out of their hollow ships,
> Mild-looking middle class boys
> Who read the comic strips;
> One baseball game is more
> To them than fifty Troys. . . .
>
> (W. H. Auden, 'Fleet Visit')

In the 1930s, when there were stands to be taken, issues to be sorted out, verse like this fulfilled a valid social function. Today, this elegant pandering to an intelligentsia left high and dry by the tidal wave of progress is indeed, in my opinion, fiddling while Rome burns, as Auden seemed himself to recognize in the end. No doubt (assuming the story true) Nero, too, had an audience (it is hard to imagine him as a solitary Romantic pitting his fiddle against the engulfing flames). No doubt, a cultural élite, conscious of its powerlessness to control anything any more, easily persuades itself that fiddling is a correct attitude, preferable to crude despair. It is the mood Auden expressed when he wrote to Louis MacNeice:

> Even a limerick
>   ought to be something a man of
> honour, awaiting death from cancer or a firing squad,
>   could read without contempt.
>   (W. H. Auden, 'The Cave of Making')

In times like ours, the Romantic intensity of a Coleridge or a Keats is easily felt as unseemly; the simple sincerity of a Wordsworth or a Robert Frost, folksy. Passionate poems *are* still written, but poets seem to prefer to keep passion under firm intellectual control. We seem to be moving through a period when poetry can learn from prose (as well as prose from poetry). Take Fleur Adcock's 'Advice to a Discarded Lover':

> Think, now: if you have found a dead bird,
> Not only dead, not only fallen
> But full of maggots: what do you feel —
> More pity or more revulsion? . . .

Five more stylish stanzas follow, each sizzling with fury and contempt. Yet, however tight the control, this is poetry working in its proper element. You just can't get away with that degree of compression in prose. If you choose prose, you find yourself working with a structure (whether short story or full-length novel) whose ostensible function must be to tell a story: that need not be the most important function, but it's a

function that can't be evaded. Poems and novels work to
different rules, impose a different etiquette. Patrick White is a
novelist who depends heavily on the adaptation of poetic
technique to prose narrative; he achieves a quite extraordinary level of emotional intensity in his narrative on the death of
Voss and his companions. But the emotional level has to be
built up step by step, diffused through an elaborate structure
of prose running into many pages. Though the best modern
fiction is in many respects more poetic than older prose
fiction, the acceptable conventions for the representation of
emotion in poetry and in prose must always be different.

A poem can get off to a flying start: it needs no structure of
narrative to prepare the way. Nor does the reader have to be
(as Frank O'Connor once put it) brought back again from
Heaven by a slow train. Verse can retain an archaic simplicity
which invites from the reader a maximum of surrender to the
subconscious; verse suggests a timelessness, a universality of
significance. The supra-logical immediacy of statement in
verse can be reinforced by rhyme, rhythm, repetition of key
words and phrases with an insistence impossible in prose. The
sense of emotion contained, pent up by the constraining form
is the secret of much of the poetry of Hardy, Housman and
Yeats.

Take Hardy's 'Ten Years Since': the poem is fourteen lines
long — once again, a kind of sonnet, therefore. But, as it is set
out on the printed page, it swells from a single four-syllable
line — ''Tis ten years since' to three lines each three iambs
long (six syllables), all three rhyming, to three slightly longer
lines (all three again rhyming); the process is then reversed
until we come to the fourteenth line, 'Those ten years since',
which is an echo of the first line:

> 'Tis ten years since
> I saw her on the stairs,
> Heard her in house-affairs,
> And listened to her cares;
> And the trees are ten feet taller,
> And the sunny spaces smaller
> Whose bloomage would enthrall her;
> And the piano wires are rustier,

> The smell of bindings mustier,
> And lofts and lumber dustier
>   Than when, with casual look
>   And ear, light note I took
>   Of what shut like a book
>   Those ten years since!

You can't hope to do anything like that in prose. The decision to write in prose imposes a different mimesis, different rules for the representation of reality. Timeless archaism is not acceptable, a simple, rigid pattern not possible. Because the speaking voice is a contemporary voice, we expect of the narrator a sophistication of narrative structure commensurate with the sophistication of thought. It seems a necessary part of the literary experience of reading a contemporary novel to feel we are surrendering ourselves to a detached, analytic mind; however much the writing in fact transcends normal exposition, the writer is expected to maintain the illusion of reporting the intensely moving or the fantastic as accurately and as dispassionately as the writer can.

Of my two uses for poetry in contemporary Western society, the first — to convey that which is too emotionally charged to be expressed in prose — seems to me temporarily in eclipse. Few poets load their verbal structure with emotion to breaking-point as Dylan Thomas did in the 1940s; Ted Hughes is exceptional among contemporary English poets in the emotional charge with which he loads his rugged, sinewy verse. The prevailing fashion, as I said, is very much that of the 1930s — tight-lipped restraint in the expression of emotion. Poets have become suspicious of emotion.

My second use of verse — to express thought too complex to be dealt with effectively by prose — seems to me to stand a better chance. By 'too complex' I mean that which seems beyond words: either because, as we say, 'words fail us'; or because saying what we mean clearly, in, as we say, 'as many words', means too many words — so many words, we lose control, and lapse into what Robert Graves called 'brininess and volubility'; or else, while struggling to retain control, we feel the sense, the point, of what we want to say elude us. You can't capture an image by piling up words till you've got it just right; it's not always the most effective procedure with an idea — often a poet does better to let the idea take shape in the reader's mind with as little assistance as possible. All truly great writing, perhaps, depends — not just on impressing us with words (though there is a place for what is often dismissed as 'mere rhetoric'), but on drawing your reader to the point where a flash of insight reveals the way it must have been, or to the point where a flash of intuition makes clear what it is you are driving at.

* * *

Consider Ezra Pound's poem 'The Garden', written in 1916:

> Like a skein of loose silk blown against a wall
> She walks by the railing of a path in Kensington Gardens,
> And she is dying piece-meal
>   of a sort of emotional anemia.

The success of Pound's poem lies in the clear images conjured up; what makes it *more* than a string of images is the unresolved conflict of attitudes which the words used set in motion. You may say that such poems are minor poems, trivial uses for poetry, you may feel they adorn life instead of striking at the heart of life; poetry does this sort of thing well, you may say, but it's hardly a justification for poetry. I'm inclined to agree. Let's take something more ambitious. Consider the range of experience represented in four short poems by the New Zealand poet Charles Brasch. First, a poem written in the first wry realization of what it means to be getting old — not just the physical decay, but the loss of that sense of contact with others on which, as a poet, you had relied, and the coming to terms which that represents:

> In middle life when the skin slackens
> Its loving clasp of our loose volumes,
> When the bone tree stiffens and its well-joined branches
> Begin to creak, to droop a little,
> May the spirit hold out no longer for

Old impossible terms, demanding
Rent-free futures where all, all is ripeness,
But cry pax to its equivocal nature and stretch
At ease with wry destiny,
Supple as wind bowing in every reed. . . .

('Ambulando')

'Ambulando' was published in 1964 when Brasch was in his mid-fifties. A decade later he lay dying in hospital: there is now a more desperate situation to cope with; he must come to terms with the fact that he is no longer free (as he could still pride himself in 'Ambulando') to face the world alone. The routine of his day is now for others to dictate:

Farewell the careless days.
Now I enter another rule. . . .

('*Tempora Mutantur*')

Contact with the world outside is reduced to such things as listening to the distant bark of a dog at night:

Gnawing, gnawing the edge of night,
Black barking dog. . . .

('Watch-Dog')

But to the end Brasch was able to summon up courage and mental energy to confront what lay ahead. He is no innocent, surprised by death, expecting the world to make sense. When death comes, when it is only a matter of brief moments left, the question all ask is asked with a bitter residual irony. The last words of Brasch's last poem are a reminiscence (unconscious, or perhaps conscious?) of Conrad's *Amy Foster*:

He was muddy. I covered him up and stood waiting in silence, catching a painfully gasped word now and then. They were no longer in his own language. The fever had left him, taking with it the heat of life. And with his panting breath and lustrous eyes he reminded me again of a wild creature under the net; of a bird caught in a snare. She had

left him. She had left him — sick — helpless — thirsty. The
spear of the hunter had entered his very soul. 'Why?' he
cried, in the penetrating and indignant voice of a man
calling to a responsible Maker. A gust of wind and a swish
of rain answered.

But where Conrad is telling a tale, painting a picture (not
attempting to get down what he yet wants to say in as few
words as he can), is grand and explicit, Brasch is utterly
simple:

> . . . To go out
> On the waves of the last pain
> Finally;
> It cannot be long,
> Not as long as my question, life –
> Why?
> Why?

('Why?')

VI

Poetry is a place for experiment, a kind of laboratory. But the
experiments conducted aren't just aimed at exploring the
possibilities of language: they are aimed also at finding new
ways of articulating experience, at finding new ways of
structuring statement about experience. A successful poem is
an organization of words representing a perceived organization of experience.

If we are sensible, we must allow prose a place alongside
poetry. Creative writing that sharpens and extends our perception of the world around us and the human beings in it,
that can push language, when the occasion warrants it, to the
limits of ingenuity and cleverness, is possible in prose also.
Prose no longer needs any apology. Where fiction is concerned, prose is the senior partner, enjoys by far the wider
audience.

The highly structured style is available to the writer today
whether the writer chooses prose or verse. And yet it makes a

difference which is chosen. When the perceived organization of experience takes on the structure of a novel, the organization becomes less personal, less immediate — less visible on the printed page. A novel is almost as much an entertainment as it is a freshly articulated organization of experience. I like to think that it is in poetry that we find the creative process fully alive. Poetry is the place for experiment, prose is the place for consolidation. I am not now speaking of course of plot, but of how writers use words to achieve their ends. Naturally, every successful experiment is, in a sense, a consolidation: a poem which does something new for the first time means that others can go on doing it for all time. And every consolidation is, in a sense, a fresh experiment — no good novel is simply a repetition of ways of doing things that have been found to work. It's a question of degree. In poetry, words can be made to work harder; a poet's words can demand more of the poem's readers. It is from poetry that we learn, whether as writer or as reader, how words work, what can be done with words; if, having learnt that, we then take our knowledge to writing or reading novels, the chances are that we shall be better writers and better readers.

5

The Writer as Moralist: the Social Function of Literary Texts

---

I

Every text has an author, every text implies an audience. Authors die, however, audiences keep changing; we are tempted to seize upon the text (the novel we've just read, the poem we have in front of us) as the only accessible reality, the only hard fact, in this transaction and confine ourselves to that.

The reality of the text is, however, something of an illusion. A Shakespearean sonnet — even, say, Keats's 'Ode to a Nightingale' — if we pick up the text and read it aloud, must sound very different from the way it sounded to the poet who made it or to a contemporary audience. My silent reading of a novel by Dickens or Henry James, my attempt to read meaning into the string of words, to bring the text to life in my own mind, is prone to all sorts of misunderstandings; a reading in a more ambitious sense (one designed to *bring out* the text's significance for others) is even more precarious and elusive. And must be: the meaning a text takes on for me exists only in my mind; its significance isn't there to be pointed to for all to see; the significance of a text is something that builds up around the text as I read it; something that builds up in your mind as you listen to me read it.

Even a short poem is a complex structure: a structure of words and syntax; understanding the way it works involves seeing the way it has been put together. But that's only a beginning: we have to take account as well of the sideways expansion of the text in our minds as we read it (or when it is read to us by a reader competent to communicate his understanding of it); we catch the resonances of the verbal structure; we feel ourselves caught up in the field of significance which the text generates while we listen, as it were, to the author's speaking voice.

Part of our response is to hold ourselves alert for more going on than agreeable mental exercise. The text, if it is one to be taken seriously, is the author's reorganization of experience. As well as an invitation to flex our mental muscles, it is a challenge to accept a view, projected by the text, of the way the world works. There is involved an assault upon our opinions, our prejudices; a strategy is deployed to make the unexpected, the unconventional, the outrageous even, somehow acceptable. That assault is more likely to be oblique than direct, the strategy elaborate; we may be uncertain how far the author is committed to the view put forward. Is Mary Gilmore's 'I have grown past hate and bitterness' just good rhetoric, saved from sentimentality by the strong clean rhythms? Or does it express a moral position we can take seriously? If so, what is that position?

> I have grown past hate and bitterness,
> I see the world as one;
> But though I can no longer hate,
> My son is still my son.
>
> All men at God's round table sit,
> And all men must be fed;
> But this loaf in my hand,
> This loaf is my son's bread.
>
> (Mary Gilmore, 'Nationality')

Is this only a mother's admission that she always puts her son first? Or does the hard-hitting rhythm of the last line challenge us to admit that there's nothing for a mother to be ashamed of if she puts her son first? Who is speaking, anyway? Does Mary Gilmore speak only for herself? Or does she speak in the

persona of some old-fashioned socialist-internationalist — are
her words a wry admission that there are limits to her
idealism?

How far are we to take seriously as statement of a moral
position the words Umberto Eco puts on Casaubon's lips at
the end of his long novel:

> I should be at peace. I have understood. Don't some say
> that peace comes when you understand? I have understood.
> I should be at peace. Who said that peace derives from the
> contemplation of order, order understood, enjoyed, realized
> without residuum, in joy and triumph, the end of effort? . . .
>
> I should be at peace. From the window of Uncle Carlo's
> study I look at the hill, and the little slice of rising moon.
> The Bricco's broad hump, the more tempered ridges of the
> hills in the background tell the story of the slow and drowsy
> stirrings of Mother Earth, who stretches and yawns, mak-
> ing and unmaking blue plains in the dread flash of a
> hundred volcanoes . . .
>
> (Umberto Eco, *Foucault's Pendulum*, Chapter 120)

How far is the theory of the inevitable corruption of
capitalist society attributed by Conrad to a character in his
novel a theory seriously held by Conrad, and how far the
distorted opinion of a character in a novel — an English
doctor warped in mind and body by the political thugs who
tortured him?

> 'No!' interrupted the doctor. 'There is no peace and no
> rest in the development of material interests. They have
> their law, and their justice. But it is founded on expediency,
> and is inhuman; it is without rectitude, without the conti-
> nuity and the force that can be found only in a moral
> principle. Mrs Gould, the time approaches when all the
> Gould Concession stands for shall weigh as heavily upon
> the people as the barbarism, cruelty and misrule of a few
> years back.'
>
> 'How can you say that, Dr Monygham?' she cried out, as
> if hurt in the most sensitive place of her soul.

'I can say what is true', the doctor insisted, obstinately. 'It'll weigh as heavily, and provoke resentment, bloodshed, and vengeance, because the men have grown different.'

(Conrad, *Nostromo*, Part III, Chapter 11)

In this final chapter the focus widens: discussion of the moral impact of a text brings the author back into the picture, however disposed we may be to regard the author's presence with suspicion, or as an intrusion.

II

A novel or a poem is not a moral treatise; it is not the raw material for a textbook reprocessed in different form. Even when its moral impact is obvious, our primary object in reading a novel isn't to understand the world around us better; we don't set out to unmask the moral propagandist, to strip away the fiction in order to discover what D. H. Lawrence, or Patrick White, or Margaret Drabble 'really believes', any more than we read Keats's 'Ode to a Nightingale' to discover what it feels like to be 'half in love with easeful Death'; or his 'Ode on a Grecian Urn' in order to be convinced (or in order to reject the view, for that matter) that

Beauty is truth, truth beauty, — that is all
    Ye know on earth, and all ye need to know.

We read a novel or a poem for what it is, for the pleasure those words, in that order, working that way, give us as we read them. And yet, because most novels, most poems, demand recognition, in some degree, as a reorganization of experience, their status as, somehow, a statement about reality, a fresh presentation of reality we have to come to terms with, cannot be ignored.

The preacher who puts pen to paper is a different case; so is the social critic, such as Matthew Arnold, or T. S. Eliot; so are philosophers like Thomas Hobbes or Karl Popper; so, indeed, are all who lay their cards openly on the table; such writers say what they mean, or try to. We read them for their ideas, the theories they express; we don't today think of what they write as literary texts; we work on the assumption that they mean what they say. Their ideas and theories are part of their public lives, accessible to us; their writings merely express those ideas and theories more forcibly, more effectively than we should expect if we were to meet them casually, over a drink or at the dinner table, when our interest may be only a token interest. It would surprise us, supposing we pressed them, made clear our interest was genuine, if we were to discover they held opinions different from those set out in their books, or claimed to hold no opinions on these subjects at all.

Yet poets often claim just this; they are cagey, reticent about their opinions when pressed. If we express our surprise when a poet does not seem willing to defend the opinions advanced in a poem, we are likely to be told that a poem is only a poem and that we shouldn't assume that what poets say in a poem represents what they really think. Novelists are only slightly less cagey. Some make no bones about assuming the role of moralist, would agree whole-heartedly with Mordecai Richler's forthright assertion (in a radio interview in 1990) that 'every serious novelist is primarily a moralist and only incidentally an entertainer'. Most are more deprecating: a novelist will tell us we shouldn't assume, because his novels deal with death, or extramarital sex, that the novelist in private life is obsessed with these subjects; if we complain that such novels present a distorted view of society, the answer is likely to be that novels have to be treated as novels, just as poems have to be treated as poems.

If this is so, if ideas are for a poet only something to weave a poem round, moral issues only for a novelist devices for constructing interesting novels, how can we talk about their moral impact? Is reading them that way to misread them? — to accord the writers who wrote them a status they don't deserve?

Many twentieth-century poets and novelists accept this view, or say they do. They profess no moral authority, are content to surrender, with more or less transparent irony, to the experts. It is, of course, a position which resulted, as we shall see, from the availability of experts ready to profess authority. There is also the more recent rebellion against all intellectual authority in support of what is usually called moral relativism: a conviction that, where ideas are concerned, perhaps where all issues other than those of simple fact (the calculable truths of mathematics, the measurable truths of the physical universe) are concerned, there are only opinions — yours as good as mine; mine as good as yours. No possibility of true statement, because at every turn we are stuck with our metaphor-ridden, ambiguous language. And, of course, in a society that holds that conviction, poets, novelists, even critics, are apt to hold it too.

* * *

The issue, in short, is one that has provoked much controversy in recent years. Let me make my own position clear. I believe a novel or a poem (if we feel when we read it that irresistible impulse to take it seriously as a work of art), perhaps if it is to work at all as a novel or a poem, will always have a moral impact. We can usually point to where, and how, the moral idea is built in. A harder question is how seriously we are to take that idea.

Clearly, there are cases where the status of the moral idea is pretty much (as T. S. Eliot once put it — in a critical essay, not a poem) that of the juicy steak thrown to the watchdog by a burglar, to keep the dog happy while he gets ahead with cracking the safe. Hamlet's soliloquy isn't designed to arouse our interest in the rival merits of patient submission to tyranny and the impulse to throw one's life away in a useless gesture of defiance (though it may have that effect in passing), but as a poetic exploration of that dilemma designed to arouse our interest in the workings of the mind of a dramatic character reduced to the anguish of indecision. But there are plainly different cases. It is surely a misreading of D. H. Lawrence's 'Moonrise' to neglect the last five and a half lines: the poem is constructed to bring out forcefully the moral idea these lines express. We are talking once again — not about an idea in the writer's mind, but the realization of the idea in the writer's text. Is that idea merely a structuring device (an enactment of a state of mind, for example) or is it so worked into the text as to demand serious attention?

It can be argued that all art (being a human artifact, the product of a thinking intelligence) has a moral component (except, perhaps, those works of art which are concerned only with solving problems of technique). But a painting or a symphony, whatever feelings it may arouse, whatever ideas it may suggest or imply, does not actually *say* anything. Novels, poems, plays work through the medium of language: they make statements; every statement, whether made by a character in a fiction, or by the author in the author's own speaking voice, implies an attitude, invites a reaction, anticipates a moral judgement. Not to react, not to judge, is to misread; 'judge' of course in the sense of 'appraise' (form your own opinion about), not the dispassionate, authoritarian judgement of a court of law. The mental set we adopt for reading a novel or a poem conditions our reaction to all that is said; prompts the question '*Why* am I being told this?' instead of suppressing it.

* * *

Reality, being infinite, has no conceivable structure; our private everyday structuring of the reality around us, in thought or in observation, is more often random than consciously controlled. A literary text is the result of a decision: we are told what we are told because the author has decided to tell us these things — and these things only. Why? The reason may be obvious; if not, we read on, the question lurking at the back of our minds, seldom fully formulated, but focusing our curiosity as we read. The mental set we have adopted resists the conclusion that the text before us is morally neutral. Even a newspaper headline, or an advertising slogan, once incorporated in a poem or a novel, is felt to acquire significance, as one element in some chosen total effect; we read it with a different rhythm, the rhythm dictated by its new context. Often the effect aimed at is ironic: the text works in such a way as partly to detach the reader from the value system it apparently takes for granted. But of course the speaking voice may equally well (if less commonly in twentieth-century writing) imply warm, sincere approval, emotional commitment.

Our impulse to take the poem or the novel as a whole as a serious comment on the way the world works may be immediate and uncomplicated; or it may be reluctant, almost against our will. We can't say that the tougher going a poem or a novel is philosophically, the better it is as literature. The contrary is more likely: to submit consciously to the manipulation of our opinions, to surrender to the reorganization of experience which the novel or poem offers, may be sheer delight.

* * *

In talking about the moral function of literature, I have in mind the status of the poet or novelist as *moralist* rather than as one who *moralizes*. By moralizing I mean preaching, laying down the moral law. 'Moralist', as I am using the term, implies concern with men and women and the way they behave (their joys and sorrows, their anxieties and triumphs); *representing* the way the world works. Some novelists and poets who recognize their role as moralists mix moralizing with imaginative creation. Mostly, novelists and poets are moralists who have chosen not to preach; the form they have chosen exempts them from the obligation to say what they mean in as many words; a novel or a poem is a representation of the writer's understanding of the human condition, a reorganization of experience which can be felt as essentially true, but doesn't have to be true as it stands — and usually isn't. Concern, and the understanding which emerges from concern, are essential to the concept of 'moralist' as I am using the term; explicit moralizing is not. Normally, a poet or a novelist moralizes only with overtones of irony: the novel or the poem is an expression of the writer's moral insight, but it is not a statement of it, and is not, therefore, detachable without loss or distortion from the work which embodies it. When a critic separates form from content for the purpose of critical discussion, the novel or the poem falls apart in our minds until we can put it together again in a new improved reading.

We don't usually have much trouble in deciding whether we are being preached at. If we are reading a sermon, we expect it. If we are reading a novel and a moralizing note intrudes upon the fiction, we detect the moralizing note at once, and usually resent it. A poem which moralizes openly is usually a bad poem. It just is not the business of literary texts to tell us what we should or shouldn't do.

A moral attitude is a different matter. We find puzzling a novel or poem that seems to imply no moral attitude; a literary text that proclaims moral neutrality strikes us as almost immoral. We have to turn to non-literary texts (the minutes of a meeting, a medical case-history, a scientific paper) for examples of texts where the absence of any discernible moral attitude (except the determination to imply no moral attitude to the subject under discussion other than a recognition that the subject is important enough to be discussed) seems to us acceptable.

The questions which arise with literary texts are the quality of the moral attitude (the force with which it is implied, the direction it points in) and the conviction it compels (or fails to compel) that the moral attitude implied both controls and is kept under control by the verbal structure which embodies or enacts it. If the moral impulse gets out of hand, we feel we are being preached at. If there seems no coherent moral attitude controlling the poet's fancy or the novelist's fiction, we feel that the poem or novel doesn't live up to the pretensions it makes, that we are being trifled with: the demand made upon our time and understanding entitles us, we feel, to expect the challenge of some fresh, worthwhile organization of experience — not just in isolated statements, but in the work as a whole.

To something so complex, the reader's reaction must also be complex. Suppose we are reading A. E. Housman's poem 'When I watch the living meet':

> When I watch the living meet,
>   And the moving pageant file
> Warm and breathing through the street
>   Where I lodge a little while,
>
> If the heats of hate and lust
>   In the house of flesh are strong,
> Let me mind the house of dust
>   Where my sojourn shall be long.

In the nation that is not
  Nothing stands that stood before;
There revenges are forgot,
  And the hater hates no more;

Lovers lying two and two
  Ask not whom they sleep beside,
And the bridegroom all night through
  Never turns him to the bride.

Our reaction isn't likely to be that what Housman says is true
(or untrue); or that Housman's obsession with death is
absurd. Readers who react that way don't know how to read
poems. And yet we feel the poem establishes a serious claim
upon our moral concern; that it is an organization of experience which can't be dismissed out of hand, treated as a joke,
or read only for the simple pleasure we take in words well put
together; that it implies after all an attitude to life which
demands to be taken seriously.

III
THE TRAGIC AND THE COMIC VIEW

To us today it seems obvious that writers have to be free to
show the world the way it is — must, indeed, be free to
represent it any way they want, provided they can carry us
along with them into their fiction or their fantasy; are under
no obligation to represent the world the way it should be. But
that wasn't always obvious. Society long believed that poets
were teachers and that their duty as teachers, even if it didn't
entail actual preaching, must prevent them from showing vice
triumphant or virtue unrewarded. There resulted what seems
to us a distortion of both the tragic and the comic view of life.
  When disaster overwhelmed the tragic hero, it had always
to be, to some extent, the hero's fault, or the fault of his
parents; to show human beings as the undeserving victims of a
malevolent universe, or of mindless, random chance, is a later
development. The comic view of the world, if less starkly
simplistic, was equally subject to conventions that seem to us
to deny the reality of the human condition. The heroes and the

heroines of comedy inhabited a world that was constantly
threatening to get out of control as a result of human folly or
incompetence; and yet things always came out for the best in
the end; the boy got his girl, they were married and left to live
happily ever after. Over the centuries, the writer of tragedy
has tended to construct a world too starkly cruel for us to
endure. It is the comic view of the world which has prevailed.

It is a view that the writer of comedy puts forward more for
our entertainment than as a direct assault upon our opinions
about how the world works. The terms of the comic poet's
licence have varied a good deal; but, provided the convention
requiring a happy ending was respected, the right to show
people frankly, honestly, the way they are was most often
conceded.

More stable societies were more cynical, or more realistic,
than societies made sensitive to moral iniquity by religious
fervour; or in which intellectual freedom had been swept away
by the winds of social change. Chaucer's Pardoner is a
thoroughgoing rogue, a moralizing hypocrite — and, within
the limits of his modest ambitions, thoroughly successful:

'Lordlings', quoth he, 'in churches when I preach,
I adopt a high and mighty kind of speech,
And ring it out as roundly as a bell,
For I know by heart all I have to tell.
My theme is always one, and ever was:
Of every evil the root is avarice.
First, I proclaim whence it is I come,
And then my bulls I show, each and every one.
Our liege lord's seal upon my papal licence
I first display as assurance against harm,
That no man be so bold, neither priest nor clerk,
To interfere with one engaged in Christ's holy work.
And then after that I tell forth my tales.
Bulls of popes and cardinals,
Of patriarchs and bishops I display,
And in Latin I speak a word or two
To add a little savour to my preaching
And to stir them up to their devotion.
Then show I forth my long glass jars —

Crammed full, they are, with rags and bones,
Holy relics, the lot of them, as all suppose. . . .
Of avarice and such accursedness is all
My preaching, to make their purses free.
Out come the pence, and especially to me.
For profit is everywhere my purpose,
No thought for correction of their sins.
What concern of mine when they are dead and buried?
They can go blackberrying for all I care. . . .
(Chaucer, *Pardoner's Prologue*, 1–21; 72–8 [modernized])

To represent an official of the Church like this was not held, in Chaucer's day, to be subverting religion. Chaucer is not attacking the Church or society: to have us see the world about us as it is, to have us accept life with warm, open-eyed, indulgent cheerfulness is a thoroughly moral purpose. One could say the same of Boccaccio or Rabelais.

The first English novelists of the seventeenth and eighteenth centuries write in the comic, not the tragic, tradition. As in Chaucer, the basis is a pseudo-realism: an optimistic view of the world, in which characters and their actions are none the less presented for our moral appraisal; it is the process of deciding where we stand with a character that gives the narrative its interest; the process of revising our judgement as the narrative advances. Defoe and Fielding had to watch their step, however. They were less free than Chaucer to show the world the way they saw it: in eighteenth-century England, a determination to show that vice was always punished and virtue always triumphant was as much expected of a writer as belief in God. Defoe's defence of *Moll Flanders* shows the tongue-in-cheek moralizing to which he was obliged to have recourse in order to make his tale acceptable. He appeals to the precedent of the comic stage, since the novel had as yet no tradition of its own:

The advocates for the stage have, in all ages, made this the great argument to persuade people that their plays are useful, and that they ought to be allowed in the most civilized and in the most religious government; namely, that they are applied to virtuous purposes, and that, by the most lively representations, they fail not to recommend virtue and generous principles, and to discourage and expose all sorts of vice and corruption of manners. . . .

Throughout the infinite variety of this book, this fundamental is most strictly adhered to; there is not a wicked action in any part of it, but is first or last rendered unhappy and unfortunate; there is not a superlative villain brought upon the stage, but either he is brought to an unhappy end, or brought to be a penitent; there is not an ill thing mentioned but it is condemned, even in the relation, nor a virtuous, just thing but it carries its praise along with it. What can more exactly answer the rule laid down, to recommend even those representations of things which have so many other just objections lying against them? namely, of example of bad company, obscene language, and the like.

Upon this foundation this book is recommended to the reader, as a work from every part of which something may be learned, and some just and religious inference is drawn, by which the reader will have something of instruction if he pleases to make use of it.

(Defoe, *Moll Flanders*, 'Author's Preface')

Fielding makes a similar claim in introducing his novel *Amelia* to its public:

The following book is sincerely designed to promote the course of virtue, and to expose some of the most glaring evils, as well public as private, which at present infest this country.

Defoe's claim to show that virtue always wins and the singlemindedness of Fielding's exposure of social evils are alike called in question by the narrative which follows. Moll's unshakeable belief in her own essential virtue is neatly undermined: we are meant to see her moralizing as self-deception. *Amelia* is more a comedy of manners than a tract: Fielding writes for an upper-middle-class audience only recently grown to importance, committed to optimism by the evidence of its own success under the new regime, willing to accept that vice still existed, but anxious to believe progress would correct the evil of public institutions and that those whom the new social mobility left at the bottom deserved their fate. That belief cannot be openly challenged. Fielding's moralizing is offered as a gesture of high-minded purpose, intended to reassure those who expect reassurance. We find the same technique in the novels of Voltaire: because the eighteenth century would not have endured the bawdy mix of fantasy and realism of Rabelais, it had instead to endure the diabolic urbanity of *Candide*.

The convention that a story must end happily has a curious history. It began as a device of comedy, a way of rounding off the plot when the playwright had got out of it all the fun he wanted. The happy endings which round off the plots of Plautus, of Shakespeare and Molière are innocent of any moralizing purpose. In Jane Austen's *Emma* the triple marriage which abruptly sorts out the tangled skeins of romance is an example of structural irony, an elegant refusal by the author to allow the moral impact of her tale to be weakened by an over-dutiful realism. The eighteenth-century notion that middle-class morality demands a seemly, if not a happy ending lingers on among the makers of even serious films. In the film version of Graham Greene's *The Heart of the Matter*, Scobie's suicide, which he had carefully planned to look like a heart attack, is tactfully turned into something more conventionally acceptable as a hero's death.

IV
MAKING SENSE OF LIFE

Moralizing is straightforward: the moralizer deals in precepts — it's wrong to do that, right to do this; the precepts have the backing of accepted authority — the Church, public opinion of the day, or the like.

The role of the writer-moralist is less clear. Poets and novelists aren't there to tell us what to do, but to reorganize thoughts and emotions into that representation of a poet's mental life which we call a poem; to reorganize the raw material of life into that representation of reality which we call a story. Often, a bit of both. Any attempt to prove to us that, in this life at any rate, the good are rewarded and the bad punished (unless the proof is openly ironical) is not acceptable, since it is plain the world does not work that way. The writer's business is to *make sense of life* as it is.

As the phrase suggests, it is a two-sided process. Looked at one way, making sense of life is a process of turning experience, observation, the writer's feelings, intuitions, ideas, perceptions into intelligible statements about the human condition. The statements 'make sense' because they have been put together according to the conventions of syntax; we, the writer's readers know how to deal with them — know the way to take them, the degree of seriousness (for example) to attribute to them, because they have been put together according to the larger conventions of a literary form with which we are familiar and can adjust our mental set accordingly.

But that is only one side of the process. 'Making sense' is equally a process of generating in others (the writer's readers) a way of looking at the world we live in, or a world (past or present) outside our immediate personal experience. It is a process which may involve making sense of things that do not, on their own, make sense, but only do so because we choose to look at them that way. What reason is there, after all, for supposing we live in a world that can be expected to make sense, in all but a limited way, to our merely human intelligence?

There seems little question that most writers think of themselves as engaged in the sort of twin-faceted activity I have described. What they may, and we should, call into question is the value, as some kind of knowledge or truth, of the poem or novel which is the result. If we speak of truth to the human condition as a product of this activity, we have to remember that all truths about the human condition are provisional. And seldom simple or straightforward. A poet or a novelist may make things too neat: the novel or poem, however striking, may have little more to offer than a 'fresh confusion of our understanding'. But, ordinarily, we can hope for better when we surrender to the attraction of a novel or a poem; even if (to extend the quotation from Robert Graves's poem 'In Broken Images') the result is only a 'fresh understanding of our confusion', that is better than confusion unperceived or supinely accepted. Or so most of us would say.

* * *

Making sense of life is also the business of historians; they too have a tale to tell that invites moral appraisal; such at any rate is the view most historians have taken of the matter. The major ancient historians had no doubt on the score. They saw themselves as rivalling the poets. Indeed, they came closer to moralizing than to acting as moralists in their fondness for anecdotes intended to inspire their readers to virtue, or to warn them against the misuse of power — the consul who killed his own son for disobeying orders, the noble whore who saved Rome from attempted revolution, mad Nero's monstrous assassination of his mother. Modern historians approach their task more circumspectly: their first obligation, they insist, is to sort out what happened from the jumble of recorded fact, but if they think of themselves at all seriously as historians, the job doesn't stop there. They will attempt to impress on their narrative their intuitive understanding of the human beings involved, their vision of how the world works. As Manning Clark put it in his Boyer Lectures in 1976, looking back on his massive history of Australia, it was the historian's task to impose order on the chaos of fact:

> The most difficult thing of all for a historian is to learn how to tell his story so that something is added to the facts, something about the mystery at the heart of things.
>
> (Boyer Lecture 3, pp. 43–4)

Not all modern historians would agree. Not all would accept that imaginative reconstruction of the past is their business. There are historians who think of themselves as the practitioners of a science, dispassionate, logical, objective. Clark prefers to align himself with those who think of themselves as artists as well as researchers — scholars whose vision of the past depends ultimately on supralogical processes: on intuition, on the ability to see how it must have been — or might easily have been.

But what *right* has the historian to set up as an authority on the human condition? what right to claim the power to see into the minds of other human beings (human beings that actually existed, are not the creation of the historian), to infer their motives, to judge their characters and their actions? Isn't this the business of those with some claim to expert knowledge: the philosophers, and their modern collaborators, the psychologists, sociologists, political scientists and others?

The historians' justification is that these things happened: they aren't making it up; their narrative, unlike a novelist's, is fact, not fiction. Explanation of why what happened happened is called for; the truth should be discoverable; it is at any rate of sufficient importance to justify reasonable conjecture. The why and the wherefor of what happened is a legitimate concern because it is *our* past; because similar things might happen again — *are* happening again; the same problems keep recurring, to confront us. If psychologists complain that they know more about what makes men and women tick, philosophers that they understand moral issues better, sociologists and political scientists that they know better how societies function, logicians that only they can argue straight, historians are entitled to reply that only they have made it their business to find out what happened; they have perhaps made it part of their business to gain a working competence in these other disciplines; but it is in their role as artists (assuming they are that kind of historians) that they claim this special authority, for the business of making sense of the past needs the intuition of an artist, an artist who has mastered the facts.

What, however, are we to say in defence of a novelist or poet whose raw material is not fact, but only pseudo-fact? In older societies, where there were no experts to claim special knowledge of what made human beings tick, poets, because of their special skill with words, their ability to put into words what it was beyond the ability of others to put into words, could pass for the only source of authority; their skill, indeed, so surpassed ordinary ability with words as to seem inspired. That's not the position today. In a society abundantly supplied with experts on human beings and their behaviour, isn't perhaps the poet or the novelist a mere amateur whose status as moralist has been stripped away by the progress of science?

Plainly, the basis of any claim to make sense of life can't be that the novelist or poet has studied history or philosophy or psychology or politics. It can only be that, like the social scientist, the writer is a trained observer of human beings, even if, most likely, self-trained; that, like the philosopher, the writer is a persistent thinker about the meaning of human existence; like the historian of the traditional school, has developed a special facility of the imagination. Imagination in the case of the historian is an ability to impose order on chaos; the ability to see the facts spring to life; to see it *how it was*. In the case of the novelist or the poet, it is an ability to impart life to a fiction; to see *how it would have been*, and thus make the fiction ring true. Not historically true, but true to the human condition.

*   *   *

Putting it like that makes the parallel too neat. The historian's is a soberer craft: the objection 'that wasn't the way it happened', if substantiated, invalidates the work of reconstruction. The novelist or the poet is engaged in creating what never was, in getting us thinking about cases that never arose.

Truth to the human condition does not mean the narrative must always be plausible: it may contain elements of the fantastic without sacrificing its essential truth. Conrad's novel *Nostromo* is an extraordinary story crowded with extraordinary men and women in an extraordinary setting. The characters, the action, go far beyond what is plausible; the natural setting (the bay constantly wrapped in cloud, the inexhaustibly rich silver mine perched high on a remote mountain) is perceived by the reader as symbolic rather than realistic. Yet the fantastic structure of Conrad's fiction is built around an inner core of truth to the human condition, giving it vigour and life.

The formal conventions which govern the poet and the novelist are less inhibiting, in short, than those which the historian must respect. There are always two sides to the novelist's fiction: it is a structure of significant events — significant in themselves (worth relating, worth our attention), significant because of the insight they seem to provide into the personalities of the characters created; it is also a structure of words, images, syntactical and rhythmical patterns, which is the representation of that story. Because it is not a reproduction of reality, but a representation of it, the structure of words can be more audacious, more aimed at arousing a response in the reader, at generating a powerful field of significance around the fiction. Like the painter, the poet or the novelist aims at an illusion: words can make us see what the writer wants us to see no less than paint on canvas.

This is true even when the writer undertakes representation of actual historical events. Take this reconstruction from Byron's *Childe Harold* of Brussels on the eve of the Battle of Waterloo:

XXI

There was a sound of revelry by night,
And Belgium's capital had gather'd then
Her Beauty and her Chivalry, and bright
The lamps shone o'er fair women and brave men;
A thousand hearts beat happily; and when
Music arose with its voluptuous swell,
Soft eyes look'd love to eyes which spake again,
And all went merry as a marriage-bell;
But hush! hark! a deep sound strikes like a rising knell!

XXII

Did ye not hear it? — No; 'twas but the wind,
Or the car rattling o'er stony street;
On with the dance! let joy be unconfined;
No sleep till morn, when Youth and Pleasure meet
To chase the glowing Hours with flying feet —
But, hark! — that heavy sound breaks in once more,
As if the clouds its echo would repeat;
And nearer, clearer, deadlier than before!
Arm! Arm! it is — it is — the cannon's opening roar!

XXIII

Within a window'd niche of that high hall
Sate Brunswick's fated chieftain; he did hear
That sound the first amidst the festival,
And caught its tone with Death's prophetic ear;
And when they smiled because he deem'd it near,
His heart more truly knew that peal too well
Which stretch'd his father on a bloody bier,
And roused the vengeance blood alone could quell:
He rush'd into the field, and, foremost fighting, fell.

XXIV

Ah! then and there was hurrying to and fro,
And gathering tears, and tremblings of distress,
And cheeks all pale, which but an hour ago
Blush'd at the praise of their own loveliness;
And there were sudden partings, such as press
The life from out young hearts, and choking sighs
Which ne'er might be repeated; who could guess
If ever more should meet those mutual eyes,
Since upon night so sweet such awful morn could rise!

XXV

And there was mounting in hot haste: the steed,
The mustering squadron, and the clattering car,
Went pouring forward with impetuous speed,
And swiftly forming in the ranks of war;
And the deep thunder peal on peal afar;
And near, the beat of the alarming drum
Roused up the soldier ere the morning star;
While throng'd the citizens with terror dumb,
Or whispering, with white lips — 'The foe! They come!
                                    they come!'

Or take this imaginative reconstruction of another memorable historic occasion: Abraham Lincoln was assassinated on 14 April 1865; his body was conveyed from Washington to Springfield, Illinois, by train, stopping at each wayside station for the local population to pay their last respects. You can imagine various ways in which a responsible historian might organize these facts to round off his account of Lincoln. We should not expect anything like what Walt Whitman made of them. His reconstruction conjures up details of scene which even the most daring historian could no more than discreetly evoke. The background becomes an intense, vivid background, matching the challenging, plangent rhythms of the verse, the obsessive patterning of the syntax. The whole is built around the reactions of the narrating poet:

> . . . Over the breast of the spring, the land, amid cities,
> Amid lanes and through old woods, where lately the violets peep'd from the ground, spotting the gray debris,
> Amid the grass in the fields each side of the lanes, passing the endless grass,
> Passing the yellow-spear'd wheat, every grain from its shroud in the dark-brown fields uprisen,
> Passing the apple-tree blows of white and pink in the orchards,
> Carrying a corpse to where it shall rest in the grave,
> Night and day journeys a coffin.
>
> Coffin that passes through lanes and streets,
> Through day and night with the great cloud darkening the land,
> With the pomp of the inloop'd flags with the cities draped in black,
> With the show of the States themselves as of crape-veil'd women standing,
> With processions long and winding and the flambeaus of the night,
> With countless torches lit, with the silent sea of faces and the unbared heads,
> With the waiting depot, the arriving coffin, and the sombre faces,
> With dirges through the night, with the thousand voices rising strong and solemn,
> With all the mournful voices of the dirges pour'd around the coffin,

The dim-lit churches and the shuddering organs – where
    amid these you journey,
With the tolling tolling bells' perpetual clang,
Here, coffin that slowly passes,
I give you my sprig of lilac.

(Nor for you, for one alone,
Blossoms and branches green to coffins all I bring,
For fresh as the morning, thus would I chant a song for
    you O sane and sacred death).
  (Whitman, 'When Lilacs Last in the Dooryard Bloom'd',
                        Stanzas 5–7)

*   *   *

Take now a drier case, lest Whitman's open (and entirely
successful) emotional incitement, or the thought that in the
case of Whitman's 'When Lilacs Last in the Dooryard
Bloom'd' it all really happened, cloud the issue. We are near
the end of Jane Austen's *Emma*. The occasion is, by comparison with the Battle of Waterloo or the funeral of Lincoln, quite
insignificant; we have left history and the 'famous deeds of
men' behind, to enter into a structure of pure fiction. Mr
Knightley has just unexpectedly proposed to Emma; the two
return to take tea with Emma's father, a dear old man, frail,
slightly dotty, whom all change upsets, whom even the
thought that he himself or those dear to him might venture out
of doors reduces to agitated concern for their health and
safety:

    What totally different feelings did Emma take back into
the house from what she had brought out! — she had then
been only daring to hope for a little respite of suffering; —
she was now in an exquisite flutter of happiness, and such
happiness moreover as she believed must still be greater
when the flutter should have passed away.
    They sat down to tea — the same party round the same
table — how often it had been collected! — and how often
had her eyes fallen on the same shrubs in the lawn, and
observed the same beautiful effect of the western sun! —
But never in such a state of spirits, never in anything like it;

and it was with difficulty that she could summon enough of her usual self to be the attentive lady of the house, or even the attentive daughter.

Poor Mr Woodhouse little suspected what was plotting against him in the breast of that man whom he was so cordially welcoming, and so anxiously hoping might not have taken cold from his ride. — Could he have seen the heart, he would have cared very little for the lungs; but without the most distant imagination of the impending evil, without the slightest perception of anything extraordinary in the looks or ways of either, he repeated to them very comfortably all the articles of news he had received from Mr Perry, and talked on with much self-contentment, totally unsuspicious of what they could have told him in return.

You are perhaps tempted to say that Jane Austen's prose captures the scene? There isn't, however, a scene to capture: the tea party never occurred; its existence is only in the mind of Jane Austen and in ours. We have moved from imaginative reconstruction of history to pure fiction. Jane Austen's prose doesn't simply report, record, put into words, a scene which the novelist's imagination had independently created. Her words are that scene. Imprinted in the verbal structure is the novelist's moral evaluation of her own fiction. Her way of telling it, which would be objectionable if reality were being recorded (the record is too long, too archly ironic), isn't merely the vehicle, it is the essence as well as the fabric of her representation of reality; the words in which the imagined scene is expressed become the starting point for a parallel, but not identical, act of creation in the reader's mind. Because the words make us see it that way, they elicit those moral judgements.

* * *

The fact remains that the novelist or poet can, normally, claim no more than amateur status as a psychologist, or a sociologist. We haven't really answered the question: what right has a novelist, or a poet, to make, or imply, moral judgements? We've seen how it's done: what are the judgements worth?

There are those who hold that a novel or a poem, like a *New Yorker* cartoon, merely reinforces our prejudices (derived from other novels, poems, *New Yorker* cartoons); that our thoughts and ideas about how the world works are the product of the literary form, the mode of expression we choose (*New Yorker* cartoons project one view of life, *Punch* cartoons another): what answer can we make to that? Where many modern novels are concerned (those critics label as post-modern fiction), the word 'judgement', and the attitude implied in those who write them to their fiction, seem out of place. What can we say about these?

It's not altogether an answer to say that poets and novelists, if they know their business (or their place, perhaps) don't judge openly, but stop at implicit judgements, leaving us to make up our own minds, or draw our own conclusions. We can still question their right to imply judgements, especially when they are in a position to make them seem compelling by a fiction in which they are all-powerful, can make anything happen.

A better answer is that the truths of the social scientists aren't like the truths of mathematics, or even the truths of physics. The psychologist or the sociologist uses procedures of analysis and reaches conclusions which are expressed in the objective language of science; as a consequence, their conclusions wear an air of detachment and impartiality, and, therefore, of finality. In fact, the truths of social science are imperfect truths, neither wholly objective nor wholly final, and necessarily so. Usually, they are at best statistically true. Often, what they have to tell us is trivial rather than profound, since, inevitably, the social scientist concentrates observation and discussion on those things which lend themselves to observation by the procedures adopted. They are procedures for dealing with problems that can be accurately defined; the conclusions reached seldom strike directly at the heart of human conduct and experience. A psychologist's understanding of human beings, though it perhaps equips the psychologist to deal with practical or immediate problems effectively, is limited. The psychologist's understanding of the human condition may be coherent and systematic; that does not make it either complete or comprehensive; there are things on earth, as well as in heaven, not dreamed of in the psychologist's philosophy. A novelist's understanding, or a poet's, though largely intuitive, ranges wider, and tends to strike deeper.

Who knows what happens when a man, or a woman, goes mad? Or perhaps only half-mad, partly crazy — not like the rest of us, happily trundling along the rails of normal existence, or so we believe? The psychologist or the psychiatrist can tell us something; can describe particular cases according to professional conventions of what merits description. The resultant case-history, though ostentatiously objective, is still shaped by prior assumptions about significance and relevance. Such histories are like the documents ordinary political or social historians use: they need interpretation, training, insight to make much of them, to extract meaning from the chaos of fact — and may mislead. There's no denying, all the same, that this is knowledge of a kind. What is the status, alongside this kind of knowledge, of a poet's insight (or a novelist's) into what it must have been like in a particular case, had that case existed?

Madness, the onset of madness, the behaviour of those who are dramatically unlike the rest of us, are themes that have something of a fascination for poets. For novelists, too, for that matter, even if it is only the mildly crazy behaviour of Ruth and her zany aunts in that minor masterpiece of the 1980s, Marilynne Robinson's *Housekeeping*. We might take A. D. Hope's poem 'Last Look':

> His mind as he was going out of it,
> Looked emptier, shabbier than it used to be:
> A secret lock to which he had no key,
> Something misplaced, something that did not fit. . . .

Or Elizabeth Bishop's poem beginning 'This is the house of Bedlam . . .' discussed in the previous chapter. Suppose we take instead Robert Graves's magnificent, moving poem about the City man tortured, and at the same time aroused, his imagination excited, by premonitions of madness:

Forewarned of madness:
In three days' time at dusk
The fit masters him.

How to endure those days?
(Forewarned is foremad)
— 'Normally, normally.'

He will gossip with children
Argue with elders,
Check the cash account.

'I shall go mad that day —'
The gossip, the argument,
The neat marginal entry.

His case is not uncommon,
The doctors pronounce;
But prescribe no cure.

To be mad is not easy,
Will earn him no more
Than a niche in the news.

Then to-morrow, children,
To-morrow or the next day
He resigns from the firm.

His boyhood's ambition
Was to become an artist —
Like any City man's.

To the walls and halls of Bedlam
The artist is welcome —
Bold brush and full palette.

Through the cell's grating
He will watch his children
To and from school.

'Suffer the little children
To come unto me
With their Florentine hair!'

A very special story
For their very special friends —
They burst in the telling:

Of an evil thing, armed,
Tap-tapping on the door,
Tap-tapping on the floor,
'On the third day at dusk.'

Father in his shirt-sleeves
Flourishing a hatchet —
Run, children, run!

No one could stop him,
No one understood;
And in the evening papers . . .

(Imminent genius,
Troubles at the office,
Normally, normally,
As if already mad.)

                    (Robert Graves, 'The Halls of Bedlam')

Suppose you were to read Graves's poem to a group of
social scientists (none of them, as it happened, literary critics).
The sixteen stanzas would take no more than a minute or so.
Imagine the reaction: it was a layman's notion of madness;
simplistic; out of date; it wasn't scientific; it was all expressed
in traditional literary concepts, not the precise language of
science; there were no data, no real facts; how could you
predict, three days before the event, that a man would go
mad?

Many of them would probably misconstruct the hypothesis
of Graves's diabolically clever poem. The onset of the
fit . . . the children fleeing from the lunatic who pursues them,
hatchet raised . . . the lunatic watching the children 'with
their Florentine hair' (his boyhood ambition had been to be
an artist) through the grating of his cell . . . the brief notice in
the evening papers — none of this is Graves's account of what
occurred. It is all in the mind and the imagination of the
victim waiting for the onset of the attack (for whom, of course,
the 'third day', like the 'little children' they will not 'suffer to

come unto' him, has a special resonance). Whether any of this happened, whether the attack came at all, we are not told. The victim has had such premonitions, it seems, before, since there has been time for doctors to be consulted. Whether the 'case' of the businessman and frustrated artist *is* 'not uncommon', as the doctors 'pronounce', or whether we are to take their pronouncement as an ironical echo of what doctors say when there is nothing they can do, is likewise left open to the reader to deconstruct as the reader chooses.

Suppose a psychiatrist's case history recording an actual case. It would be long on fact, such facts as were available; the patient's version would get only a brief, objective summary. From the case history and from Graves's poem we reach, or fail to reach, a different understanding of what it is to be mad. That Graves's poem communicates the horror of it more effectively than the case history is surely undeniable.

To suggest that a poet's fiction can constitute a more firmly grasped kind of knowledge than the unemotional, abstract, evasive objective language of science permits is a case one would think twice before putting to a group of psychologists. Put like that, to them, it would have to seem needlessly provocative. But I put it here. It seems to me we need the novelist's and the poet's understanding of the human condition at least as much as we need the scientist's; that perhaps we live already in a world where we have too little of the one and too much of the other; too many data, and too little insight; too much information, and too little wisdom.

* * *

I'm not setting up poets or novelists as experts in anything except words: words structured into sentences that work, rhythmically as well as imaginatively, as an embodiment of what the writer chose to see. I expect more, however, than competence with words. To be taken seriously, they need an ability to construct with words what Aristotle called a representation of reality; a structure of words which becomes, for them and for us, their readers, a reorganization of experience. I am convinced this is still in our modern world a legitimate role for poets and novelists to play. Still? I'm inclined to say the attempts modern society, infatuated with objectivity, bewitched by technology, has made to dispense with this kind of knowledge are misguided. Misguided because the consequence is to put concern with the complicatedly trivial too often before the things that matter. I'm not denying the achievements of modern medicine or technology. What worries me is that a very human tendency to concentrate on what we're good at, and to treat as unimportant what we can't so easily cope with, has got out of hand.

You may not want to come so far with me. Even if you don't, I hope you will agree that poets and novelists have a role to play as moralists: an important role; one we should be the worse off for having to do without. That does not make them teachers. A teacher teaches: we expect a teacher to be reasonable, able to keep things in perspective, strong on common sense. A poet or a novelist may be slightly crazy — has to be slightly crazy, perhaps, or at any rate not too much under the thumb of common sense. It's almost part of the business to over-react. Common sense and vision are irreconcilable. The masterpieces of literature, like the masterpieces of painting, are not the product of common sense. Virgil's *Aeneid* represents a poet's reaction to the brutality of war, the hypersensitive reaction of a man who had lived through and detested war; who had seen the harm done by those who believed they were dying nobly when they were throwing their lives away to no purpose, or to a silly purpose. Though himself no soldier, though hardly cut out for hero worship, Virgil could not help knowing what war was like; it was part of the common experience of his time. At most we might make the kind of reservations we make about D. H. Lawrence's reactions to industrial ugliness:

Morel made the meal alone, brutally. He ate and drank more noisily than he had need. No one spoke to him. The family life withdrew, shrank away, and became hushed as he entered. But he cared no longer about his alienation.

Immediately he had finished tea he rose with alacrity to go out. It was this alacrity, this haste to be gone, which so sickened Mrs Morel. As she heard him sousing heartily in cold water, heard the eager scratch of the steel comb on the side of the bowl, as he wetted his hair, she closed her eyes in disgust. As he bent over, lacing his boots, there was a certain vulgar gusto in his movement that divided him from the reserved, watchful rest of the family. He always ran away from the battle with himself. Even in his own heart's privacy, he excused himself, saying, 'If she hadn't said so-and-so, it would never have happened. She asked for what she's got.' The children waited in restraint during his preparations. When he had gone, they sighed with relief.

He closed the door behind him, and was glad. It was a rainy evening. The Palmerston would be the cosier. He hastened forward in anticipation. All the slate roofs of the Bottoms shone black with wet. The roads, always dark with coal-dust, were full of blackish mud. He hastened along. The Palmerston windows were steamed over. The passage was paddled with wet feet. But the air was warm, if foul, and full of the sound of voices and the smell of beer and smoke.

(D. H. Lawrence, *Sons and Lovers*, Part 1, Chapter 2)

There is no objectivity in this selection of detail: we are in no doubt which are the relevant data (*all* are relevant), in no doubt whether a detail is chosen as background colour or as significant (*all* are significant, *all* signal their coded message to the experienced reader). The fact that Lawrence was clearly the man to feel this mixture of fascination and revulsion with life in an English mining town at the end of the Victorian era does not invalidate the reaction. It is part of the writer's job to react, to the edge of morbidity, to things to which the reactions of the rest of us have been blunted by common sense; to challenge our unthinking acceptance, call in question our prejudices.

Take a less violent, blander example: a more opulent Victorian interior, where the evasions are more discreetly muted than in Morel's kitchen. Here is a paragraph from *Our Mutual Friend*. Dickens is never in a hurry: his story is as yet still taking shape, still expanding in a fresh direction after the gruesome fishing by night for corpses in the Thames which is the subject of Chapter 1. The following example, from Chapter 3, shows how conversation can build up the picture the novelist wants as effectively as description of scene:

> As the disappearing skirts of the ladies ascended the Veneering staircase, Mortimer following them forth from the dining-room, turned into a library of bran-new books, in bran-new bindings liberally gilded, and requested to see the messenger who had brought the paper. He was a boy of about fifteen. Mortimer looked at the boy, and the boy looked at the bran-new pilgrims on the wall, going to Canterbury in more gold frame than procession, and more carving than country.
> 'Whose writing is this?'
> 'Mine, sir.'
> 'Who told you to write it?'
> 'My father, Jesse Hexam.'
> 'Is it he who found the body?'
> 'Yes, sir.'
> 'What is your father?'
> The boy hesitated, looked reproachfully at the pilgrims as if they had involved him in a little difficulty, then said, folding a plait in the right leg of his trousers, 'He gets his living along-shore.'
> 'Is it far?'
> 'Is which far?' asked the boy, upon his guard, and again upon the road to Canterbury.
> 'To your father's?'
> 'It's a goodish stretch, sir. I come up in a cab, and the cab's waiting to be paid. We could go back in it before you paid it, if you liked. I went first to your office, according to the direction of the papers found in the pockets, and there I see nobody but a chap of about my age who sent me on here.'
> There was a curious mixture in the boy, of uncompleted savagery, and uncompleted civilisation. His voice was hoarse and coarse, and his face was coarse, and his stunted figure was coarse; but he was cleaner than other boys of his type; and his writing, though large and round, was good; and he glanced at the backs of the books, with an awakened curiosity that went below the binding. No one who can read, ever looks at a book, even unopened on a shelf, like one who cannot.

* * *

Let's agree that the role of the creative writer as moralist derives its authority from an ability to present a reorganization of experience which we accept as essentially true. That raises a further question: aren't we being deceived? How can a made-up story, a *fiction*, really tell us anything about how the world works when the novelist or poet has complete control over what happens? — can show that virtue is always rewarded (or never rewarded)? That all women are promiscuous, all capitalists vile? Or, for that matter, that prostitutes always have hearts of gold? that capitalists are responsible, sensible citizens, fond of dumb animals, if impatient with intellectuals, especially Marxists? That God looks after us (or doesn't)? that there is (or isn't) a divinity which shapes our ends, rough-hew them how we will?

There's no denying authors can do as they like: it's their plot, they're their characters. There are two aspects of all narrative, however: there is the forward movement along the line of narrative (the sequence of events) and there's the sideways expansion into a field of significance. We read to find out 'what happened', but we read also surrendering to the pull of the sideways expansion which gives the narrative its significance. 'What happens' is completely under the author's control; if the narrative is crudely implausible, an absurd, worthless distortion of how the world works, how human beings behave, we probably rebel — unless we are reading that kind of modern novel where we are being *made* to feel that the fiction has been deliberately contrived to provoke our rebellion; mostly, we accept the fiction for what it is, a story which in itself proves nothing. Its moral significance is generated by the sideways expansion: the pattern of existence, the representation of a way of life, which is built up as the characters act, speak, are talked about by the narrator and by one another. The narrative creates a situation, a sequence of events; the sideways expansion creates an imagined reality for us to react to. The author's own attitude is more often implicit than explicit: we feel sympathies anticipated, created, whittled away, as the narrative proceeds. The sense of involvement generated by the onward thrust of the narrative impels us to decide whether approval or disapproval, or a mixture of the two, is expected of us — and to decide how far we are prepared to react in the way expected, to surrender to the provocation to which our involvement with the narrative exposes us.

It is something as old as literature itself. Homer's *Iliad* sets up a way of life for our general approval (the way of life of the warrior aristocrats of the heroic age); but within that framework of approval, the behaviour of Achilles, or Agamemnon, is called in question, exposed to constant reappraisal. It is a game in which the rules are far from straightforward: to see Achilles' treatment of Hector as barbarous is to fail to adjust our thinking to the codes of behaviour open to members of a society where revenge for a friend killed overruled all other codes of behaviour. To see Jane Austen's *Emma* as a witty, entertaining novel in which only perfectly trivial events take place is to misjudge the literary experience the novel offers. I don't mean the way of life of Emma Woodhouse and her friends is satirized — or for that matter that it is presented for our approval, put forward as the proper way for people to behave. What we have is a reorganization of experience: the novel is both a simplification and an intensification of the reality it purports to represent (the way of life of a section of English middle-class society in the year of the Battle of Waterloo); everything is seen coolly from a distance, with a force and a truth we shouldn't ever see it with from studying newspapers and documents of the period; even Mrs Elton, the absurd, snobbish woman whom the local parson marries when Emma rejects him, has the essential truth of a good caricature — or a painting by Modigliani.

V
THE SOCIAL FUNCTION OF LITERATURE

What I've just been saying stresses too much one aspect only of the role of the poet-novelist, that of presenting life for our judgement. You may feel I'm suggesting you should read Graves's poem 'The Halls of Bedlam' and say, 'Yes, Graves has got it right; it would be like that'. You may feel that Jane Austen, if not satirizing the way of life of comfortably-off middle-class folk in her day, isn't neutral either. As for Dickens and Lawrence, given the subjects they write about, how can they be neutral? must it not be their object to arouse our moral indignation?

I'm not going to say we don't feel like this when we read these texts, or shouldn't. But to read them only in this way is to misread them. It is fundamental to the literary experience that you are always sorting out how far poets and novelists mean what they say; and how they get that meaning across, for the meaning we take out of a literary text is often a meaning that isn't stated in as many words. Poems and novels aren't sermons or tracts, disguised to take them palatable. They are more often, to use that old phrase, a 'mirror held up to life'; except, of course, that a mirror simply reflects, and the reorganization of experience offered by a well-written poem or novel (into words held together by syntax and rhythm) is a total restructuring of that experience.

But why is the mirror held up? Well, partly, of course, for our entertainment. But not only for our entertainment. Take the novels of Fielding, the most successful of English eighteenth-century novelists. Who was Fielding's audience? It was apparently a large one: eight thousand copies of *Amelia*, the last of Fielding's novels, were printed in the year of publication, 1751. Who read them? Why did they read them?

The middle of the eighteenth century was a period of great upward social mobility. In addition to an audience which read to be entertained by Fielding's representation of a way of life that was familiar to it, there was an audience (probably a much larger audience) interested also in learning the manners of the class into which they had recently graduated. The members of that second audience didn't read expecting to be told, in any simple, straightforward sense, how well-to-do middle-class people behaved; sorting out was part of the game for them too — sorting out what was correct, sensible, generous, and what was mean, snobbish, ridiculous according to the standard of that class; judging the representation of that class in action as the narrative unfolded.

This accounts for what seems to us the sentimental indulgence with which Fielding treats the well-disposed lower orders, such as the sergeant in *Amelia*, the loyal friend of Fielding's hero. The sergeant is commissioned and becomes an officer; by his innate decency he wins his way into the middle class, where, on the whole, decent behaviour prevails, and is recognized and rewarded. In the eighteenth century the army was a great instrument of social mobility; the officer class, a large one. By the end of the century, it was the turn of the navy (as we see in Jane Austen's *Persuasion*): the take-over of the middle class by an urban commercial bourgeoisie (whom we meet in Balzac and Flaubert, as in Dickens) is a nineteenth-century phenomenon. The symbol of eighteenth-century middle-class decency is the country clergyman: often himself the beneficiary of social mobility, he represents a culture respected for its way of life more than its wealth. His decency stands out against a backdrop of the rascally, unscrupulous mob. Worse treated, however, than the undeserving poor are the old aristocrats, who are represented as corrupt, effete womanizers: in a regime dominated by middle-class standards, the aristocracy had lost political power and the sympathies of those who thought of themselves as decent people.

Jane Austen works in the same tradition as Fielding, though with her the tradition has become more refined: as well as writing for readers interested in seeing the manners of gentlefolk dextrously represented, she wrote for readers curious to find out how such people judged, or appeared to judge, the behaviour of one another. When we come to Dickens, there is a redistribution of sympathies: by the mid-1830s, the social system is once more stable; a reasonably literate, comfortably well-off middle class can have its interest aroused in the way of life of a lower class that lives by its wits as much as by hard work, and towards which those who have arrived are beginning to develop a social conscience. The mirror held up to life now caters for a rather different curiosity.

Until the present century, getting ahead in life meant acquiring the manners and social attitudes of the class you aspired to join. The heroine of Patrick White's *A Fringe of Leaves* is a nicely imagined example of one kind of nineteenth-century success story: born and bred a farmer's daughter, she becomes the wife of a gentleman and has to acquire gentle speech and the manners and way of life of gentlefolk; Ellen Gluyas, by a stroke of fortune, is transformed into Mrs Roxburgh, without ever losing the ability to lapse back into her Cornish patois when moved by a flood of sympathy for a fellow victim of the way of life that has been thrust upon her. White writes in the tradition of Jane Austen, but the appeal is now to our modern conscience in respect to past inequalities, rather than to any felt need to right present wrongs, as in D. H. Lawrence's *Sons and Lovers*.

We like to think ours is approaching a classless society; if workers do not live and behave quite like management, we prefer to think they choose not to. Status is a matter of money and the material possessions money can buy; the apparatus of status is available to all who have the money; no reprocessing of the individual is necessary, unless the individual submits voluntarily to reprocessing, as part of his or her new idea of himself or herself. Almost nobody sets out to be a gentleman; gentlemen unwilling or unable to disguise the fact are treated as odd survivals.

The social attitudes and habits of the tribe have still to be learnt. The equivalent of the eighteenth-century novel in this respect in modern technological society is probably TV soap opera. To make them interesting, the characters of soap opera are made to live a little more comfortably than average: their lives are filled to overflowing with the petty dramas of life in the affluent society; these provide an acceptable intensification of the experience of most of those who watch, while remaining essentially trivial; death or major calamity is not allowed to strike too frequently. People are interested in soap because it is easily consumed: it appeals to what Matthew Arnold in *Culture and Anarchy* called the 'taste of the bathos' (as opposed to the taste of the sublime); but they are interested also because it is from soap that people learn, agreeably (almost surreptitiously), how to behave in the petty dramas of life, as well as how to adjust to death or calamity; or, at any rate, how they are conventionally expected to adjust. There are curious formal similarities with the novels of Fielding: great length; the string of loosely connected episodes (it sometimes seems everything conceivable must happen to the main characters before they are through); the episodes are short, and fragmented further by the way they are presented — the chunks of soap transmitted between two commercials demand about the same attention span as the chapters of a

Fielding novel. The difference lies in the medium: TV deals in the directly visible; there can be no structure of manipulation or distancing comment.

* * *

All texts are designed for a particular audience. Some can adapt better than others to a new audience. Novels wear out more than poems: the eighteenth-century novel hasn't lasted well because its simple moral function (presentation of the manners of gentlefolk) is no longer required. Or rather, that brand is no longer required. Jane Austen, Dickens have lasted better: the reorganization of experience which they offer is more drastic, the writer's vision more penetrating.

We don't read novels any more to learn the manners of gentlefolk. We still read, however, to learn about life. The need is met only very imperfectly by social science. We read to sharpen our awareness of moral issues. To understand what it feels like to be involved in the crises of human existence: love, death, murder and the rest. Soap shows us conventional people behaving conventionally in such crises, learning to cope, to forgive and forget what has never really penetrated below the conventional surface, learning socially acceptable evasions of reality. Literature attempts to represent these crises in their shattering, catastrophic individuality. It attempts to enlarge our human sympathy in a world increasingly dominated by complicated triviality. If Ezra Pound was right in his prediction (in *Hugh Selwyn Mauberley*) that a 'tawdry cheapness shall outlast our days', it will be the poets and the novelists who will have held out longest. They can at least claim to have done something to restore our human dignity in a world where we feel more and more the frustration of human contacts, the degradation of the quality of life by the need to behave in such a way that machines can cope with our transactions.

* * *

The people who read novels today read them because they enjoy them: the same applies to that smaller group who read poems. I'm speaking of course of those who read of their own free will — not students, professional reviewers, publishers' readers and the like. However disturbing the literary experience, it offers a kind of pleasure. Anyone with a feeling for words reacts with pleasure to words well handled. It may be the pleasure we get from the grand rhetoric of *Paradise Lost*:

> Of Mans First Disobedience, and the Fruit
> Of that Forbidd'n Tree, whose mortal tast
> Brought Death into the World, and all our woe,
> With loss of *Eden*, till one greater Man
> Restore us, and regain the blissful Seat,
> Sing Heav'nly Muse, that on the secret top
> Of *Oreb*, or of *Sinai*, didst inspire
> That Shepherd, who first taught the chosen Seed,
> In the Beginning how the Heav'ns and Earth
> Rose out of *Chaos*: Or if *Sion* Hill
> Delight thee more, and *Siloa's* Brook that flowd
> Fast by the Oracle of God; I thence
> Invoke thy aid to my adventrous Song,
> That with no middle flight, intends to soar
> Above th' *Aonian* Mount; while it persues
> Things unattempted yet in Prose or Rime.

Or it may be the pleasure we get from the crisp, cool craftsmanship of Jane Austen:

> About thirty years ago, Miss Maria Ward of Huntingdon, with only seven thousand pounds, had the good luck to captivate Sir Thomas Bertram, of Mansfield Park, in the county of Northampton, and to be thereby raised to the rank of a baronet's lady, with all the comforts and consequences of an handsome house and large income. All Huntingdon exclaimed on the greatness of the match, and her uncle, the lawyer, himself, allowed her to be at least three thousand pounds short of any equitable claim to it. She had two sisters to be benefited by her elevation; and such of their acquaintance as thought Miss Ward and Miss Frances quite as handsome as Miss Maria, did not scruple to predict their marrying with almost equal advantage. But

there certainly are not so many men of large fortune in the world, as there are pretty women to deserve them. Miss Ward, at the end of half a dozen years, found herself obliged to be attached to the Rev. Mr Norris, a friend of her brother-in-law, with scarcely any private fortune, and Miss Frances fared yet worse. Miss Ward's match, indeed, when it came to the point, was not contemptible, Sir Thomas being happily able to give his friend an income in the living of Mansfield, and Mr and Mrs Norris began their career of conjugal felicity with very little less than a thousand a year. But Miss Frances married, in the common phrase, to disoblige her family, and by fixing on a Lieutenant of Marines, without education, fortune, or connections, did it very thoroughly.

(Jane Austen, *Mansfield Park*, opening lines)

But there is also the pleasure of anticipation: where is Milton heading? How is Jane Austen going to get her novel off the ground after so matter-of-fact a beginning, however drily and elegantly expressed? There is the æsthetic pleasure we take in a sensuously vivid image:

O wild West Wind, thou breath of autumn's being,
Thou, from whose unseen presence the leaves dead
Are driven, like ghosts from an enchanter fleeing,

Yellow, and black, and pale, and hectic red,
Pestilence-stricken multitudes . . .

(Shelley, 'Ode to the West Wind')

Or the more complex pleasure of a striking, intriguing image:

Let us go then, you and I,
When the evening is spread out against the sky
Like a patient etherised upon a table . . .

(T. S. Eliot, 'The Love Song of J. Alfred Prufrock')

It's easy to make a long list. We don't, however, just measure books by the pleasure they give. It's not possible, or desirable, to devote our lives, or that part of our lives we are free to dispose of, to the pursuit of pleasure, choosing or rejecting solely on the basis of the degree of pleasure which an activity seems to offer. Pleasures cloy. We may, at the moment of intensest pleasure, surrender completely. Mostly, however, built into the experience of pleasure is an evaluation of it: this is a sensible way, we feel, to spend our time; an experience we can reflect on afterwards, chew over; or a senseless way to spend our time; an experience we're going to remember with shame, prefer to forget about.

The experience of literature comes out high on this scale. Not just because it is more demanding to read a novel by Henry James than to watch a bad thriller on TV. True, many modern novels depend heavily on verbal, syntactical and rhetorical brilliance. But if difficulty were all, solving a crossword puzzle would rank with reading a poem we have to rack our brains over. A good poem, a good novel has the paradoxical quality of *testability*: despite the sorting out of fantasy and truth to life it involves us in, it is ultimately by truth to life that we select the good (want to keep on reading them, to read again and again) and reject the bad, the spurious, the novel or poem which is only verbally attractive.

We might argue about this for a long time; but in the end,I think, we should come back to the conviction that what makes a novel or a poem worth reading isn't that it is well written, but that it has to do with life. Not, oddly enough, that it shows life the way it is: more often, the novel or the poem somehow focuses upon reality, but does so from a perspective of art that makes the novel or the poem, not just more pleasurable than crude, unorganized reality, but somehow more deeply, more permanently, true. It is a striking property of a work of art that we perceive it — not as less true, but as more true than reality itself: the Venus de Milo, as she catches our eye from her pedestal in the Louvre, is in all sorts of ways not a bit like reality; Dido's speech (in Virgil's *Aeneid*) confessing her love for Aeneas isn't a bit like reality:

> If it were not settled in my mind, unshakable,
> never again to bind myself with the marriage bond,
> after my first love failed me, deceived me by his death,
> if I did not loathe marriage beds, marriage torches,

I might perhaps have surrendered and failed this once . . .
                                    (*Aeneid* 4, 15–19)

Claudio's speech in *Measure for Measure* pleading with his sister
to prostitute herself to the man who threatens to have him
executed if she does not submit to his lust isn't a bit like
reality:

Isabella: What says my brother?
Claudio: Death is a fearful thing.
Isabella: And shameful life — a hateful.
Claudio: Ay, but to die, and go we know not where;
           To lie in cold obstruction, and to rot;
           This sensible warm motion to become
           A kneaded clod; and the delighted spirit
           To bathe in fiery floods, or to reside
           In thrilling region of thick-ribbed ice;
           To be imprison'd in the viewless winds,
           And blown with restless violence round about
           The pendent world; or to be worse than worst
           Of those that lawless and incertain thought
           Imagine howling! — 'tis too horrible!
           The weariest and most loathed wordly life
           That age, ache, penury, and imprisonment
           Can lay on nature, is a paradise
           To what we fear of death.
           (Shakespeare, *Measure for Measure*, Act III, Scene 1)

Women (even queens) don't talk to their sisters in long set
speeches that scan, any more than men talk in poetry to their
sisters about death when death stares them in the face. We
know that in moments of emotional crisis our feelings are,
most often, beyond expression ('words fail us', as we say); or
else what we say is trite, a string of clichés that fall short of, or
go absurdly beyond, the ineffable truth, like the poor, shop-
soiled clichés with which Emma Bovary stumbles to express
her passionate love for her cynical seducer (who has heard
them all before, from more practised lips, and takes it for
granted that Emma no more means her protestations of love
than the others did). It is on such occasions that we feel, as

Flaubert (that great artist in words) drily comments, that 'human speech is like a cracked copper cauldron on which we beat out tunes for bears to dance to, when what we would like is to win the compassion of the stars' (*Madame Bovary*, Part II, Chapter 12).

Poetry, however, *can* set out to win, if not the compassion of the stars, the compassion of the responsive reader. It does this, not by imitating reality, but by transforming it. The odd thing is that Dido's speech or Claudio's speech somehow seems more real than anything Dido or Claudio might conceivably have said if it had happened in real life. It is the business of cold hard marble to seem more real than flesh and blood; it is the business of painted sky, sea and stones to seem more real in a picture than in ordinary life; the business of words in a poem (or a novel) to seem more real than speech in ordinary life.

* * *

I perhaps sound as if I would have you read in a spirit of connoisseurship — savouring a novel or a poem, as you might savour a good wine, or the pattern of light on a polished table-top. Deep in the literary experience, however, there is a compulsion to go along with this reorganized, intensified reality; we feel the challenge to revise our understanding of life in the light of what we perceive as the essential truth of the intensification.

I don't mean we get our understanding of life from literature: we get our understanding of life from living. I don't mean either that we understand life first and then turn to literature for a pleasurable confirmation of what we already know. What I am prepared to argue is that our experience of life is enhanced (extended, made deeper, more intense, richer) by literature. We need some experience of life to have the capacity to respond to the experience of literature: we have to have something on which to build. Those who can bring little experience of life have little on which to build: there may not be enough for the literary experience to activate. You remember Yeats's lines?

Bald heads forgetful of their sins,
Old, learned, respectable bald heads
Edit and annotate the lines
That young men, tossing on their beds,
Rhymed out in love's despair

To flatter beauty's ignorant ear.
All shuffle there; all cough in ink;
All wear the carpet with their shoes;
All think what other people think;
All know the man their neighbour knows.
Lord, what would they say
Did their Catullus walk that way?

(W. B. Yeats, 'The Scholars')

Before we join Yeats in deriding the dons he despised, let us be clear about the basis for our derision. Yeats's dons weren't necessarily stupid. They doubtless enjoyed their Catullus, after their fashion. It was that what Catullus wrote about simply fell outside their experience: they had been trained in a tradition of scholarship in which the connection between literature and life had been lost. Many less learned read what they read with a casual, limited capacity to respond: for them, literature is, as we say, an escape from life, not an enrichment of it.

There are times when life around us feels too trivial, too boring, too brutal, too hopeless to endure; perhaps, then, the best thing to do is to escape. There needn't be anything wrong with the man or the woman who feels sometimes an overpowering compulsion to escape; having escaped for a while into literature, we may come back refreshed, ready to confront reality. It's the full-time refugee from reality who is in trouble, the man or the woman whose thoughts never re-establish contact with reality (or never made contact with reality except at the level of meaningless routine). It's the people who read only to escape from that routine, who never connect what they read with the world of their own experience whom we should pity: pity for what they are missing, in life as well as in what they read.

* * *

I'm suggesting, in short, a two-way relationship between life and literature: life is the starting point; but life with no understanding of life is uncomprehending routine. Religion, science each offer an understanding of a kind: a framework which can do something to give coherent shape to our guesses about the meaning of life. A novel or a poem can make us feel we are able to come to terms with life on a more satisfactory basis than we could otherwise. There seems no reason to suppose human life has a meaning, in the sense of something that we could write down in objective prose and agree about. We are all today such fluent speakers of objective prose, we are apt to forget how limited the area of human experience is with which objective prose can cope adequately: outside that area, we deceive ourselves — or cheat; we persuade ourselves objective prose is the only instrument at our disposal, when in many areas it is only a starting point.

A poem or a novel does not have to be constructed around a settled philosophy of life; it is a better poem or novel, perhaps, when it isn't. The role of the poet and the novelist is more to raise questions than to provide explicit answers. They deal more in essential truth than objective truth. Nor is it necessary for a novel or a poem, in order to have this quality of essential truth, to be about the contemporary world and contemporary problems as is the case with the novels of Dickens or D. H. Lawrence, or Eliot's *Waste Land*. There is nothing wrong with frontal attack; but often transposition into a different context in time or place sharpens the contemporary relevance by leaving it for the reader to see for himself. A novel like Patrick White's *Voss*, or *The Riders in the Chariot*, or *The Twyborn Affair* is only incidentally concerned with describing the typical, the everyday, though the fiction keeps re-establishing contact with the typical and the everyday within a framework closer to fantasy. White's novels are an exploration of the way it would have to be when those human beings got into those situations. They convince because of their essential truth to life, as Coleridge's *Ancient Mariner* convinces.

That may not be enough for many people. It is enough for me. Those who ask 'What use is literature?' seem to me not to have begun to understand life. What use is painting? What use is music? What use is life? We don't have to be able to answer these questions in terms of measurable, 'quantifiable'

usefulness to feel that life would be unspeakably the poorer
without the stimulus to our minds, the challenge not to fall
into uncomprehending routine, which literature provides. I
keep coming back to the idea of a poem or a novel as a vision
of life. Does that make it sound too grand? Visions vary. Some
approach the mystic, the apocalyptic. Wordsworth's ode
'Intimations of Immortality from Recollections of Early
Childhood' operates at that level:

> Our birth is but a sleep and a forgetting:
> The Soul that rises with us, our life's Star,
>   Hath had elsewhere its setting,
>   And cometh from afar:
>
>   Not in entire forgetfulness,
>   And not in utter nakedness,
> But trailing clouds of glory do we come
>   From God, who is our home.

A poem like Lawrence Ferlinghetti's San Francisco rooftop
scene is also a vision of life, however:

> Away above a harbourful
>   of caulkless houses
> among the charley noble chimney pots
>   of a rooftop rigged with
>   clotheslines
>   a woman pastes up sails
>   upon the wind
>   hanging out her morning sheets
>   with wooden pins
>   O lovely mammal
>   her nearly naked teats
>   throw taut shadows
>   when she stretches up
>   to hang at last the last of her
>   so white washed sins. . . .

(Lawrence Ferlinghetti, from *A Coney Island of the Mind*)

Or take this description of Emma Bovary and her lover after their first ride together had ended in surrender to her seducer. The young doctor's wife, whose emotional life has been fed more by the romances she read as a girl than by experience of life, is deep in a romantic dream; the process of return to reality is slow. Her lover has been through all this before with others: he feels only sensual satisfaction, his mood does not rise beyond complacent possession of a new, attractive mistress; a connoisseur's pride in her appearance, no thought of how she may feel. The final image of Emma's horse rearing on the cobbles as they enter the small provincial town where she lives, while the neighbours watch from the windows, sums up the reality with which she has temporarily lost contact:

> They returned to Yonville by the same path. They could see the tracks which their horses had left in the mud, side by side; there were the same bushes, the same stones in the grass. Nothing around them had changed; yet for her something more momentous had happened than if mountains had moved. Rodolphe lent forward from time to time and took her hand, in order to kiss it. How charming she was on horseback! Straight, slim-waisted, her knee folded over the mane of her mount, her colour a little heightened by the open air, in the red of the evening.
>
> As they came into the town, her horse rose in a caper on the cobblestones.
>
> People were watching from the windows.
>
> (Flaubert, *Madame Bovary*, Part II, Chapter 9)

Madame Bovary is an intensely moral work. Yet it ends with the total degradation of its heroine and the triumph of petty shrewdness (in the person of the shopkeeper Lheureux) and fatuous mediocrity (in the person of the pharmacist Homais); its noblest character is the fool Bovary, whose simple passionate love for his faithless wife shines through the contempt Flaubert builds up for his other characters, for the political and social system under which they flourish. What gives his novel its moral strength is Flaubert's concern, the integrity of his vision, the extraordinary skill with which that vision is transposed into the medium of words — the delicate, impres-

sionistic feeling for the misty colours of Normandy countryside — and, at the same time, its comic stylishness: a whole
society is re-created with a terrible, austere authority.

VI

What of the future? There are powerful and original novelists
writing today, there are good poets. What the future holds, as
far as individual genius is concerned, is unforeseeable. Who,
at a time when tragedy seemed worked out, dead, could have
foreseen the emergence of Ibsen — in Norway? Who, when
critics were predicting the end of the novel, could have
foreseen Carlos Fuentes or García Márquez, or Patrick
White? could have foreseen, a generation later, Margaret
Drabble, Umberto Eco, Milan Kundera, Marilynne Robinson, Michel Tournier? Anywhere round the world writers of
genius may now be writing. The question is, who will read
them?

As always, I'm talking primarily about literature written to
be read — read in private by individual readers: not plays
written for performance on the stage; not novels used as raw
material for television. I'm not talking about the physical
survival of the great classics of the past: they will survive as
long as there are libraries to house them, even if there is no
one to read them. I'm talking of the survival, as a significant
part of our thinking lives, of the literary experience. What is
its future? I think it more likely that economic factors will
decide the matter than the drying up, or the resurgence, of
creative genius. My guess is that economic changes will
impose a more brutal process of simplification and elimination
of the weaker than we have yet seen. As books get dearer, the
danger is that the kind of books I have been talking about will
be published in such small editions as to reach only a tiny
fraction of their potential readers, or will be only read in the
way that you can read a book you can borrow for a couple of
weeks from a library; or will disappear altogether because this
kind of publishing ceases to be worth any publisher's while.
There is a real danger that the only novel to be published will
be the bestseller launched on a wave of publicity.

We have to reckon with the likelihood that, as long as our present culture survives, the number of people who feel starved for good books will almost certainly diminish in importance: to be read and liked here and there by individuals scattered across the face of the earth, however large the total when you add them up, isn't comparable to being a writer in London or Paris in 1780 or 1880 or even 1930. It is hard to imagine a society at all like that now emerging in which the service done literature, music, the arts generally at any serious level by technology can be more than a marginal spin-off; the emphasis in television must be on the sensational, the trivial and the commercially rewarding. The literary experience no longer occupies the centre of civilized life: it has been expelled from that position by organized sport, by complicated activities that do more to gratify the ego of the owner of expensive equipment and stimulate the economy than ownership of books; it has had to fight for a place alongside a succession of rivals that demand less mental effort: cinema, radio, TV — how can it be other than a losing battle?

More real, however, than the threat from the electronic media, is the threat represented by objective prose and the mental set, the assumptions about the way the world works, which constant exposure to objective prose implants in our minds. The danger is that science will be accorded general acceptance as the only authoritative interpretation of experience, and objective prose (ostensibly objective prose) will become the only acceptable form of discourse about how the world really works. The danger is progressive: literature is first denied the role it long played uncontested of interpreting experience; is denied next even the role of providing an alternative interpretation; is relegated then to the status of an entertainment (a purveyor of clichés about how the world works, not generating truth); either a popular entertainment, agreeable but no longer perceived as essentially true, or else (for some reject that status) an esoteric form of trifling.

We need courage to say the world is not like the social scientists' account of it; that their painstaking measurements of the trivial encourage a distortion of reality; that the principles governing the universe are not perhaps such as to surrender their secrets to patient, systematic inquiry; that objective truth, in the area of human relations, is an illusion; that hope, if not happiness, for civilized society lies more in the tiny, peculiar sanity of poets than in the immense, compassionless folly of technology left to its own devices. And yet that is perhaps the case. I am not contemptuous of the achievements of the social sciences. I don't seriously expect technology put at the service of the arts. All I want is respect for the arts, as providing a wholesome alternative to technical ingenuity, to total preoccupation with the mechanics and electronics of staying alive comfortably and the trivialization of life which advertising and the media urge upon us.

'Poets', said Shelley, 'are the legislators of the world.' Plainly, they are not. And just as well: there is every indication they would make very bad legislators. Let them stick to poetry. We can learn from them to take a joy in words that reaches out beyond the sentimental ingenuity of advertising; and perhaps learn while we are about it to shake ourselves free from sentimental attitudes to life; attitudes that are facile, tawdry, sterile. A few good poets will be enough. Let's only hope there will be readers — readers who have learnt how to read. As well as being read for their own sake, the poets will then serve as a challenge, as a source of invigoration for those who write creatively in prose: the novelists, the playwrights, writers for the cinema, for radio and for television who take their responsibilities as writers seriously. A world worth living in needs something worth living for.

List of Critical Terms

The object of this List is to indicate how a number of important terms which are used in different (often widely different) ways in current practice are used in this book. There is no suggestion that the practice adopted here might be generally adopted. For terms not listed, see Index.

COMMENTARY: The traditional term for a series of notes on a literary text covering points of grammatical difficulty, historical and literary background, etc. Unlike INTERPRETA-TION, which, in modern usage, is continuous and critical, *commentary* is discontinuous and avoids critical issues. E.g., A. Norman Jeffares's *Commentary on the Collected Poems of W. B. Yeats*, 1968.

DECONSTRUCTION: A term invented as a reaction against structuralist criticism, intended to emphasize that reading is not wholly a process of synthesis and submission to a text. See Harold Bloom *et al.*, *Deconstruction in Criticism*, 1979.

DISTANCING: Originally, a term used by psychologists to denote the relationship between emotional involvement and actual physical involvement. E. Bullough's classical paper '"Psychical distance" as a factor in art and an aesthetic principle', *British Journal of Psychology* 5, 1912, 87–98, is often referred to. In literary criticism, the term denotes the degree of detachment set up in certain texts by the author's speaking voice as well as the corresponding detachment generated in the reader.

FORM: In this book, *form* denotes the conventions which govern the layout and manner of treatment of a literary work. See Chapter 2, Section IV. It is thus opposed to *structure*, which is the working out of those conventions in a particular text. *Form* is what a text has in common with other texts sufficiently like it to be seen as a single family or tradition; *structure* is what is unique to a particular text. In contemporary critical usage, the two terms are often used as more or less interchangeable. For *form*, as used here, some critics substitute 'genre', a term which has disparaging overtones (tending to imply over-adherence to formal conventions). Many English speakers, moreover, find genre difficult to pronounce in a way that is not disagreeable in the ear.

INTERPRETATION: 1(a) The mental process by which we apprehend statement as meaningful. The activity of communicating this understanding to others — telling them what the statement means (a sense taken over from actual translation by an interpreter). (b) In particular, the process of reading meaning into a text, either silently, or in oral performance. 2 The emerging understanding of a text which accompanies 1(a) and leads normally to a more or less coherent understanding of the text as a whole. That understanding serves as a basis for subsequent readings, which often expand or correct earlier readings.

Interpretation Sense 2 is thus a product of Sense 1. It is a mental state, not something tangible or concrete. The traditional metaphors employed when we speak of 'building' or 'constructing' an interpretation (derived from the Greek concept of a literary text as a *poiema* — a 'made thing') are misleading in so far as they suggest something fixed or static. An interpretation of a particular text is better regarded as a tension in the mind, holding together an understanding of that text which is flexible, open to correction, threatened, even, by the fresh evidence of a further reading. There is an evident analogy here with modern concepts of the nature of philosophical or scientific theories. See Thomas Kuhn, *The Structure of Scientific Revolutions*, 2nd edn, 1970.

The term *interpretation* is also used by some critics of a more or less drastic brief restatement of a text which purports to isolate its essential meaning. Here, as with Sense 2, a temptation exists to regard the activity of *interpretation* as teleological, a form of problem-solving.

INWARD EAR: A term often used by critics to denote the mental process enabling the silent reader to catch the rhythm, etc., which the reader's interpretation would give the text in performance aloud. Perhaps an adaptation of Wordsworth's 'inward eye' which is described in his poem 'I wandered lonely as a cloud' as 'the bliss of solitude', enabling him to reconstruct in thought what he had seen.

MEANING: A term prone to confusion but which it would be unnatural to avoid in a book like the present. Umberto Eco offers a useful brief historical survey of the problem:

> Classical criticism aimed at finding in a text either (a) what the author intended to say, or (b) what the text says independently of its author. Only after accepting the second principle can one ask if what is found is (i) what the text says by virtue of its textual coherence and of an original underlying signification system, or (ii) what the addressees found in it by virtue of their own system of expectations.
>
> (Umberto Eco, 'Some paranoid readings', *Times Lit. Suppl.*, 1990, 706)

As the term is used in this book, *meaning* is a property of verbal structures, the product of (1) syntax, which draws out an appropriate sense for the words and indicates a grammatical relation between them, and (2) rhythm, which controls the distribution of emphases, and, in more complicated verbal structures, serves as an indicator and determinant of the way what is said is to be taken (see RHYTHM).

The reading of meaning into a literary text is an operation which takes place within the mind of the reader. The indications of rhythm and even of syntax in a text, like all linguistic indicators, are frequently ambiguous (language does not work like mathematics); there are those who argue, therefore, that this is a process in which the writer of the text is left behind, and the reading in of meaning left in the control of the reader, who is free to read an infinite variety of meanings into the verbal structure. The view is gaining ground in contemporary literary theory that this freedom has been exaggerated by postmodernist critics.

The position adopted in this book is that (1) an implicit social contract exists between writer and reader which allows considerable freedom (since two minds are involved, the writer's and the reader's, not one), but which it is irresponsible to repudiate; (2) the freedom of the reader as interpreter is limited by the rhythm built into any complex text by the writer, which establishes an authorial voice heard by the reader's INWARD EAR. See SOUND OF SENSE.

Talk of the 'meaning' of a symphony or a painting, while well established by usage, is better regarded as involving a metaphor; compare the metaphor we employ when we speak of a building as 'making a statement'.

MENTAL SET: A focusing of the attention determining the attitude or frame of mind in which we read a text. Mental set implies a prior assumption that the text will form a coherent whole. See Chapter 1, Section III. For 'set' as a term of Gestalt Psychology ('a pre-established attitude which determines what is to be perceived and how we shall react') see Allport, 1955 in Bibliography.

PERFORMANCE: A particular reading of a text, especially one embodying the performer's interpretation, usually aloud. Most often, of actors, though a distinction between 'reading' as tentative or exploratory and 'performance' as something more definitive would be useful, if it could be supported by usage.

POSTMODERNISM: A term current in the 1970s and 80s, used most often to denote the work of novelists whose chief common characteristic was a determination to break free from traditional conventions of plot structure. Proclaimed as successors of the 'Moderns', who were considered to end, in English literature, with Joyce and Virginia Woolf and their experiments with stream of consciousness technique. Also applied to critics sympathetic to postmodern writing. The difficulty with 'modern' and 'postmodern' is that the assertion of contemporaneity quickly becomes out of date. In the 1980s 'Postmodernism' lost ground to 'Magic Realism', a term taken over from German critics of the 1920s, and now used to describe the massive complex plot structures of García Márquez, Umberto Eco and others. See Gerald Graff, *Literature Against Itself*, 1979; David Lodge, *After Bakhtin*, 1990.

READING (noun): Most often, in this book, of the act of reading meaning into a printed text; the process whereby the text becomes a more or less coherent experience in the mind of the reader.

Since 'a reading' in this sense is the outcome of an interpretation of the text, or forms the basis for subsequent interpretation, 'reading' and 'interpretation' are often treated as synonyms.

A reading may be either silent or aloud. Most would agree, however, that a reading aloud, since it forces decisions upon us, or warns us more plainly that the text will not work the way we try to take it, is the 'truer' interpretative act.

RECEPTION: A term for the understanding or popularity of a literary work, at a given moment, past or present (e.g., at the moment of publication), or across subsequent centuries (Shakespeare, e.g., was little understood, as it seems to us, in the eighteenth century — hence Johnson's forthright, down-to-earth, patronizing appraisals; was rediscovered by Romantic critics, German as well as English; then drastically reinterpreted by twentieth-century critics. Donne, after being neglected throughout the eighteenth and nineteenth centuries, was rediscovered in the twentieth century).

The concept of a constantly changing reception serves as a corrective to that implied by the term 'survival' of an author's works, which suggests that a work is best understood in the author's lifetime or at the moment of publication; that its impact can only fade or wither; that the role of the critic is analogous to that of the restorer of Old Masters. In fact, many works take time to permeate to understanding and appreciation (the metaphor of the time-bomb might be more appropriate in these cases); or the understanding of them

wanes, and then revives in different circumstances and in a
new light, so that the appropriate metaphor is perhaps that of
a virus passing through a series of mutations (e.g., Virgil's
Aeneid, after a long period of rejection by Romantic critics as
second-rate and imperialistic, suddenly increased in popularity and understanding in the USA during the Vietnam War,
when Virgil's view of war as a progressive corruption of moral
standards evoked a response that would have been impossible
in Victorian England).

RHYTHM: A convenient, if imprecise, name for an elusive
property of all speaking and writing; in texts where the
meaning is not explicit, the ultimate vehicle of meaning.

The most obvious component of rhythm is the distribution
of the stresses: both the individual 'natural' stress that falls on
a particular syllable of most of the words in a phrase or
sentence (giving, as it were, the beat of the phrase, and in
verse serving as the basis of metre) and the additional
'affective' stress given certain syllables (not necessarily the
syllable normally stressed), so that these act as indicators and
determinants of tone, attitude, nuance, etc., and thus of
meaning. For metrical purposes, syllables are usually treated
simply as stressed or unstressed; in actual speech or careful
reading aloud, the degrees of stress possible are numerous and
complicated, and the effect produced by a minor variation
often subtle.

Rhythm, as used in this book, includes other features of
spoken (or heard) language besides stress. In addition to the
phonetic properties of individual words (length and weight of
vowels and consonants and consonant-grouping — properties
exploited, e.g., by Edith Sitwell in *Façade*) rhythm is to be
taken as including variations in pitch (sentence intonation),
tempo, attack, phrasing; variations in the spacing of words in
a phrase, in the insistence on words related by sense, sound or
grammatical form. A mistake in any of these can instantly be
felt as a misreading threatening the meaning of a line or
sentence by the reader or the listener.

In addition to selecting an appropriate reading from the
possibilities offered by the syntactical structure, *rhythm* can
offer a wide range of overtones or modifiers of the selected

meaning, virtually ensuring that every reading of a text can be fresh or experimental, opening up new possibilities, and therefore unique.

In a well-written text, the *rhythm* varies almost constantly as it follows and sustains the meaning, forming a complex unity. Translators of such texts, by neglecting *rhythm* in pursuit of an apt translation of individual phrases, often end up with a *rhythm* which is disjointed, or vaguely chaotic. It is obvious that paraphrase, by destroying *rhythm*, can be even more destructive of meaning.

See MEANING, SOUND OF SENSE; more in Chapter 1, Section II; also Bibliography under Berry, Bolinger, Harding. On *Façade* see Edith Sitwell, *Taken Care of*, 1965, 139–44.

SIGNIFICANCE: A term devised to stress the capacity of a literary work to place itself in some larger context which enhances or extends its verbal or translatable meaning; the structure of reference which builds up in our minds as we read. For 'significance' opposed to 'meaning' see Hirsch, 1967 and 1976 in Bibliography.

MEANING is what the text says. *Significance* is what we make of what the text says. The distinction is obviously useful and important. The problem is in the terms used to express the polarity. 'Meaning' is used by some critics as a blanket term, covering everything; others oppose 'verbal meaning' and 'total meaning'. The problem is made worse by the fact that *meaning* is a concept confined to the English language. The corresponding French word is *signification*, usually translated as *significance*, especially by linguists trained in the tradition of Ferdinand de Saussure; others use *sens* (cf. German *Sinn*) which, if translated as 'sense', introduces further confusion.

In this book, *significance* occurs mainly in the phrase 'Field of Significance', employed to oppose the sideways expansion of, e.g., a narrative text in our mind to the onward thrust of the narrative itself. For 'Field' as a term of Gestalt Psychology, see Allport, 1955 in Bibliography. See MEANING.

SOUND OF SENSE: Robert Frost in a letter to John T. Bartlett dated 4 July 1913 (written during Frost's visit to England), after remarking 'I alone of English writers have consciously set out to make music out of what I may call the sound of sense', goes on:

> An ear and an appetite for these sounds of sense is the first qualification of a writer, be it of prose or verse. But if one is to be a poet he must learn to get cadences by skillfully breaking the sounds of sense across the regular beat of the metre. Verse in which there is nothing but the beat of the metre furnished by the accents of the polysyllabic words we call doggerel. Verse is not that. It is a resultant from these two.

It is clear from the examples Frost quotes that by the *sound of sense* he has in mind patterns of stress, pitch, intonation, etc. as they occur in natural speech. It is only by attending to these that a writer can implant the imprint of the thinking mind of the speaker upon the syntactical patterns he employs. In a letter to Sidney Cox dated 2 February 1915, Frost takes the theory a stage further, arguing that the number of such patterns is limited:

> Remember, a certain fixed number of sentences (sentence sounds) belong to the human throat just as a certain fixed number of vocal runs belong to the throat of a given kind of bird. These are fixed I say. Imagination cannot create them. It can only call them up for those who write with their ear on the speaking voice.

In this second passage, Frost anticipates modern linguistic theories of 'deep' syntactical structures advanced by the proponents of transformational grammar.

Verse based on a tension between the rhythm of the natural speaking voice and the beat of the metre is at least as old as the sixteenth century in English. It is a natural development once verse is freed from the necessarily more regular cadences of song. See Chapter 3 for the theory developed there of the difference between the singing and the speaking voice. Shakespeare is usually credited with being the first to exploit this tension in his dramatic verse. Frost seems to have hammered at his theory for a year or so at the beginning of his poetic career; reference then drops from his correspondence, perhaps as part of a growing dislike for theoretical discussion. But it is clear that the theory continued to underlie his practice as a poet. The effect is not simply an easy colloquial note; more important is the illusion of a speaker actually thinking his way along the line of statement as he speaks. What Edward Thomas (who perhaps discussed the theory with Frost during their meetings in England in 1913–14) seems to have meant when he wrote of 'the patterns of stress and pause which reflect a mind actually engaged in the act of thinking, rather than offering concluded thoughts' (quoted by Andrew Motion, *The Poetry of Edward Thomas*, 1980, 82).

In this book, the term RHYTHM is used (1) as roughly equivalent to Frost's 'the sound of sense'; (2) as roughly equivalent to the tension described above by Frost between the natural sound of the sense and the metrical beat. See RHYTHM.

STRUCTURE: See FORM.

TEXT: As used by literary critics, the term implies a piece of writing complete in itself, the structure of which has been fixed, normally by publication (it is those words, in that order, making those statements, etc.), as opposed to an oral composition (an oral epic, or an anecdote, e.g.), the form of which is fixed, while the structure remains fluid. The original metaphor is from weaving (a text is a woven thing), implying pattern, organized structure, as well as finality.

Texts are commonly spoken of as having a 'context' (the literary, intellectual, political, etc., circumstances which surround their composition and publication or which they evoke; the setting in which the story unfolds, or to which the argument of a poem has reference, whether explicit or left unstated). Two further related terms, both borrowed from contemporary French critics, are frequently used. One is 'Subtext' the pattern of implication which underlies what is actually said; the message, as we say in everyday speech, is incomplete unless we can 'read between the lines'. The other is 'Intertextuality', a term used to describe a property of density or complexity which a literary text acquires as a result of the relationship which the text sets up (by direct reference or quotation, or more obliquely) between itself and other texts. Poems are made out of other poems, novels out of other novels, and this property of intertextuality can be part of the pleasure of reading them rather than a basis for accusations of plagiarism.

In this book, the term 'Field of Significance' is used to cover appropriate aspects of these three terms.

Further Reading

Books about literary theory start with Aristotle's *Poetics*, and end with the latest new book to bring to the subject — not a definitive answer to all our questions, but perhaps (to quote again a line from Robert Graves) a fresh understanding of our confusion.

For older standard works the reader can be referred to the comprehensive Bibliography (arranged under subject headings) in Warren and Wellek, *Theory of Literature*, 1949. For more recent works (particularly those giving emphasis to structuralist theories of literature), the very full Bibliography in Jonathan Culler, *Structuralist Poetics*, 1975, can be recommended; for a bibliography of works compiled strictly from the point of view of contemporary literary theory, see Josef Bleicher, *Contemporary Hermeneutics*, 1980. The following list comprises (1) a sprinkling of standard works outside the area of literary theory proper; (2) books which I have found useful; (3) recent books which have attracted attention; these are cited more as an indication of current trends than as items in a basic reading list; many have been the subject of controversy; some exemplify the almost impenetrable prose which has become fashionable in certain quarters among those who discuss literature. Only works available in English have been listed.

Books dealing with the criticism of particular texts (and not concerning themselves, except incidentally, with the theory of interpretation) have in general been left out.

ALLPORT, Floyd Henry, *Theories of Perception and the Concept of Structure*, 1955

AUERBACH, Erich, *Mimesis: The Representation of Reality in Western Literature*, 1945; English translation 1953

AUSTIN, J. L., *How To Do Things With Words*, 1962

BARTHES, Roland, *S/Z: An Essay*, 1970; English translation 1974

BATESON, F. W., *A Guide to English Literature*, 1965

BERRY, Cicely, *The Actor and his Text*, 1987

BLEICHER, Josef, *Contemporary Hermeneutics*, 1980

BLOOM, Harold, *Kabbalah and Criticism*, 1975

—— and others, *Deconstruction in Criticism*, 1979

BOLINGER, Dwight, *Intonation and its Parts: Melody in Spoken English*, 1986

BOOTH, Wayne C., *A Rhetoric of Irony*, 1974

——, *The Rhetoric of Fiction*, 1961

——, *Critical Understanding*, 1979

BOWRA, C. M., *Primitive Song*, 1962

CHOMSKY, Noam, *Aspects of the Theory of Syntax*, 1965

COHEN, Ralph (ed.), *New Directions in Literary History*, 1974

CRANE, R. S., *The Languages of Criticism and the Structure of Poetry*, 1953

CULLER, Jonathan, *Structuralist Poetics*, 1975

——, *The Pursuit of Signs*, 1981

ECO, Umberto, 'After Secret Knowledge' and 'Some Paranoid Readings', *Times Lit. Suppl.* 1990, 666 and 678; 694 and 706 (= Tanner Lectures, 1990)

FISH, Stanley, *Doing What Comes Naturally*, 1990

FORSTER, E. M., *Aspects of the Novel*, 1927

FOWLER, Roger, *A Dictionary of Modern Critical Terms*, 1973

FRYE, Northrop, *Anatomy of Criticism*, 1957

FUSSELL, Paul, *Poetic Meter and Poetic Form*, revised edition 1979

GOODMAN, Nelson, *Ways of Worldmaking*, 1968

GOODMAN, Paul, *The Structure of Literature*, 1954

GRAFF, Gerald, *Literature Against Itself: Literary Ideas in Modern Society*, 1979

HARDING, D. W., *Words into Rhythm*, 1976

HARTMAN, Geoffrey H., *Criticism in the Wilderness*, 1980

HIRSCH, E. D. Jr, *Validity in Interpretation*, 1967

——, *The Aims of Interpretation*, 1976

ISER, Wolfgang, *The Implied Reader: Patterns in Communication in Prose Fiction from Bunyon to Beckett*, 1974
———, *The Act of Reading: A Theory of Aesthetic Response*, 1978
JAMESON, Fredric, *The Prison-House of Language*, 1972
KERMODE, Frank, *The Sense of an Ending: Studies in the Theory of Fiction*, 1966
———, *The Genesis of Secrecy*, 1979
LAKOFF, George & JOHNSON, Mark, *Metaphors We Live By*, 1980
LANGER, Suzanne K., *Form and Feeling*, 1953
LEAVIS, F. R., *The Great Tradition*, 1948
LEAVIS, Q. D., *Fiction and the Reading Public*, 1932
LEGOUIS and CAZAMIAN, *History of English Literature* (The Middle Ages and the Renaissance, by Legouis, originally published 1926; many times reprinted)
LODGE, David (ed.), *Language of Fiction: Essays in Criticism and Verbal Analysis of the English Novel*, 1966
———, *After Bakhtin: Essays in Fiction and Criticism*, 1990
MUECKE, D. C., *Irony*, 1970
POPPER, Karl, *The Logic of Scientific Discovery*, 1959
RICHARDS, I. A., *Practical Criticism*, 1929
RICOEUR, Paul, *The Conflict of Interpretations*, 1969; English translation 1974
RUTHVEN, K. K., *Critical Assumptions*, 1979
SARTRE, Jean-Paul, *What is Literature?* 1948; English translation 1950
SAUSSURE, Ferdinand de, *Course in General Linguistics*, 1915; English translation 1959
SCHOLES, Robert, *Structuralism in Literature: An Introduction*, 1974
SEARLE, John R., *Speech Acts: An Essay in the Philosophy of Language*, 1969
SONTAG, Susan, *'Against Interpretation' and Other Essays*, 1966
STEIN, Jack, *Poem and Music in the German Lied from Gluck to Hugo Wolf*, 1971
STEINER, George, *Real Presences* (Stephen Lecture), 1986
TODOROV, Tzvetan, *The Poetics of Prose*, 1977
VALDES, Mario and MILLER, Owen (eds), *Interpretation of Narrative*, 1976
WARREN, Austin & WELLEK, René, *Theory of Literature*, 1949

WATSON, George, *Concise Cambridge Bibliography of English Literature*, 2nd edn 1965
——, *The Study of Literature*, 1969
——, *The Story of the Novel*, 1979
WATT, Ian, *The Rise of the Novel*, 1957
—— (ed.), *The Victorian Novel*, 1971
WHITE, Hayden, *Metahistory: The Historical Imagination in Nineteenth-Century Europe*, 1973

Index

CHESTER COLLEGE LIBRARY

CHESTER COLLEGE LIBRARY